How Personal & Internet Security Work

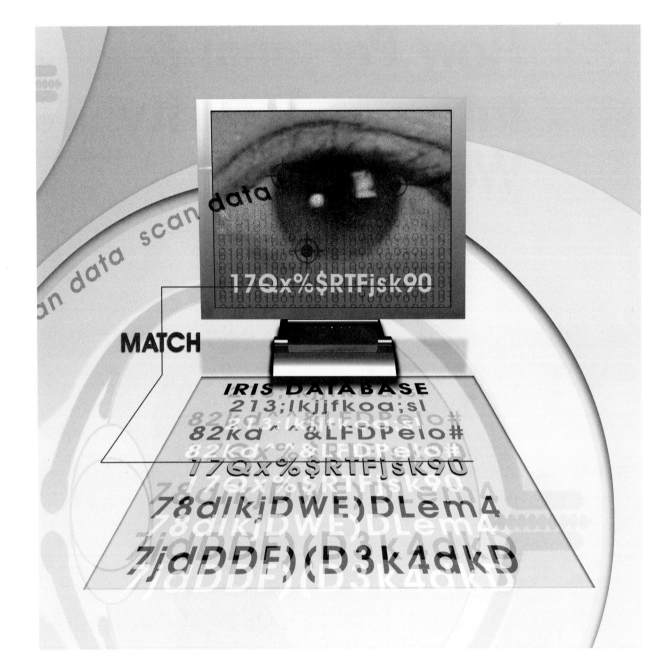

How Personal & Internet Security Work

Preston Gralla

800 East 96th Street
Indianapolis, Indiana 46240 USA

How Personal & Internet Security Work

Copyright © 2006 by Que Publishing

International Standard Book Number: 0-7897-3553-9

Library of Congress Catalog Card Number: 2006922248

Printed in the United States of America

First Printing: June 2006

09 08   4 3 2

Trademarks

Warning and Disclaimer

Bulk Sales

Que Publishing offers excellent discounts on this book when ordered in quantity for bulk purchases or special sales. For more information, please contact

U.S. Corporate and Government Sales
1-800-382-3419
corpsales@pearsontechgroup.com

For sales outside the United States, please contact

International Sales
international@pearsoned.com

Associate Publisher	Greg Wiegand
Acquisitions Editor	Stephanie J. McComb
Development Editor	Kevin Howard
Managing Editor	Patrick Kanouse
Project Editor	Tonya Simpson
Production Editor	Megan Wade
Indexer	Erika Millen
Technical Editor	Marc Charney
Publishing Coordinator	Sharry Lee Gregory
Book Designer	Anne Jones
Page Layout	TnT Design, Inc.

Table of Contents

About the Author

PRESTON GRALLA is a best-selling author of more than 30 books that have been translated into 20 languages, including *How the Internet Works*, *How Wireless Works*, *Google Search and Tools in a Snap*, and many others. A well-known technology guru, he has made many television and radio appearances, including on the *CBS Early Show*, CNN, MSNBC, and *ABC World News Now*. He has also done occasional commentaries about technology for National Public Radio's *All Things Considered*.

Gralla has published articles about technology for many national newspapers and magazines, including *USA Today*, the *Los Angeles Times*, the *Dallas Morning News* (for which he was a technology columnist), and *PC Magazine*. He was the founding managing editor of *PC Week* and founding editor, editor, and editorial director of *PC/Computing*. He also received the award for the Best Feature in a Computer Publication from the Computer Press Association.

Gralla is editor-in-chief of the Case Study Forum, which specializes in writing case studies for technology companies. He lives in Cambridge, Massachusetts, with his wife Lydia, son Gabe, and daughter Mia, who occasionally visits from college.

Acknowledgments

THANKS, as always, to my wife Lydia, son Gabe, and daughter Mia. Also, many thanks to the numerous organizations, from the Electronic Frontier Foundation to the Electronic Privacy Information Center (EPIC), to the American Civil Liberties Union (ACLU) and others who are on the front lines of protecting our rights to privacy, on the Internet and off.

Thanks also to Stephanie McComb for entrusting me with the project, Eric and Seth Lindley at Partners Photography & Illustration for the excellent illustrations, and thanks to Kevin Howard, Tonya Simpson, Megan Wade, and Erika Millen.

We Want to Hear from You!

AS the reader of this book, *you* are our most important critic and commentator. We value your opinion and want to know what we're doing right, what we could do better, what areas you'd like to see us publish in, and any other words of wisdom you're willing to pass our way.

As an associate publisher for Que Publishing, I welcome your comments. You can email or write me directly to let me know what you did or didn't like about this book—as well as what we can do to make our books better.

Please note that I cannot help you with technical problems related to the topic of this book. We do have a User Services group, however, where I will forward specific technical questions related to the book.

When you write, please be sure to include this book's title and author as well as your name, email address, and phone number. I will carefully review your comments and share them with the author and editors who worked on the book.

Email: feedback@quepublishing.com

Mail: Greg Wiegand
             Associate Publisher
             Que Publishing
             800 East 96th Street
             Indianapolis, IN 46240 USA

Reader Services

VISIT our website and register this book at www.quepublishing.com/register for convenient access to any updates, downloads, or errata that might be available for this book.

Introduction

TO live in a modern society is to walk the delicate tightrope between a need for security and the right to privacy. The events of September 11, 2001, might have made that tightrope thinner than ever, but the truth is that this tension between security and privacy has been with us a long time.

In fact, it has been there since at least the days of the founding of the United States when the founding fathers, recognizing the need for both security and privacy, wrote the Constitution, which established a powerful federal government but also added the Bill of Rights, which added protections against that very government, including the right to privacy.

In its zeal to provide for security, government at times treads on the right to privacy. But it's not only governments that invade people's right to privacy. Increasingly, so do private businesses—so much so that Scot McNealy, CEO of the computing company Sun Microsystems, told a stunned assemblage, "You have no privacy, now get over it."

It's no surprise that the statement would come from the executive of a technology company because, increasingly, security and privacy issues play out on the Internet.

Most of the privacy threats of the last several years have come via the Internet. Spyware, hackers, snoopers, and people who break into private computers and networks are everywhere. Your every move online is tracked; your Internet service provider (ISP) might be forced to turn over records about your surfing to a law enforcement agency; even search sites such as Google track your online activity and may also have to turn over information about you.

This book is dedicated to examining security and privacy issues, in cyberspace as well as in the real world. It takes the basic point of view that there are no easy answers to how to balance the rights of privacy and security. Its purpose is to show you, in vivid, easy-to-follow, step-by-step instructions, the security dangers in today's world, as well as the threats to your privacy.

It seemed at times when writing this book that the day's news and headlines followed the book's outline. The book covers all the major security and privacy issues of our day. It shows you how controversial eavesdropping programs work, including those done by the super-secret National Security Agency (NSA). It details how your credit card and identity can be stolen. It describes how hackers break in to networks, how spyware snoops on you when you use your computer, and how "zombie" networks spew spam and scams. It shows how terrorist-tracking systems work...and on the other end of the spectrum, how Paris Hilton's cell phone was hacked.

In short, this book is dedicated to the proposition that the more you know about security and privacy, the better you'll be able to make your own personal decisions about how to balance the two.

P A R T

Internet Security

WHEN you go onto the Internet, your life is an open book. Its very nature makes you vulnerable to attack. It was designed to allow for the freest possible exchange of information, data, and files—and it has succeeded admirably, far beyond its designers' wildest expectations. However, that freedom carries a price. Hackers and virus writers try to attack the Internet and computers connected to the Internet; those who want to invade others' privacy attempt to crack databases of sensitive information or snoop information as it travels across Internet routes; spyware is everywhere; wireless snoopers can easily jump onto your network; and distasteful and pornographic sites have sprung up on the Web.

In this section of the book, we look at dangers to your privacy and computer when you connect online. You'll first learn about the basic protocols that make up the Internet and that make you vulnerable to attack. Then you'll see how hackers can invade your PC, how spyware worms its way in, how websites and others can invade your privacy, and much more. Along the way, you'll also see how technologies have been developed that can protect your privacy and security.

Chapter 1, "How the Internet Works," delves into TCP/IP, the protocol that makes Internet communications possible. In addition, the chapter shows you how the Web works. By learning about the underpinnings of Internet communications, you'll see exactly why your computer is vulnerable whenever you connect.

Chapter 2, "How Hackers Break In to Your PC—and How to Protect Against Them," shows you all the ways in which hackers and other digital malcontents target your computer and attack you. You'll also learn about how "script kiddies"—often bored, adolescent boys—target your PC. And finally, you'll see all the ways in which computers can be protected against hackers and script kiddies.

Chapter 3, "How Spyware and Anti-Spyware Work," explains how the most devious of privacy-invaders and security threats—spyware—works. You'll learn how it invades your PC, the damage it does, and how it morphs to evade detection. You'll also see illustrations of some of the more dangerous forms of spyware, such as keyloggers and dialers. And you'll also see how anti-spyware protects computers from invasions.

Chapter 4, "How Websites Invade Your Privacy," discusses controversial technologies that enable websites to track what you do when you're online. It covers cookies, web tracking, and web bugs, as well as a technology that can help preserve people's privacy: Internet passports. Some people worry that cookies and web tracking can invade their privacy. Others disagree, saying that cookies and web tracking can help customize the Web to users' interests. Cookies are bits of data put on a hard disk when someone visits certain websites. That data can be used for many purposes. One common use is to make it easier for people to use websites that require a username and password by storing that information and then automatically sending the information whenever it's requested. Passports enable people to decide what type of information about them can be tracked by websites. Web tracking enables those who run websites to see how people use their sites. Web bugs are another technique for tracking people's Internet use.

In Chapter 5, "The Dangers of Internet Search," you'll see that searching on a site such as Google is not as risk-free as it may at first seem. Search sites can amass tremendous amounts of personal information about you, as you'll learn in this chapter.

Chapter 6, "How 'Phishing' Attacks Can Steal Your Identity—and How to Protect Against Them," details one of the greatest online threats to your privacy. In a phishing attack, you get what appears to be a legitimate email from a bank, a financial institution, or eBay and are told you need to log on to your account. But it's a spoof email that leads you to a spoofed site, and your information is stolen—and personal identity may be stolen as well. The chapter shows you how phishing and phishing protection work.

Chapter 7, "How Zombies and Trojan Horses Attack You—and How to Protect Against Them," details one of the strangest and well-hidden Internet threats: the use of zombies and entire zombie networks to launch massive attacks and send millions of pieces of spam. *Zombies* are PCs that can be remotely controlled by hackers, and you'll find out how PCs become zombies and how to protect against it happening to yours.

Chapter 8, "The Security Dangers in Browsers," details all the ways that browsers, in particular Internet Explorer, are vulnerable to attack. It also shows ways to protect yourself when browsing the Web.

Chapter 9, "How Worms and Viruses Do Their Damage—and How to Protect Against Them," looks at viruses and worms and how they are detected. Any program you download from the Internet has the potential to be infected with a virus, and it could, in turn, infect your computer. You'll see just how these nasty data killers work and look at antivirus tools that can detect and kill them. This chapter also examines how worms move from computer to computer, wreaking havoc along the way.

Chapter 10, "Wi-Fi Security Dangers and Protections," takes an in-depth look at the wireless technology that has become nearly ubiquitous. Whether you have a home Wi-Fi network, use it at work, or connect to a public hot spot, you're in danger every time you connect. This chapter shows you all the ways you can be attacked, including "Evil Twin" hacking and more. It also details how anyone can protect himself no matter where he connects.

Chapter 11, "Bluetooth Security Dangers," examines another popular wireless networking technology: Bluetooth. Bluetooth is used in PCs as well as personal digital assistants and cell phones, and as this chapter shows, as it becomes more popular, it becomes more vulnerable as well.

In Chapter 12, "How Instant Messaging Pests Work," you'll find out that this simple means of communication on computers can be every bit as dangerous as any other kind of digital communication. It can be used to send you spyware, Trojans, and other pieces of malware.

Chapter 13, "How Spam Works—and How to Fight It," details how spam is more than a mere annoyance because it can also be used to plant spyware, Trojans, and viruses on your PC. The chapter also shows ways in which spam can be combated.

Chapter 14, "How Denial-of-Service Attacks Bring Down Websites," delves into how hackers can bring down massive websites such as CNN and can attack small businesses as well. As you'll see, these kinds of attacks have changed from being purely malicious and are now often part of cyberextortion schemes.

In Chapter 15, "How Virtual Private Networks and Encryption Keep You Safe," you'll learn how these sometimes-obscure technologies can ensure that whatever information you send online can't be read except by you and the intended recipient.

Chapter 16, "How Web Blocking and Parental Controls Work," takes a detailed look at the issues of pornography and free speech on the Internet. Explicit sexual material is posted on the Internet, and some people would like to fine and jail people and organizations that allow such material to be posted. Passing those types of laws raises a host of constitutional issues about free speech. As a way to solve the problem, companies create and sell software for parents that enables them to block their children from seeing obscene and violent material on the Internet. In this chapter, you'll see how one of the most popular pieces of parental control software works.

Finally, Chapter 17, "How Personal Firewalls and Proxy Servers Protect You," looks at firewalls and the related technology of proxy servers. Many companies whose networks are connected to the Internet have a great deal of sensitive information on their networks and want to ensure that their data and computers are safe from attack. The answer is to use firewalls—systems that allow people from inside a company to use the Internet but also stop people on the Internet from getting at the company's computers. This chapter also discusses personal firewalls—software people can use at home to ensure that hackers can't invade their own computers.

CHAPTER

1

How the Internet Works

THE very thing that makes the Internet such an open place, and a great way to communicate with the world and gather information, also makes it easy to attack your computer and potentially invade your privacy. The Internet's open communications protocols make the security dangers possible.

These protocols do something very simple. They break up every piece of information and message into pieces called *packets*, deliver those packets to the proper destinations, and then reassemble the packets into their original form after they've been delivered so the receiving computer can view and use them. Two protocols do this—the Transmission Control Protocol (TCP) and the Internet Protocol (IP). They are frequently referred to as *TCP/IP*. TCP breaks down and reassembles the packets, and IP is responsible for ensuring the packets are sent to the right destination.

TCP/IP is used because the Internet is what is known as a packet-switched network. In a *packet-switched network*, there is no single, unbroken connection between sender and receiver. Instead, when information is sent, it is broken into small packets, sent over many routes at the same time, and then reassembled at the receiving end. By contrast, the telephone system is a circuit-switched network. In a *circuit-switched network*, after a connection is made (as with a telephone call, for example), that part of the network is dedicated only to that single connection for a finite period of time.

The Web uses these protocols, and others, as a way to deliver web pages and other information to your PC. It works on a *client/server* model. The client is your web browser; the server is a web server that delivers pages to you.

Why do these protocols make the Internet such an unsafe place? Because they were designed for openness and simplicity, so the packets that are sent back and forth over email and over the Web are open to inspection by anyone with a little bit of technical know-how. All someone needs is a piece of free software and a bit of knowledge, and he can examine the packets. Additionally, the various Internet protocols make it easy for someone to hide his true identity or even pose as someone else.

How TCP/IP Works

1 The Internet is a packet-switched network, which means that when you send information across the Internet from your computer to another computer, the data is broken into small packets. A series of devices called *routers* send each packet across the Net individually. After all the packets arrive at the receiving computer, they are recombined into their original, unified form. Two protocols do the work of breaking the data into packets, routing the packets across the Internet, and then recombining them on the other end: The Internet Protocol (IP), which routes the data, and the Transmission Control Protocol (TCP), which breaks the data into packets and recombines them on the computer that receives the information.

3 Each packet is put into separate IP envelopes, which contain addressing information that tells the Internet where to send the data. All the envelopes for a given piece of data have the same addressing information, so they all can be sent to the same location to be reassembled. IP envelopes contain headers that include information such as the sender's address, the destination address, the amount of time the packet should be kept before discarding it, and many other kinds of information.

2 For many reasons, including hardware limitations, data sent across the Internet must be broken up into packets of fewer than 1,500 characters each. Each packet is given a header that contains a variety of information, such as the order in which the packets should be assembled with other related packets. As TCP creates each packet, it also calculates and adds to the header a *checksum*, which is a number TCP uses on the receiving end to determine whether any errors have been introduced into the packet during transmission. The checksum is based on the precise amount of data in the packet.

4 As the packets are sent across the Internet, routers along the way examine the IP envelopes and look at their addresses. These routers determine the most efficient path for sending each packet to the next router closest to its final destination. The packets arrive after traveling through a series of routers. Because the traffic load on the Internet changes constantly, the packets might be sent along different routes and might arrive out of order.

Router

Original packet retransmitted

CORRUPT

18,713

To: 137.42.6.72

6 When all the non-corrupt packets are received by the computer to which the information is being sent, TCP assembles them into their original, unified form.

To: 137.42.6.72   17,136

To: 137.42.6.72   14,132

To: 137.42.6.72   12,333

To: 137.42.6.72   23,578

TCP

5 As the packets arrive at their destination, TCP calculates a checksum for each packet. It then compares this checksum with the checksum that has been sent in the packet. If the checksums don't match, TCP knows that the data in the packet has been corrupted during transmission. It then discards the packet and asks that the original packet be retransmitted.

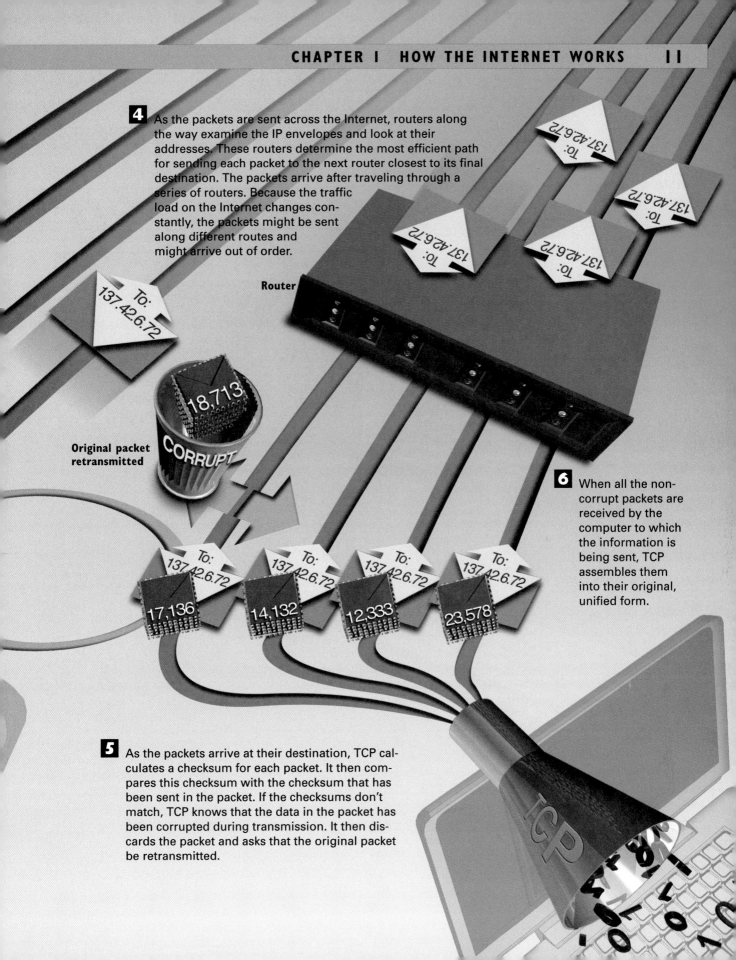

How the World Wide Web Works

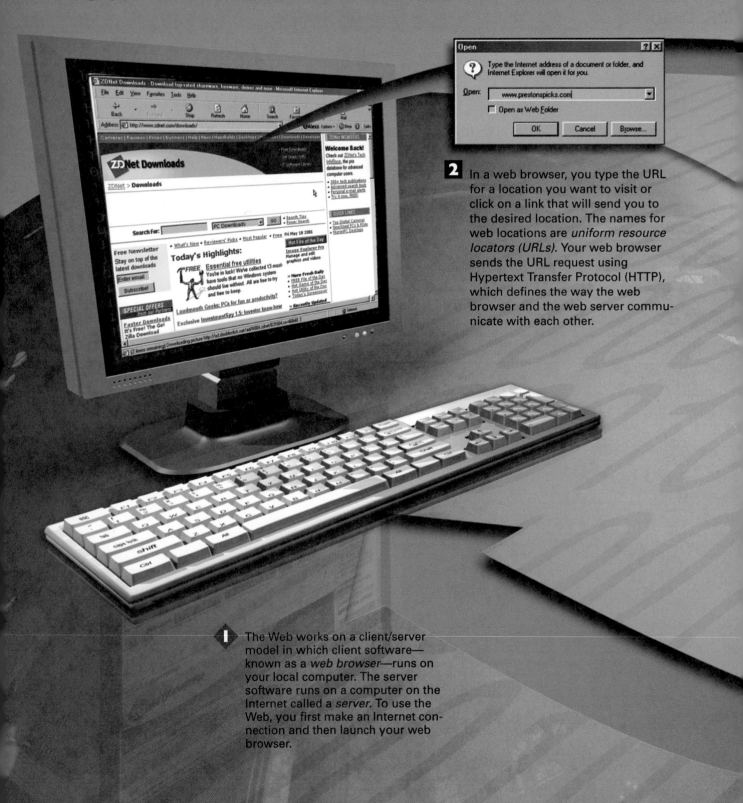

2 In a web browser, you type the URL for a location you want to visit or click on a link that will send you to the desired location. The names for web locations are *uniform resource locators (URLs)*. Your web browser sends the URL request using Hypertext Transfer Protocol (HTTP), which defines the way the web browser and the web server communicate with each other.

1 The Web works on a client/server model in which client software—known as a *web browser*—runs on your local computer. The server software runs on a computer on the Internet called a *server*. To use the Web, you first make an Internet connection and then launch your web browser.

3 URLs contain several parts. The first part—the http://—details which Internet protocol to use. The second part—the part that usually has a www in it—sometimes tells what kind of Internet resource is being contacted. The third part—such as zdnet.com—can vary in length and identifies the web server to be contacted. The final part identifies a specific directory on the server and a home page, a document, some other Internet object, or the default home page.

www.prestonspicks.com

Router

4 The request is sent to the Internet. Internet routers examine the request to determine to which server to send the request. The information just to the right of the http:// in the URL tells the Internet on which web server the requested information can be found. Routers send the request to that web server. The request is sent as a URL, like this: http://www.quebooks.com. But Internet servers can't understand letters; they can only handle numbers. So that URL needs to be translated into an IP address that servers can understand. An IP address is in the form of four numbers separated by dots, like this: 216.187.118.221. A DNS server translates the URL into IP addresses.

Web server

6 When the server finds the requested home page, document, or object, it sends that home page, document, or object back to the web browser client. The information is then displayed on the computer screen in the web browser.

5 The web server receives the request using the HTTP protocol. It is told which specific document is being requested.

CHAPTER

2

How Hackers Break In to Your PC—and How to Protect Against Them

TO connect your computer to the Internet is to be in danger. There's no way around it—the moment you get on to the Internet, you are threatened by spyware, viruses, Trojans, and more. And among the worst threats are hackers, who look for ways to break into people's PCs and do damage.

Why is the Internet so open to hackers? A big part of the reason has to do with the origins of the Internet itself. The Internet was not designed to be a massive globe-spanning network connecting hundreds of millions of people doing everything from shopping to conducting financial transactions. Instead, it was built for government and military researchers to be able to easily communicate with each other and share resources.

Because of that, the Internet was designed to be open and to allow people to do things such as allow others to take control of their computers.

It's this very openness that makes hacking so easy. When you connect to the Internet, your computer is wide open. And it needs to be that way because to accomplish anything, such as connecting to a website, it needs to send and receive information freely. This openness can be exploited by hackers, who can use it to break in to your PC.

In addition, the Internet was not designed with security in mind, so it's easy for people to *spoof* their real email addresses or locations. There's a famous *New Yorker* cartoon with the punch line, "On the Internet, no one knows you're a dog." That can be updated to, "On the Internet, no one knows you're a hacker."

This problem is made worse by the number of *script kiddies* online. Script kiddies are people, not uncommonly adolescent boys, who are bent on doing damage to people's PCs but who don't have a great deal of knowledge about the workings of the Internet, networks, or computers. But they are able to download freely available malicious software, and scripts to run that software, and can wreak havoc. Often, they work out their own emotional issues by harming other people's computers.

But all is not bleak when it comes to protecting yourself against hackers. Plenty of software and many techniques can be used to protect yourself. An entire security software industry has sprung up, so you can buy antivirus software, anti-spyware software, and firewalls that will protect you. And in many cases, the software is available for free.

Ultimately, though, just as important as using the right software is learning the proper behavior—not clicking on spam messages, responding to instant messages from people you don't know, and so on.

So while it's true that there is no absolute protection against hackers, there's a great deal that can be done so that you'll most likely be safe the next time you go online.

How Hackers Invade PCs

1 Hackers not only attack big websites and corporations, but also individual computers in homes or businesses. Hackers can do damage and use your computer in many ways. As a start to many of hackers' nefarious deeds, they need access to your computer. One common way they gain it is through the use of a program like Back Orifice. Before the hackers can use the program, you have to get it on your computer. You can unwittingly get a copy of Back Orifice on your computer in many ways—for example, you can open a file in an email message and it can be installed to your computer without you realizing it, or you can be sent it when you use Internet's IRC chat protocol.

2 Hackers have automated tools that scan thousands of computers to see which ones have Back Orifice running on them. These tools send out *port probes*—packets that look at specific virtual ports that all computers have when connected to the Internet. Back Orifice uses port 31337, among other ports, and if it's running on a computer, it opens that port. A port probe alerts the hacker that port 31337 is open so he knows he can take control of your PC.

3 The hacker can do many things when he takes control of your computer—in essence, it's as if he's sitting at your keyboard and monitor without you knowing about it. He can, for example, copy or delete all the files, data, and software on your computer.

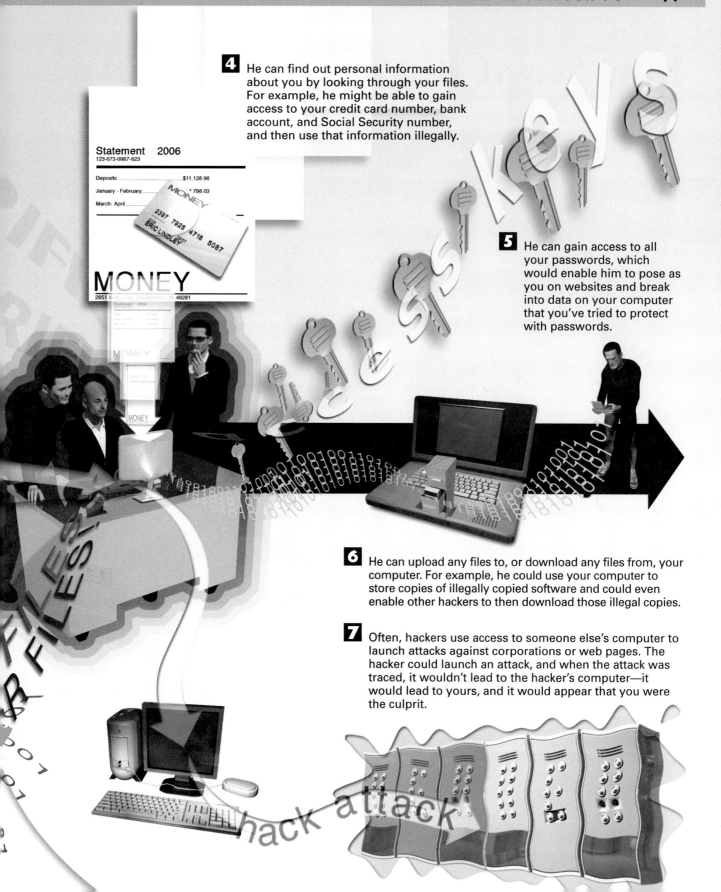

4 He can find out personal information about you by looking through your files. For example, he might be able to gain access to your credit card number, bank account, and Social Security number, and then use that information illegally.

Statement   2006
123-673-0987-623

Deposits..........................$11,128.96

January - February............... 798.03

March- April.....................

MONEY

2851 Welton Rd. Indianapolis, IN 46281

Statement   2006

MONEY

MONEY

5 He can gain access to all your passwords, which would enable him to pose as you on websites and break into data on your computer that you've tried to protect with passwords.

6 He can upload any files to, or download any files from, your computer. For example, he could use your computer to store copies of illegally copied software and could even enable other hackers to then download those illegal copies.

7 Often, hackers use access to someone else's computer to launch attacks against corporations or web pages. The hacker could launch an attack, and when the attack was traced, it wouldn't lead to the hacker's computer—it would lead to yours, and it would appear that you were the culprit.

How Script Kiddies Target PCs

1 *Script kiddie* (also called *script bunny*, *script kitty*, or *skiddie*) is a derogatory term applied to people, most frequently adolescent boys, who do damage to people's computers or to websites but with no great knowledge of computers. Instead, they merely run scripts (computer instructions, programs, and code) written by others to launch attacks, without understanding exactly what they are doing. Script kiddies are often lonely, bored, and socially outcast, and they gain a sense of worth by doing damage and bragging about it. Script kiddies do damage in many ways. In this illustration, you'll see how they use Trojans to damage PCs.

2 A script kiddie visits a website devoted to hacking and downloads a malicious piece of software and set of scripts for using the software.

3 He launches the software. The software sends out tens of thousands of probes across the Internet, looking for computers that have security holes and that have had Trojans installed on them without the knowledge of their owners.

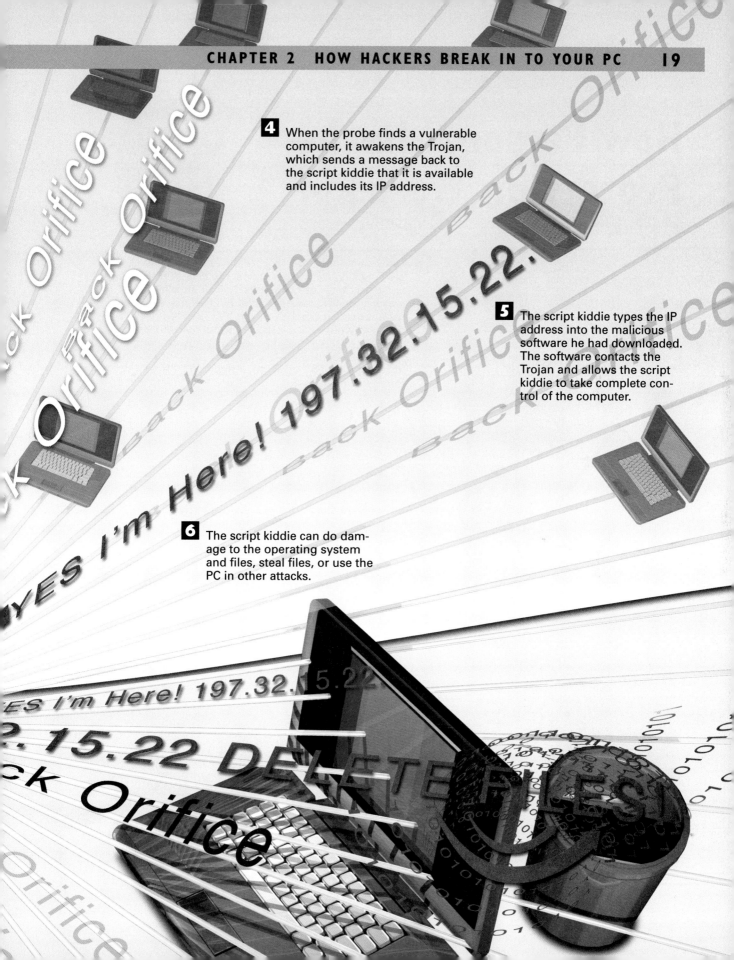

4 When the probe finds a vulnerable computer, it awakens the Trojan, which sends a message back to the script kiddie that it is available and includes its IP address.

5 The script kiddie types the IP address into the malicious software he had downloaded. The software contacts the Trojan and allows the script kiddie to take complete control of the computer.

6 The script kiddie can do damage to the operating system and files, steal files, or use the PC in other attacks.

How Personal Hacker Protection Works

HACKING

1 One of the most effective protections against hackers attacking a PC is a personal firewall—a piece of software that protects against hacker attacks in two ways. It blocks unwanted inbound traffic, so probes cannot make it through. And it blocks outbound traffic as well, so a Trojan or piece of spyware can't make an outbound connection to a hacker, telling him to take control of the PC. For more information about personal firewalls, see Chapter 17, "How Personal Firewalls and Proxy Servers Protect You."

Firewall

2 Anti-spyware software and antivirus software stop spyware and viruses from infecting a PC. They run constantly in the background, watching for infections and stopping them before they start. They also include scanners that scan a system for infections and then clean out any infections that are found.

GET PATCH
security patch download security
security patch download security

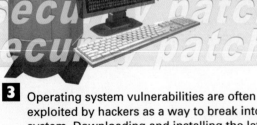

3 Operating system vulnerabilities are often exploited by hackers as a way to break into a system. Downloading and installing the latest patches ensures that the operating system is up to date and as secure as possible.

4 One way hackers gain access to a PC is through Trojans that have been installed on it. Trojans can get onto PCs in many ways, including when someone opens spam and follows a link. Anti-spam software helps protect against hacking, as well as prevents spam recipients from clicking spam links. Trojans or malicious software is also installed when people click on pop-up ads or windows that appear when they surf the Internet. A pop-up killer, such as is built in to Internet Explorer, Firefox, and other browsers, helps protect against Trojans being installed by pop-ups.

access denied

5 Unprotected wireless networks let hackers invade a network and, from there, worm their way into every computer on the network and do damage. Wireless networks can be protected in a number of ways—for example, by turning on encryption or by using settings that let only specific computers onto the network and deny access to all others

CHAPTER

3

How Spyware and Anti-Spyware Work

THESE days, the biggest danger you face when you go onto the Internet might be spyware—a type of malicious software that can invade your privacy and wreak havoc on your PC. Spyware is a relatively new phenomenon; it does not have a long history as do viruses, Trojans, and worms.

Spyware is an umbrella name for many types of malicious programs, but these kinds of programs have several things in common. First, all of them, one way or another, spy on your behavior. They may watch which web pages you visit and report that information to a server or person, or they might track your web searches. They may even allow people to record every keystroke you make or open a back door into your computer so hackers can later take control of your PC when they want.

The second thing they have in common is that they install either without your knowledge or by tricking you. One common way they get on your PC is when you install a piece of software, such as file-sharing software. When you install that software, spyware often comes along for a ride and installs itself without your knowledge or misleads you about what the program actually does.

Although some spyware is created for purely malicious reasons, other kinds are created as part of money-making schemes. One kind of spyware swarms your PC with dozens of pop-up ads, some of which you'll most likely click to close. But every time you click, the spyware purveyor makes money because he has a business arrangement with a merchant or website to drive traffic to it.

There is a fine line between spyware and what is called *adware*. They work similarly, but with adware, you download a piece of software that you can use for free, such as a weather program. In return, the adware watches your surfing habits and sends that information to a server, which then delivers ads to you based on your behavior. The ads are displayed only inside the weather program and don't appear when you don't use it. Spyware, by way of contrast, watches you all the time and displays ads whenever you surf the Web or are connected to the Internet.

Spyware can do more than just spy on you. It can do damage to your computer as well. Some spyware inundates your computer with blizzards of pop-up ads—in some instances so many that it takes away all your system resources and your PC grinds to a halt. This makes your computer unusable.

Because there is money to be made from surfing, spyware isn't going away any time soon. But as you'll see in this chapter, anti-spyware can combat it, so there are ways to keep yourself safe and protect your privacy.

How Spyware Invades Your PC

1 Spyware sits in the background of your computer, watches which websites you visit, and then reports on your activities. Based on those activities, targeted ads are delivered to you. But first, the spyware has to get onto your computer. Often, you get spyware by downloading a free program or clicking a pop-up ad. Spyware comes along for the ride without you knowing it. When you install the program you've chosen, spyware is installed as well, without your knowledge.

2 Spyware often runs whenever you turn on your computer, even when the program upon which it rides is not running. It watches your web activities and tracks every website you visit.

3 At regular intervals, the spyware phones home, reporting to the spyware website which sites you've visited.

4 Based on the sites you've visited, the spyware website creates a profile about your surfing activities.

profile

8253417 profile
- Likes sports
- cares about money

sites visited
- sportsillustrated.com
- money.com

office

FREE CELLPHONE

HURRY!

www.call005.com

Instant Mortgage Rates

BUY!
BUY!

Bad Credit?
call
817-986-2096

sports delight
24 hour sports channel 7 days a week!!!!!

5 Based on that profile, the website delivers targeted ads to you. The ads appear whenever you run the program on which the spyware piggybacked onto your system. When you delete the program on which the spyware piggybacked onto your system, the spyware typically does not get deleted. It keeps watching your surfing activities and reporting on them, although it can't deliver ads based on that information because the program on which it was piggybacked has been deleted. To delete the spyware, you need a special spyware detector and killer, such as Ad-Aware from www.lavasoft.com.

How Spyware Morphs Itself to Escape Detection

1 One of the most insidious kinds of spyware is *polymorphic* spyware, which uses a variety of tactics to evade detection and removal, including the ability to constantly change its filename and location.

2 Cool Web Search and About: Blank are two home page–hijacking pieces of shareware that morph and use other techniques to evade detection and deletion. Programs like these can install themselves to multiple locations on a hard disk.

3 When a piece of anti-spyware detects and kills the files in one of the locations, the spyware spawns a new copy of itself at another location and runs from there.

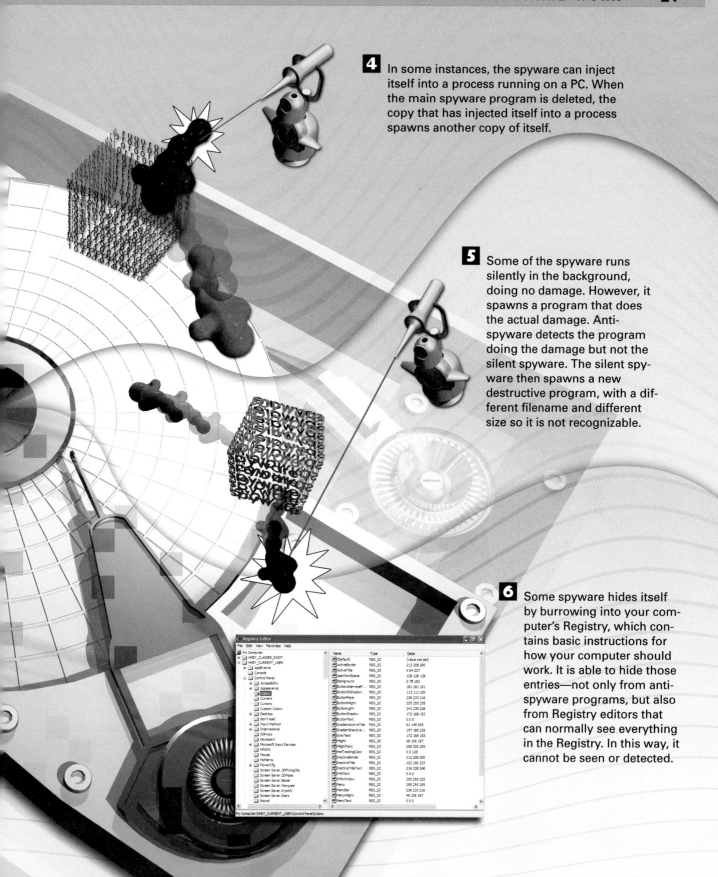

4 In some instances, the spyware can inject itself into a process running on a PC. When the main spyware program is deleted, the copy that has injected itself into a process spawns another copy of itself.

5 Some of the spyware runs silently in the background, doing no damage. However, it spawns a program that does the actual damage. Anti-spyware detects the program doing the damage but not the silent spyware. The silent spyware then spawns a new destructive program, with a different filename and different size so it is not recognizable.

6 Some spyware hides itself by burrowing into your computer's Registry, which contains basic instructions for how your computer should work. It is able to hide those entries—not only from anti-spyware programs, but also from Registry editors that can normally see everything in the Registry. In this way, it cannot be seen or detected.

How Spyware Invades Your Privacy

sports delight
24 hour sports channel 7 days a week!!!!!

BUY! BEER NOW

I There are many different types of spyware that invade your privacy in many different ways. One type monitors all your surfing habits and reports on those habits to a server on the Internet. That server may deliver ads to you based on your surfing habits, or it could sell the information to other companies.

2 A particularly privacy-invading type of spyware is called a *keylogger*. (For more information about keyloggers, see "How Keyloggers Work," later in this chapter.) Keyloggers record every keystroke you make and send that information to a hacker, who can then steal all your passwords, logins, and other information.

3 Some spyware installs other malicious software on your system. For example, some spyware installs a Trojan on your PC, which allows a hacker to take complete control of your PCs and files as if she were sitting at the keyboard. (For more details about Trojans, see Chapter 7, "How Zombies and Trojan Horses Attack You—and How to Protect Against Them.")

4 Some spyware monitors your Internet searching activity and reports that activity to servers, which can then keep track of your interests and deliver ads to you based on them or create profiles of you and sell that information to other companies.

5 Spyware is not only a danger to individuals—it can be extremely dangerous for corporations as well. Spyware can crawl into an individual's computer and then infect all the other computers and servers on a corporate network, gathering not only personal information, but also corporate information.

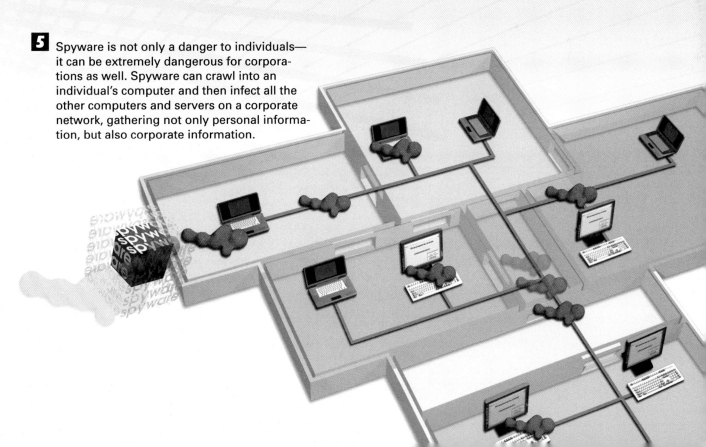

How Home Page and Search Page Hijackers Work

1 Home page hijackers and search page hijackers infect your computer in the same way that any spyware does, such as by downloading a file, with the hijacker coming along for the ride.

2 A home page hijacker changes your browser's start page so that whenever you launch your browser, you go to the new start page rather than to the one you want.

HIJACK ME NOW

Download now

Last Chance
50% OFF
Order now
Click here

BUY!
BEER
NOW

sports delight
24 hour sports channel 7 days
a week!!!!!

News Now!
24 hour news channel 7 days
a week!!!!!

Bad Credit?
call
817-986-2096

The Weather Site
www.weathernow.com

FREE CELLPHONE

3 Typically, the new home page you go to includes many pop-up ads and may inundate your PC with so many ads that your system becomes unstable and unusable. The hijacker makes money because he is paid to deliver pop-up ads, so the more ads he can deliver, the more he is paid.

4 A search page hijacker changes your normal search engine to a new one. When you do a search from your browser, that search is sent to the new search engine, not to your normal one. The search engine often delivers pop-ups in the same way as a home page hijacker does.

Some home page hijackers intercept every search you perform. For example, if you visit Google and do a search there, the hijacker sends the search to the new search engine, not Google, and then inundates you with pop-ups.

5 Some home page hijackers and search page hijackers are very difficult to eradicate. When you change your browser settings to go back to your normal search and home page, they might change them back again. They can do this by putting themselves in your startup folder and starting up every time you turn on your PC.

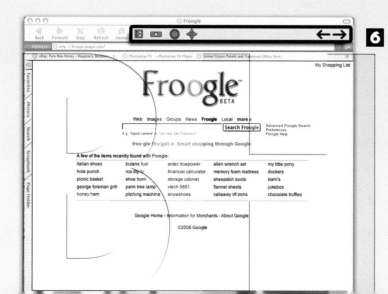

6 Some home page hijackers and search page hijackers disguise themselves as browser add-ins (called browser helper objects [BHOs]) or toolbars. So you think that the toolbar is performing a useful function, but in fact, it is hijacking your home page and search page.

How Dialers Work

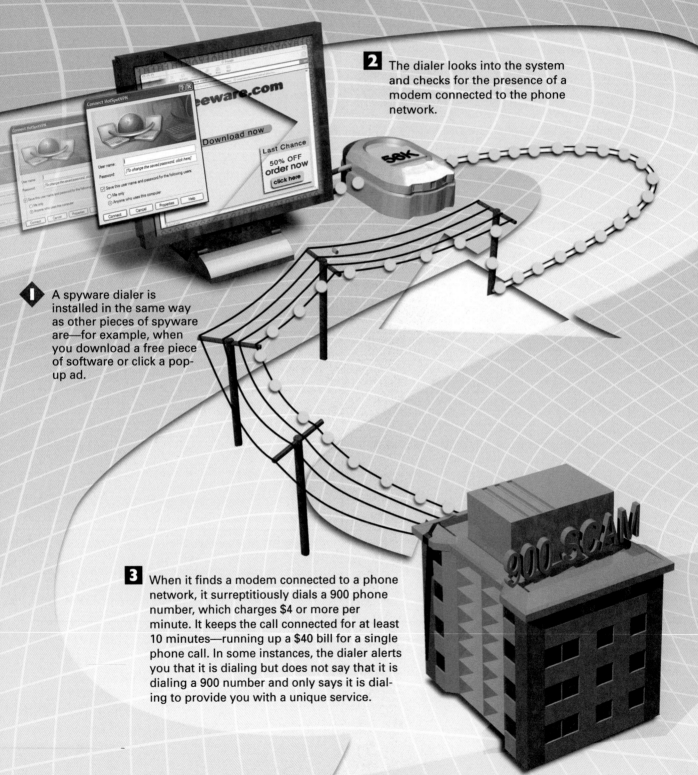

2 The dialer looks into the system and checks for the presence of a modem connected to the phone network.

1 A spyware dialer is installed in the same way as other pieces of spyware are—for example, when you download a free piece of software or click a pop-up ad.

3 When it finds a modem connected to a phone network, it surreptitiously dials a 900 phone number, which charges $4 or more per minute. It keeps the call connected for at least 10 minutes—running up a $40 bill for a single phone call. In some instances, the dialer alerts you that it is dialing but does not say that it is dialing a 900 number and only says it is dialing to provide you with a unique service.

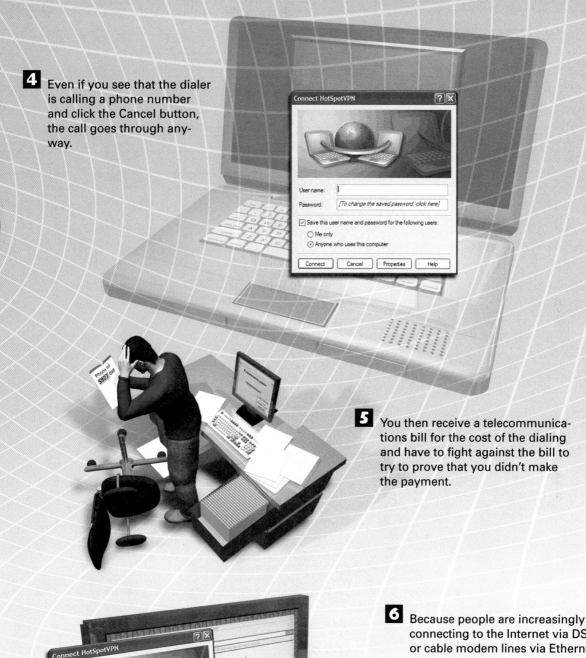

4 Even if you see that the dialer is calling a phone number and click the Cancel button, the call goes through anyway.

5 You then receive a telecommunications bill for the cost of the dialing and have to fight against the bill to try to prove that you didn't make the payment.

6 Because people are increasingly connecting to the Internet via DSL or cable modem lines via Ethernet cables, dialers are not as common as they used to be. A dialer cannot make calls via Ethernet cables over a DSL or cable modem connection.

How Keyloggers Work

1 A keylogger is installed in the same way as other pieces of spyware are—for example, when you download a free piece of software or click a pop-up ad.

2 A keylogger is often installed in two parts: a **.exe** file and a **.dll** file. When the computer starts, the **.exe** file automatically launches. The **.exe** file then launches the **.dll** file, which does most of the work.

3 The **.dll** file sits silently in the background, recording all the keystrokes you make.

intercepted data

glxt

4 In some instances, the keystrokes are sent directly to an attacker.

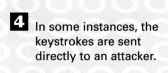

5 In other instances, the keystrokes are saved in a file that is sent at regular intervals to the attacker.

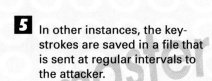

6 The attacker examines the keystrokes, looking for passwords, logins, and other information she can use—for example, to log in to your bank to steal money or to steal your identity.

BankTrust

welcome back

password: glxt

send

How Rootkits Work

1 A rootkit allows an intruder to gain access to someone's PC whenever he wants, without being detected. It is made up of a series of files and tools. It can be installed on a system in a number of ways, sometimes in the same way that shareware is installed. In the most notorious instance of a rootkit, Sony surreptitiously installed rootkits on tens of thousands or more computers by shipping it as part of software that installed on people's PCs when they put a Sony music CD into their PC's drive.

2 A rootkit can replace important components of an operating system with new software. The new software disguises itself as the original files, including the same file size, creation date, and so on, making it extremely difficult to detect.

kernel.exe

1/10/2006

537,111 bytes

kernel.exe

1/10/2006

537,111 bytes

3 A rootkit installs a backdoor *daemon*, or automatic program. This backdoor opens a hole in the system, allowing the rootkit creator to crawl in and take control of the PC whenever he wants.

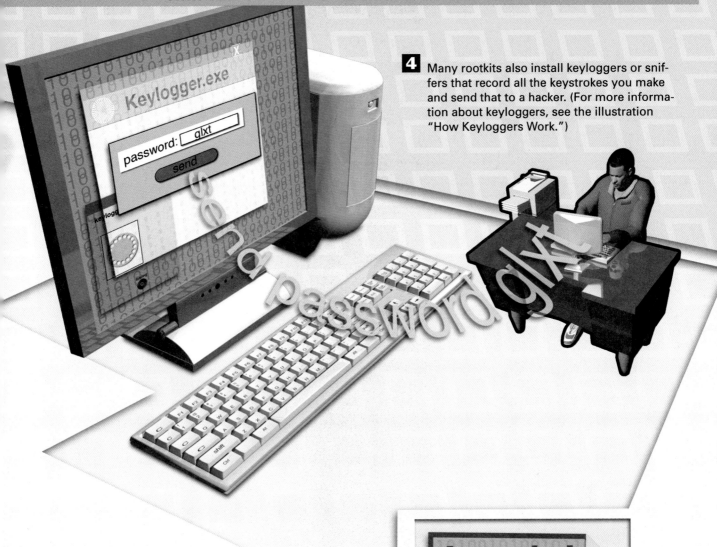

4 Many rootkits also install keyloggers or sniffers that record all the keystrokes you make and send that to a hacker. (For more information about keyloggers, see the illustration "How Keyloggers Work.")

5 A rootkit can modify a computer's system log that tracks all the activity on a PC. The system log normally includes all activity, including malicious activity, so the rootkit modifies the log to hide all traces of itself.

Following the Spyware Money Trail

1 Many types of spyware make money for spyware creators or users in many different ways. This illustration shows how a lot of spyware has a money trail that includes reputable, well-known websites and merchants.

MERCHANT SITE

ID:spyguy ID:spyguy ID:spyguy ID:spyguy

2 Much spyware is intended to make money from *affiliate programs*, in which any user can sign up to make money by delivering ads for the site or merchant. First, someone who wants to make money from spyware signs up for an affiliate program with a website or merchant. The person gets a code that identifies him, so he can be paid for every link or click to the merchant.

3 Some merchants monitor those who sign up for their affiliate programs, but many do not. Those wanting to make money from spyware look for merchants who do not do a good job of policing their affiliate programs.

4 Those wanting to make money from spyware are often not spyware authors. Instead, they make a deal with a spyware author in which spyware will include links to the person's affiliate program ID. The spyware author shares the money from the program with the person looking to make money from spyware.

Electronics.com

GREAT DEALS

Download now

Last Chance
50% OFF
order now

click here

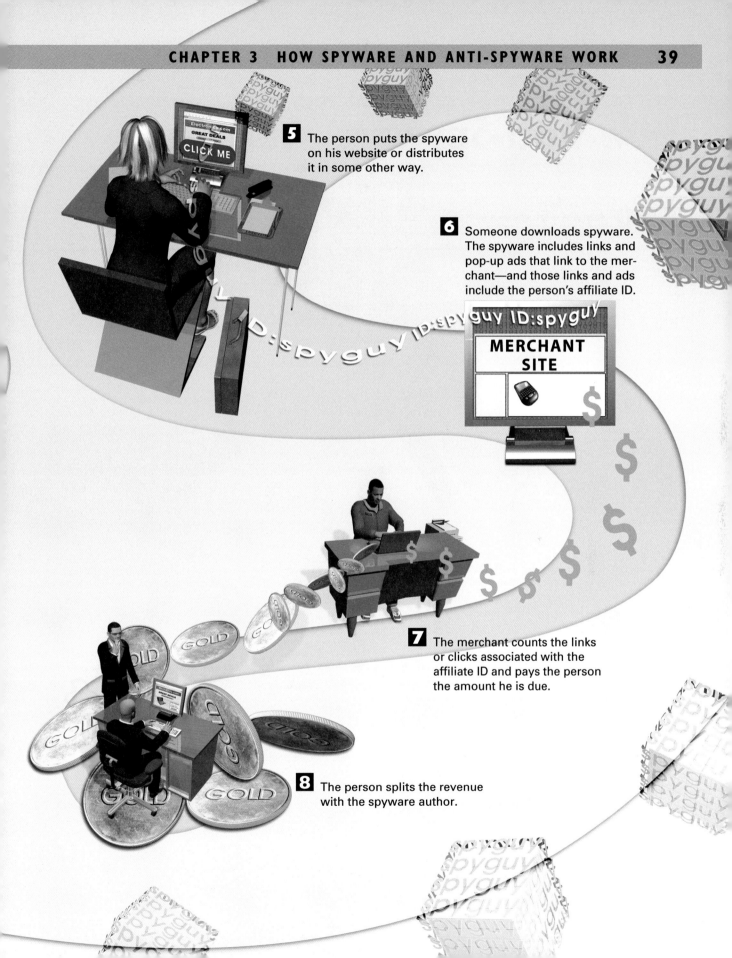

5 The person puts the spyware on his website or distributes it in some other way.

6 Someone downloads spyware. The spyware includes links and pop-up ads that link to the merchant—and those links and ads include the person's affiliate ID.

7 The merchant counts the links or clicks associated with the affiliate ID and pays the person the amount he is due.

8 The person splits the revenue with the spyware author.

How Anti-Spyware Works

1 Anti-spyware scans a system in search of bits of code called *signatures* that are telltale signs of a spyware infection.

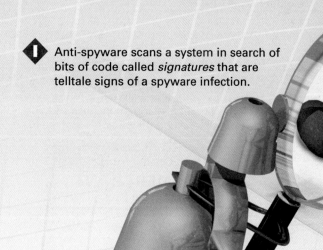

match

2 When the anti-spyware finds what it believes is a signature, it compares it to its database of signatures, called a *signature base*. If it finds a match, it knows there is a spyware infection.

3 New spyware is being released all the time, and existing spyware is often updated. To ensure that it can catch all the latest infections, anti-spyware regularly downloads the latest, updated signatures.

In some instances, particular pieces of spyware don't leave telltale signatures. In other instances, spyware constantly morphs, making detection difficult. So some anti-spyware doesn't search only for signatures, but looks for telltale suspicious behavior as well.

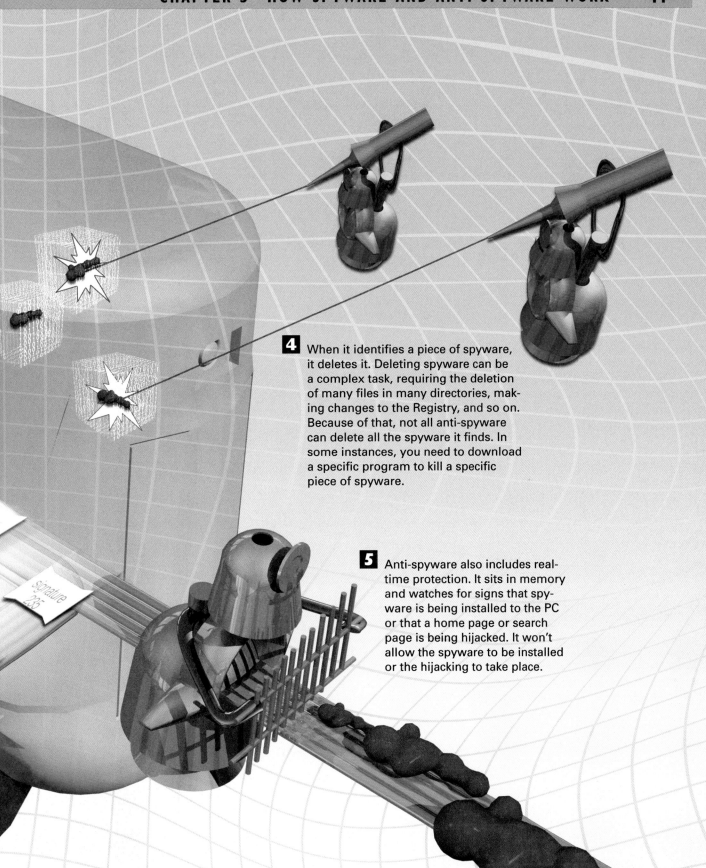

4 When it identifies a piece of spyware, it deletes it. Deleting spyware can be a complex task, requiring the deletion of many files in many directories, making changes to the Registry, and so on. Because of that, not all anti-spyware can delete all the spyware it finds. In some instances, you need to download a specific program to kill a specific piece of spyware.

5 Anti-spyware also includes real-time protection. It sits in memory and watches for signs that spyware is being installed to the PC or that a home page or search page is being hijacked. It won't allow the spyware to be installed or the hijacking to take place.

CHAPTER
4

How Websites Invade Your Privacy

SURFING the Web may feel like a solitary experience, but in fact, every time you visit a new website, that website gathers information about you. The information might be innocuous—how many pages you visit on the site, for example. But it might be not-so innocuous as well. The site may track every page you visit and the amount of time you spend on each page. It might examine your IP address and find out your geographic location and your place of work. And it may gather a lot more information and be able to put together a surprisingly sophisticated and complete profile of who you are and your personal interests. So, how is this done?

In some instances, the site may use this information to better deliver information to you—it might customize which pages it shows to you, depending on your past surfing habits on the site, for example. The site may customize the ads it delivers to you as well.

But it might do more with that information as well, which can be disturbing. It might be able to create a complete profile of you and then sell that information to advertisers, other websites, or the highest bidder. When information like this from a website is combined with offline databases with profiles about you (such as what you've bought at particular stores), an extremely complete profile about you can be built.

Three technologies are often used to track your web activities—cookies, web tracking, and web bugs.

Cookies are bits of data put on a hard disk when someone visits certain websites. There are legitimate uses for cookies—for example, they make it easier for people to use websites that require a username and password. The cookie on the hard disk has the username and password on it, so people don't have to log in to every page that requires that information. Instead, the cookie sends the information to the server and the person can visit the page freely.

Cookies can contain many kinds of information, such as the last time a person visited the site, the person's favorite sites, and similar information. They can be used to track people as they go through a website and to help gain statistics about which types of pages people like to visit.

Although cookies can be used to track how people use a website, many other methods can be used, as well. In one method, web server logs are examined in detail. This would make it possible, for example, to identify the most popular pages on the site, the sites people have just visited, how many pages people read in a typical visit, and similar information. Other methods include using software *sniffers* that examine every packet coming into or going out of a website. Webmasters can use this tracking information to help create better sites—but they can also use it to assemble demographic information to sell to advertisers.

Web bugs can also trace people's paths through a website. Web bugs get their name not in reference to an error in a program, but instead from the term *to bug*—as in "to wiretap." More dangerously, web bugs can be included in email, and they can actually enable people to view some of your email.

How Cookies Work

1 *Cookies* are pieces of data placed on a computer's hard drive by a web server; they can be used for a variety of purposes. They can store usernames and passwords, for example, so people don't have to continually log on to a site that requires registration; or they can enable people to fill electronic shopping carts with goods they want to buy. Cookies also store the name of the site that placed the cookie. Only that site can read the cookie information, so information from one site can't be shared with information from another site. Cookie information is put into a special file on a hard disk. The location and files vary according to the type of computer and the browser. On PCs using Internet Explorer, for example, cookies are often found in the folder Documents and Settings\Owner\Cookies, with each cookie in its own text file. But in Netscape, the information is put into a file called COOKIES.TXT. That single text file holds all the cookies, and each cookie is one line of data in the file.

Web server

CGI script

Password: pg
Username: who

www.buyshop.com

buyshop.com   True   123702   132

3 If no cookie is associated with the URL, the server places a cookie inside the cookie file. Some sites might first ask a series of questions, such as name and password, and then place a cookie on the hard disk with that information in it. This is typical of sites that require registration. Commonly, a CGI script on the server takes the information the user has entered and then writes the cookie onto the hard disk.

2 When you visit a site, your browser examines the URL you're visiting and looks into your cookie file. If it finds a cookie associated with that URL, it sends that cookie information to the server. The server can now use that cookie information.

4 As you travel through a website, more information might need to be put into your cookie. On a site where you can purchase goods online, for example, you might put goods into an electronic shopping cart. Every time you do this, new cookie information is added, detailing the goods you want to buy. When new cookie information is put in, a CGI script deletes the old cookie information and inserts a new cookie. When you leave a site, your cookie information remains on your hard disk so the site can recognize you the next time you decide to visit—unless the cookie has specifically been written to expire when you leave the site.

Delete old cookies: put on new cookies

5 The web server takes actions based on your cookies—for example, displaying your electronic shopping cart. If the site enables you to buy online, it might ask for your credit card number. For security reasons, that number is not stored in your cookie. Instead, it is stored on a secure server. When you decide to buy something, you enter a secure area with your browser. Your cookie then sends an ID to the server that identifies you, and the server then displays your credit card information, enabling you to buy online.

Delete old cookies: put on new cookies

6 After you order something from your electronic shopping cart—or after you decide to delete something from the shopping cart—a new cookie is put on your hard disk; this one does not include the goods you bought or decided to take out of your shopping cart.

Web server

7 Because some people don't like cookies to be placed on their hard disks, browsers give people control over whether to accept cookies, to not accept cookies, or to ask each time a cookie is being placed on the hard disk. Pictured is the message you get if you've asked to be told each time a cookie is placed on your hard disk.

The server www.amazon.com wishes to set a cookie that will be sent to any server in the domain .amazon.com The name and value of the cookie are: session-id-time=867052800

This cookie will persist until Mon Jun 23 03:55:00 1999

Do you wish to allow the cookie to be set?

[OK]   [Cancel]

How Web Bugs Track You

1 A *web bug* is a piece of HTML code placed on web pages or in email messages that can be used to silently gather information about people, track their Internet travels, and even allow the creator of the bug to secretly read a person's email. In this illustration we look at web bugs used in email. Email web bugs can be placed only in HTML email, so the person creating the bug must create an HTML-based email message.

WebMailApp

Add to email:
contents=
document.body.
in HTML;

2 In the HTML code for the message, the person inserts a small piece of JavaScript code that has the capability to read the entire contents of an email message.

Web bug hidden
in HTML message

Email

```
<img src="http://ad.doubleclick.net/
ad/pixel.mysite/NEW" width=1 height=1
border=0><IMG WIDTH=1 HEIGHT=1
border=0SRC="http://media.preferences.
com/ping? ML_SD=MySiteTE_MySite_1x1_
RunOfSite_Any&db_afcr=4B31-C2FB-
10E2C&event=reghome&group=register
&time=1999.10.27.20.5 6.37">
```

4 The person sends the email message. The recipient opens the message in an HTML-enabled email reader, such as Outlook. (Note: If the recipient doesn't have an email reader, the web bug won't work.)

3 The person also puts a web bug into the email message. The web bug is an HTML reference to a tiny graphic (the smallest possible on a computer screen is 1 pixel by 1 pixel) that is transparent so it can't be seen. This tiny graphic is also called a *clear gif* because *gif* refers to a common web graphics format. When someone reads her HTML message, her computer gets the graphic from a server—and that server then can get information about the person's computer.

5 The JavaScript runs and reads the entire email message. The person's email software contacts the remote server to get the clear gif. It does more than get the gif, though—it also sends identifying information about the computer, such as its IP address and the time the message is being read. It also sends the contents of the email message, as taken by the JavaScript. At this point, that doesn't really matter because the sender of the message knows the contents of the message because he created it. But the sender now knows identifying information about the recipient of the mail, such as his IP address.

Get graphic
IP 47.32.21.2 read
5:10 09/12/02

Web server

Get graphic
IP 47.32.21.2
read 5:10
10/13/02

Cookie

clear.gif

6 The server sends the gif but can also send a cookie along with it. It can match this cookie with the identifying information sent via the web bug and, with those pieces of information, track a person's use of the Internet. For example, if the piece of mail that set all this in motion was a piece of junk mail, the sender would be able to know who responded to the offer and track what she did in response—visiting a particular web page or buying specific products. That information could then be kept in a database.

7 If the recipient of the message sends the message along to someone else and sends a message along with it, the whole process starts all over. Now, however, when the web bug sends the contents of the email message, it contains the person's comments, so the mail has effectively been wiretapped. This can keep continuing so that every time a new person gets the message, the wiretap continues.

Forwarded Email

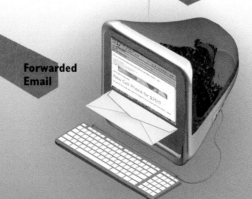

How Websites Track Your Activities

User

1 Websites track your activities in a number of ways, most frequently using special software to watch what you're doing. Frequently, a *sniffer* sits on the Internet and analyzes traffic to the site. This sniffer is a computer that runs software that examines all the TCP/IP packets coming into and out of the website.

Cookie

Packet sniffer

Web server

IP packet

2 To track traffic through a website, the sniffer must first identify who is coming to the site. The software can do this in a number of ways. If the site uses cookies, the software uses the cookie as a way to identify someone. It can also use the Open Profiling Standard (OPS) information stored on a person's web browser. OPS enables people to determine the type of information about them that can be made public. If no cookies or OPS information is present, the software uses the person's IP address.

User

3 The sniffer examines packets as they come into and leave the site. It notes any time an action is taken, such as when someone requests a web page, and whenever that action is completed, such as when the final packets from the page are delivered. It tracks who is making the requests, where they are coming from, where they are going, and similar information. This information is contained in the TCP/IP packets. The sniffer discards all the intermediate packets transmitted during each action. Only the beginning and ending packets are necessary—it discards all the intermediate packets because they provide no useful information.

End download   Begin FTP

Cookie data

4 Information is sent from the sniffer to a database, where all the information is stored.

Database

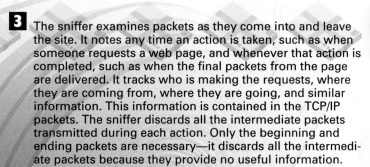

IP data

5 Many types of reports can be created out of the database, such as the average amount of time people spend on a site, the average number of pages they read per visit, the most popular pages on a site, sites people have just visited, sites they're going to visit, and other information.

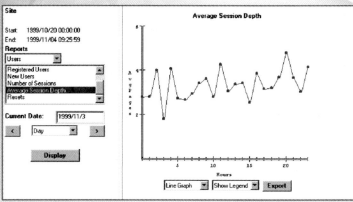

Server traffic analysis

How Websites Build Personal Profiles of You

1 Many websites ask or require you to fill out a form if you want to enter special areas or get special benefits, such as free email newsletters. Forms may only ask for basic information about you, such as email address and name, or they might ask for more complete information, including mailing address, age, occupation, salary, interests, and more. That information is put into a database.

2 The website matches your name with the cookie it puts on your hard disk. The site is able to build a more complete profile about you by using the cookie to watch which pages you visit. It puts this information into your record in the database, and so begins to build a more complete profile. Some sites have business relationships with advertising networks, which allows them to read information from multiple cookies on your hard disk. In this way, it can build a more complete profile about your web interests by gathering information from multiple sites, not just one. (For more information about cookies, refer to "How Cookies Work," earlier in this chapter.)

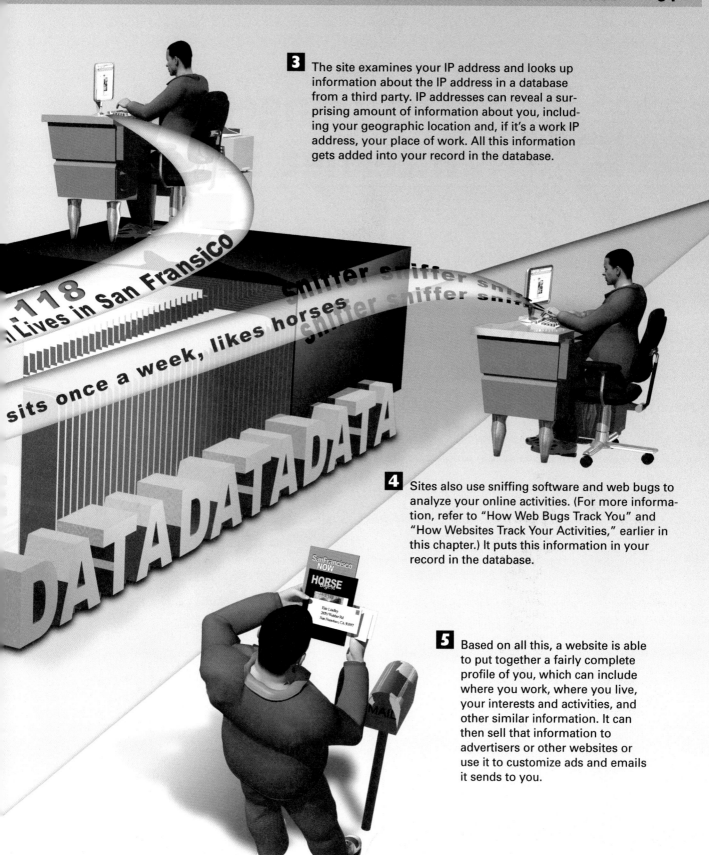

3 The site examines your IP address and looks up information about the IP address in a database from a third party. IP addresses can reveal a surprising amount of information about you, including your geographic location and, if it's a work IP address, your place of work. All this information gets added into your record in the database.

4 Sites also use sniffing software and web bugs to analyze your online activities. (For more information, refer to "How Web Bugs Track You" and "How Websites Track Your Activities," earlier in this chapter.) It puts this information in your record in the database.

5 Based on all this, a website is able to put together a fairly complete profile of you, which can include where you work, where you live, your interests and activities, and other similar information. It can then sell that information to advertisers or other websites or use it to customize ads and emails it sends to you.

CHAPTER

5

The Dangers of Internet Search

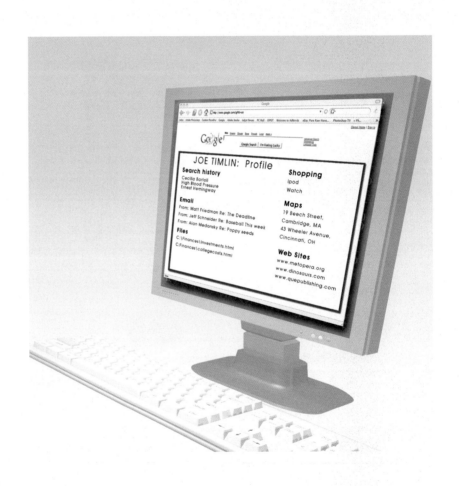

SEARCHING the Internet seems such an innocuous act. Type in your search terms, see the results, click to a few pages, and you're done. What in that process could possibly invade your privacy or endanger your security?

In the wrong hands, plenty. Consider every step of what you do during that process. First, you type in a search term(s) and send it to a search site. Some sites have ways of keeping track of your terms by keeping them in a database and matching them to cookies or logged-in users, so now, the site knows one of your interests.

Next, you view the results and click those that interest you. The site can track this as well, and now it has an even better sense of who you are and what your interests are.

One search term by itself might not mean much. But how about 10? 20? 500? By the time you enter 500 searches and click thousands of results, the site could very easily put together a pretty comprehensive profile about you. Do you frequently search for information about high blood pressure? Do you click sites that criticize the president? What kind of entertainment do you search for? In a very short time, your searches can build up a fairly definitive profile about you.

The problem has been magnified because search sites like Google and Yahoo! are no longer just search sites. They've become entire universes in which you live when you go onto the Internet. Google, for example, has an email service, a site for searching for bargains online, a mapping service, downloadable software to search your computer, an image search service, a blogging site and a way to search blogs, a toolbar that can record all the sites you visit on the Internet…the list could go on for quite some time. And that's just a start. Google and its competitors, such as Yahoo!, constantly roll out new services all the time. The more of these services you use, the more information can be gathered about you.

All this is not to say that the sites use this information for nefarious purposes, or even that they necessarily gather this information. For example, Google doesn't keep track of all your searches, unless you specifically tell it to do that. So, why do it? Because it lets you revisit that list and makes it easy to keep going back to searches you've already performed, or even search within those searches.

To date, search sites don't necessarily track everything they could about you. And they don't create personal profiles about you to sell to the highest bidder.

The point, though, is that the sites *could* gather this information if they wanted to. So, before you do another Internet search, at least be aware of what it might say about you.

To help you better understand what you reveal about yourself when you search the Internet, the following two illustrations explain how Google works and what Google could theoretically find out about you based on the services you use. Again, Google does not track your activities to identify you personally—but it's good for you to know what the search site could uncover about you, if it wished.

How Google Searches the Internet

Crawling the Web

1 When you search using Google, you're actually searching through an index of web pages. To gather the raw material for the index, Google's web-crawling robot, called Googlebot, sends a request to a web server for a web page. It then downloads the page. Googlebot runs on many computers simultaneously and constantly requests and receives web pages, making thousands of requests per second. In fact, Googlebot makes requests more slowly than its full capability because, if it operated full-throttle, it would overwhelm many web servers and the servers would not be able to deliver pages quickly enough to users.

Googlebot

Web page

Indexable text

2 When Googlebot downloads the page, it finds all the links on it and adds them to a queue, where each of those links will also be crawled and gathered. For each of those new pages it crawls, it gathers links, crawls them as well, and continues gathering pages in this manner. This technique, called *deep crawling*, lets Googlebot find every page on every site it encounters, and it also lets it find new sites to crawl.

3 To ensure that Google's index is as up-to-date as possible, Googlebot needs to crawl the same pages continually. Sites that frequently change, such as news sites, need to be crawled constantly throughout the day, while sites that rarely change might need to be crawled only once a month. Googlebot performs calculations on pages it crawls, determining how often they change; based on that, it decides how often to crawl that site. Pages that frequently change and so must be visited frequently are called *fresh crawls*.

Web server

LINK QUEUE

4 Googlebot extracts the full text of every page it visits and sends that information to the indexer.

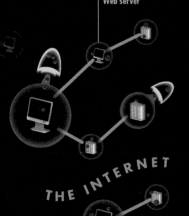

THE INTERNET

CRAWL SCHEDULE	
PAGE	**FREQUENCY**
Amazon Home	10 min.
CNN	5 min
History of Aardvarks	Monthly
New York Time Page 1	Daily

The Indexer

5 The indexer receives the text and stores it in its database. The index is sorted alphabetically by search term, and each index entry contains the list of pages on which the term appears. The indexer doesn't index commonly used words, called *stop words*, such as *the*, *on*, *is*, *or*, *of*, and *why*. It also doesn't store single digits, single letters, and some punctuation marks.

INDEXER

Aardvark

RESULTS

Performing the Search

6 When you visit Google, the page you see is delivered to you by a normal web server. When you type in your query, it's sent back to the web server. The web server then takes the query and forwards it to Google's index servers.

7 Google's index servers receive your request and match it to the most relevant documents. The method Google uses to match queries to documents is Google's "secret sauce," the key to its ability to return the most relevant results. Google uses hundreds of factors to decide which documents are most relevant, including how popular the page is (called Google's PageRank), where the search terms is found within the page, and (if you use multiple search terms) how close those terms are to one another in the page. It doesn't stop at examining the sheer popularity of a page, though. If a page is linked to from popular pages, that page has a higher rank than if it is linked to from unpopular pages.

8 When the index server determines the results of the search, it sends the query to Google's doc servers. They retrieve the stored documents, which include site names, links, and snippets that summarize each page.

9 The doc servers send the results back to the web server, which in turn sends the results to the person doing the search. The user browses through the results and can click a link to get to any page.

Aardvark Makes Public Debut at Neb. Zoo

Wed Sep 28 6:15 PM ET

OMAHA, Neb. - The Henry Doorly Zoo ha born in Omaha on Sept. 9, made its publi

AP Photo: A 2 1/2-week-old baby aardvark sniffs the lens of a television camera Wednesday, Sept 28.

The baby was born weighing only 3 pounds but grew to about 5 pounds within two and a half weeks. The animal comes out of an incubator for feedings, exercise and play each day from noon to 4 p.m., the zoo said. The animal eats a specially formulated liquid diet but will begin eating solid foods in about one month.

Add headlines to your personalized My Yahoo! page
(About My Yahoo! and RSS)

Odd News - AP

MY YAHOO!

» More News Feeds

The aardvark is a long eared, long nosed and hairless nocturnal animal that hails from throughout Africa.

Web masters who don't want their sites to be searchable via Google can instruct Google not to index their sites. To do it, they create a text file called `robots.txt` containing only these two lines and put it in the root directory:

```
User-agent: *
Disallow /
```

That tells all search engines, not just Googlebot, to stay away. They can also tell Googlebot or other search engines to not search their site by putting this HTML tag into the <head> section of the HTML for their web page:

```
<META name="ROBOTS" content="NOINDEX, NOFOLLOW" />
```

What Google Knows About You

1 This illustration shows many of the kinds of information Google can find out about you. Note that Google does not sell this information to other sites and does not use it to create personal profiles about you. But it gives you a sense of what the largest and most successful search engine in the world knows about you as you use it.

2 If you turn on the Google feature called Search History, Google will keep track of every search you perform when using the search engine and will keep that record on its servers. So, it will know the history of your Internet travels and your interests.

3 If you use Gmail, all your incoming and outgoing mail is stored on Gmail servers. In addition, Google computers examine all incoming mail and analyze their contents, to help it decide which ads to embed in the mail.

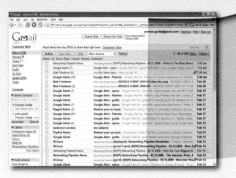

4 If you install Google Desktop, a piece of software that searches your PC in the same way Google searches the Web, Google could theoretically know all the contents of your hard disk.

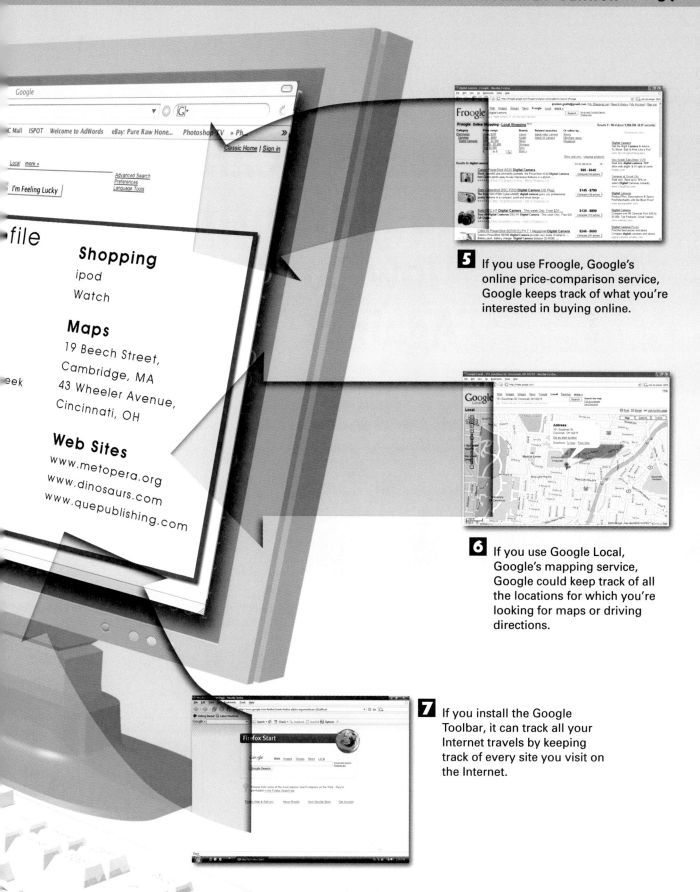

5 If you use Froogle, Google's online price-comparison service, Google keeps track of what you're interested in buying online.

6 If you use Google Local, Google's mapping service, Google could keep track of all the locations for which you're looking for maps or driving directions.

7 If you install the Google Toolbar, it can track all your Internet travels by keeping track of every site you visit on the Internet.

CHAPTER

6

How "Phishing" Attacks Can Steal Your Identity—and How to Protect Against Them

PERHAPS the most lucrative type of Internet attacks are so-called *phishing* attacks—attacks in which you're sent an email from what appears to be a bank; financial institution; or commerce site such as PayPal, Amazon, or eBay, but which is in fact forged. The term *phishing* was invented by hackers who were "fishing" to steal account information from AOL users. Hackers frequently replace the letter *f* with *ph*, and that's how the term was created. The emails warn that you must log on to your account, perhaps to verify information or perhaps to ensure your account does not expire. You're told to click a link to get to the site. When you get to the site, it looks like the real thing, but it's a spoof. Log on, and all your information is stolen.

Why has phishing become so widespread? Because it pays off, big-time. Fraudsters can collect massive amounts of revenue by draining bank accounts and participating in identity theft.

The research group Gartner, for example, claims that identity theft initiated by phishing cost U.S. banks and credit card issuers approximately $1.2 billion in 2003. And the numbers rise every year.

How widespread have the attacks become? They're nearly ubiquitous. You've probably gotten numerous phishing attempts in the past year, as has just about everyone you know.

Worse yet, people fall for them. A Gartner survey in April, 2004, found that nearly 11 million adults, or about 19% of those who have received phishing attacks, clicked a link in a phishing email. And nearly 1.8 million Americans, or 3% of those attacks, actually entered financial or personal information such as credit card numbers or billing addresses on the spoofed websites.

Phishers mostly aren't caught by the authorities, but every once in a while they are. And sometimes, victimized companies sue phishers. For example, Microsoft and Amazon filed a joint suit against Gold Disk Canada, Inc., and co-defendants Barry Head and his two sons. The suit claimed the defendants sent out millions of pieces of phishing email. The case has not yet been decided in court, as of this writing.

While phishing fraud is widespread, it's actually not that difficult to protect against. Spam filters catch most phishing attempts, and some email programs, such as Outlook, now include built-in antiphishing tools. Additionally, browsers include antiphishing tools that warn you when you're about to go to a website that is most likely a spoof. Additionally, there are browser add-ins you can install that fight spoofs and phishing.

But the best protection is the simplest: Never click a link in an email that claims to be from a financial institution, no matter how legitimate the email seems. Phishers are very clever forgers, so you can never be sure whether the email is real or not. Instead, call the financial institution yourself or use your browser to visit the site, apart from the email. That way, you'll be safe.

How Phishing Works

1 To hide the identity of the phisher, phishing attacks are not sent from the phisher's computer. Instead, a phisher uses or hires a person who controls an army of thousands of zombie PCs whose owners don't know they have been turned into zombies. The person controlling the zombie army tells them to send out the email composed by the phisher.

2 The email is sent to tens of thousands or more people; specific individuals are not targeted. The email list might be provided by the person who controls the zombie army, be bought from spammers, or have been accumulated by the phisher.

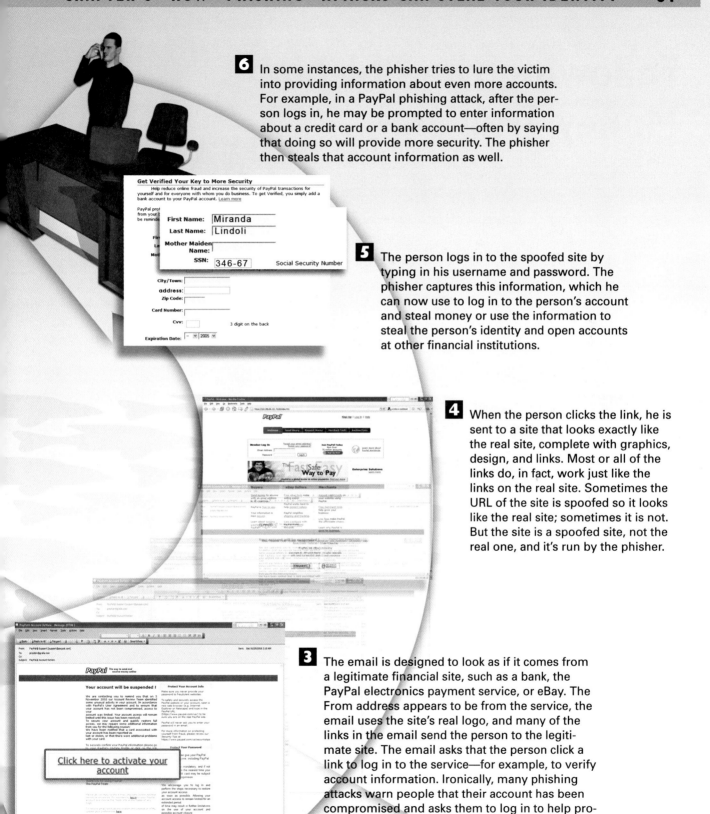

6 In some instances, the phisher tries to lure the victim into providing information about even more accounts. For example, in a PayPal phishing attack, after the person logs in, he may be prompted to enter information about a credit card or a bank account—often by saying that doing so will provide more security. The phisher then steals that account information as well.

5 The person logs in to the spoofed site by typing in his username and password. The phisher captures this information, which he can now use to log in to the person's account and steal money or use the information to steal the person's identity and open accounts at other financial institutions.

4 When the person clicks the link, he is sent to a site that looks exactly like the real site, complete with graphics, design, and links. Most or all of the links do, in fact, work just like the links on the real site. Sometimes the URL of the site is spoofed so it looks like the real site; sometimes it is not. But the site is a spoofed site, not the real one, and it's run by the phisher.

3 The email is designed to look as if it comes from a legitimate financial site, such as a bank, the PayPal electronics payment service, or eBay. The From address appears to be from the service, the email uses the site's real logo, and many of the links in the email send the person to the legitimate site. The email asks that the person click a link to log in to the service—for example, to verify account information. Ironically, many phishing attacks warn people that their account has been compromised and asks them to log in to help protect their account.

Following the Phishing Money Trail

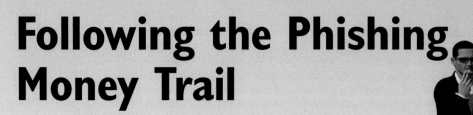

1 Phishers rarely work by themselves. They are usually part of a larger crime organization. The Russian mafia has been especially active in phishing, and is responsible for a significant number of phishing attacks.

2 The phisher pays someone who controls a fleet of zombies to send out the phishing attack from the zombie PCs.

3 The phisher compiles a large list of bank accounts, credit card information, PayPal logins, and similar information from the phishing attack.

Zombie PC

Zombie PC

Zombie PC

sending passwords and account information

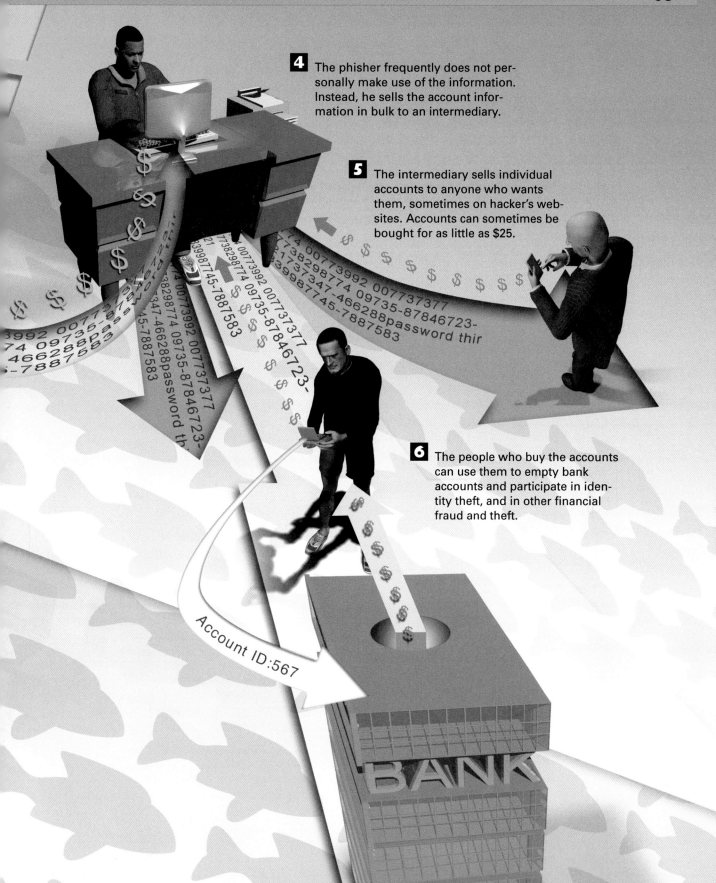

4 The phisher frequently does not personally make use of the information. Instead, he sells the account information in bulk to an intermediary.

5 The intermediary sells individual accounts to anyone who wants them, sometimes on hacker's websites. Accounts can sometimes be bought for as little as $25.

6 The people who buy the accounts can use them to empty bank accounts and participate in identity theft, and in other financial fraud and theft.

Account ID:567

BANK

How to Protect Against Phishing Attacks

1 Some email programs include built-in anti-phishing features. For example, the newest version of Microsoft Outlook will put what it believes are phishing attacks into a Junk Mail folder. It strips out all graphics from the email, and it displays the true link names, so that you can see the links are not real. In addition, the links don't work—if you click on them, nothing happens.

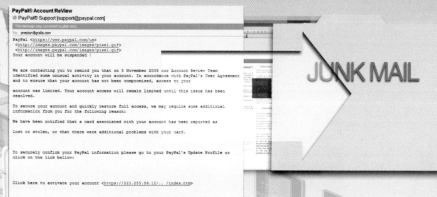

2 Some browsers, including Internet Explorer 7 and Firefox, include built-in anti-phishing tools. When you click a link in your email program, the browser will pop up a warning, telling you that you're being sent to a site which may not be a legitimate one.

DO NOT ALLOW

3 Free anti-phishing toolbars that work inside a browser can protect against phishing attacks as well. Some tool-bars, such as the Netcraft toolbar, will warn you before visiting a site that it is a phishing attempt.

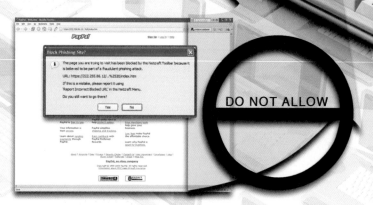

DO NOT ALLOW

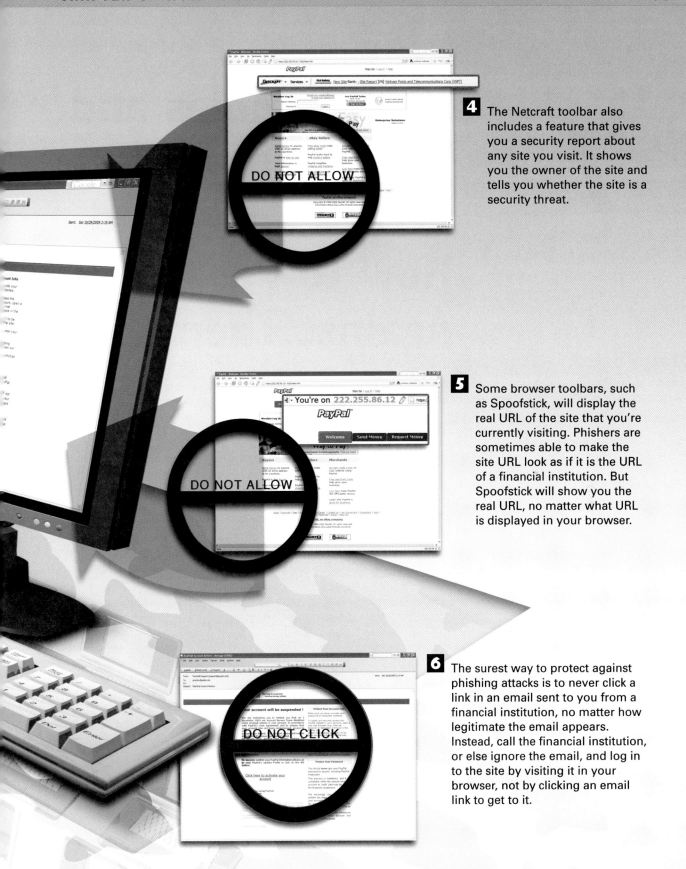

4 The Netcraft toolbar also includes a feature that gives you a security report about any site you visit. It shows you the owner of the site and tells you whether the site is a security threat.

5 Some browser toolbars, such as Spoofstick, will display the real URL of the site that you're currently visiting. Phishers are sometimes able to make the site URL look as if it is the URL of a financial institution. But Spoofstick will show you the real URL, no matter what URL is displayed in your browser.

6 The surest way to protect against phishing attacks is to never click a link in an email sent to you from a financial institution, no matter how legitimate the email appears. Instead, call the financial institution, or else ignore the email, and log in to the site by visiting it in your browser, not by clicking an email link to get to it.

CHAPTER

7

How Zombies and Trojan Horses Attack You—and How to Protect Against Them

TWO of the most insidious dangers on the Internet—zombies and Trojan horses—are so good at disguising themselves that you may never know they've infected your computer. Yet millions of computers are unknowingly infected with these pieces of malware.

Zombies and Trojan horses (generally just called *Trojans*) are related dangers, and some people lump them together. But, in fact, they are usually used for very different purposes.

A *zombie*, sometimes called a *bot* (short for *robot*), is a computer that has been taken over by someone else to do their bidding. The reason for the name is obvious—in noncomputer terms, a *zombie* is someone who has been dead and then resurrected to do the bidding of a zombie master. The zombie has to follow the commands of his master and has no will of his own.

A computer zombie operates in much the same way. First it is infected, often by opening an infected piece of email or perhaps by visiting a website that plants the infection on the PC. The PC typically shows no outward signs of infection. Most of the time, the computer acts normally. But a zombie master can issue commands, telling it to take actions. Usually, that action involves something illegal, such as sending out spam or phishing attacks or planting spyware on another PC.

A zombie on its own cannot do much damage. But zombies do not act on their own. Instead, they act in concert. People command huge networks of zombies that number in the tens of thousands—sometimes in the millions. Those who own the networks rent them out to send massive amounts of spam or phishing attacks, and these people are paid well for their work. Most of the time, the people whose PCs are infected do not even know their PCs are zombies and are sending out spam and phishing attacks.

A Trojan is slightly different from a zombie. A PC can be infected by a Trojan in the same way that a zombie can infect a PC—by email, by visiting an infected website, and so on. Often, a person might think he is downloading a useful piece of software, but in fact, a Trojan lurks within. This is where the Trojan gets its name, from the mythological Trojan Horse that appeared to be a gift to the people of Troy but in fact contained the Greek army, crouching in its belly and waiting until nightfall to come out and sack the city.

A PC infected by a Trojan often doesn't show signs of infection. But it allows someone to take over complete control of the PC, just as if she were sitting at the keyboard. So, someone can steal information and files and use the Trojan to launch attacks on other PCs and websites. Trojans can also automatically download spyware to the infected PC or steal personal information and send it in an email to a hacker.

How Zombies and Bot Networks Work

1 A *zombie*, also called a *bot*, is a computer that can be taken over and controlled by someone remotely. Typically, a single person controls a zombie network of many thousands of infected computers. In one instance, a single zombie network was made up of more than 1.5 million PCs. An unsuspecting PC can become infected in many ways, including via email, via file-sharing networks, or directly over a network if network file sharing has been turned on with no security precautions.

The zombie software is installed on the PC. It turns off the PC's antivirus software and blocks access to security sites, so the owner of the PC will not know his computer is infected.

2 The zombie connects to an Internet Relay Chat (IRC) channel and lets it be known that it is available to carry out the commands of the owner of the zombie network.

3 The owner of the zombie network sends a command over the IRC channel to tell all the PCs to perform a certain command—for example, to send spam or phishing attacks.

4 The zombies obey the command, and each zombie sends thousands of spams or phishing attacks. A single zombie network can send many hundreds of thousands of spams and phishing attacks.

5 Because the spam and phishing attacks are carried out by the zombies, and not the owner of the zombie network, the owner can't be traced to the attacks.

6 After the spam and phishing attacks have been sent, the owner of the zombie network tells the zombies to go back to sleep. At any point, he can reawaken them to do his bidding.

Note:
Those who run zombie networks look to infect computers that have broadband cable and DSL connections because they can send many more messages per minute than computers connected to the Internet via dial-up. Broadband-connected PCs are also online all the time, while dial-up PCs are available only sporadically when they have dialed in to their ISPs.

How Trojan Horses Work

I *Trojan horses* (more commonly called *Trojans*) are malware that lets an intruder take control of your PC or steal information from you without your knowledge. Trojans are commonly spread to your PC via email when you open an attachment such as a picture. However, they can also infect PCs in many other ways, such as when you visit an infected website.

2 One type of Trojan steals passwords, credit card information, and other data; puts that information into a text file; and emails it to an intruder.

3 Another type of Trojan, called a *downloader*, downloads spyware and other kinds of malware to your PC without your knowledge.

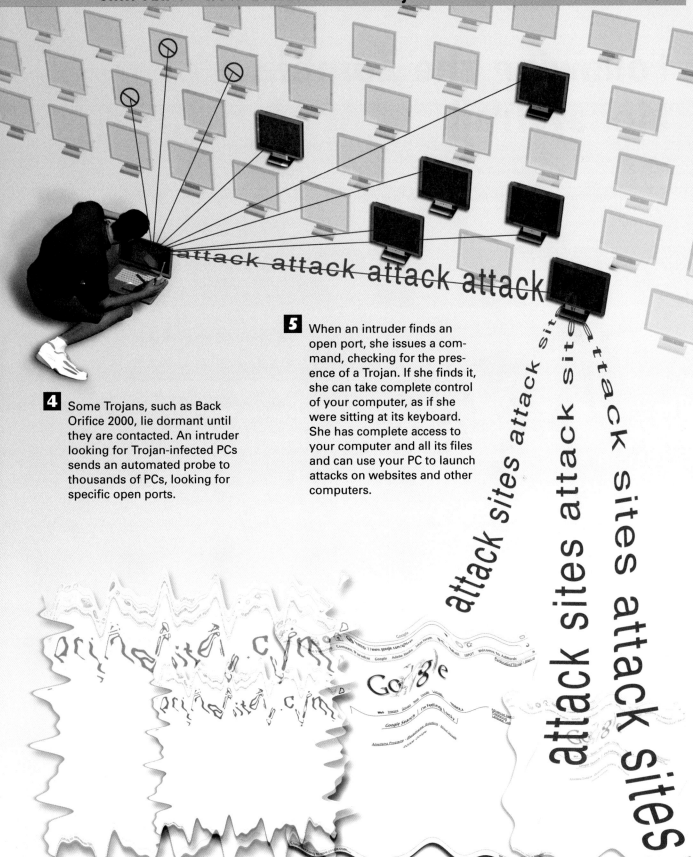

4 Some Trojans, such as Back Orifice 2000, lie dormant until they are contacted. An intruder looking for Trojan-infected PCs sends an automated probe to thousands of PCs, looking for specific open ports.

5 When an intruder finds an open port, she issues a command, checking for the presence of a Trojan. If she finds it, she can take complete control of your computer, as if she were sitting at its keyboard. She has complete access to your computer and all its files and can use your PC to launch attacks on websites and other computers.

Following the Zombie Money Trail

1 People who run zombie networks typically don't run them merely to do harm—they run them as money-making propositions. Spammers, those who launch phishing attacks, and purveyors of spyware often hire out zombie networks.

2 The amount of money paid to those who run zombie networks varies according to how many zombies the person controls and the total aggregated bandwidth of the network.

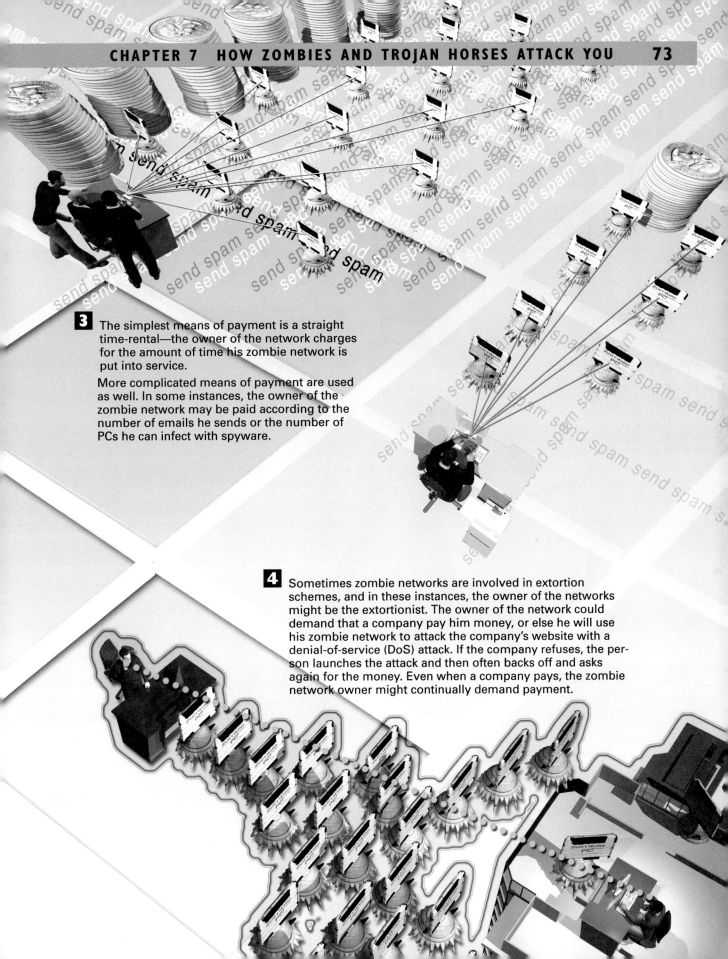

3 The simplest means of payment is a straight time-rental—the owner of the network charges for the amount of time his zombie network is put into service.

More complicated means of payment are used as well. In some instances, the owner of the zombie network may be paid according to the number of emails he sends or the number of PCs he can infect with spyware.

4 Sometimes zombie networks are involved in extortion schemes, and in these instances, the owner of the networks might be the extortionist. The owner of the network could demand that a company pay him money, or else he will use his zombie network to attack the company's website with a denial-of-service (DoS) attack. If the company refuses, the person launches the attack and then often backs off and asks again for the money. Even when a company pays, the zombie network owner might continually demand payment.

How Zombie and Trojan Protection Works

I The first line of defense against Trojans and zombies is running antivirus software on a PC and keeping the virus definitions up-to-date. Antivirus software protects against many, but not all, zombies and Trojans by detecting certain actions or tell-tale signatures the malware leaves behind. Antispyware software can also protect PCs against Trojans and zombies, and it can protect PCs against spyware that Trojans or zombies try to install on the PC. You should install more than one anti-spyware program on a PC because not all anti-spyware programs detect all kinds of spyware.

Inbound firewall

2 An inbound-blocking firewall is an especially powerful tool against Trojans and zombies. The firewall closes down incoming ports so Trojans and zombies can't crawl through them and infect a PC. Network Address Translation (NAT), which is used by home and office network routers, also provides protection. For more information about NAT, see "How Network Address Translation Protects Home Networks" in Chapter 17, "How Personal Firewalls and Proxy Servers Protect You." Some routers use another line of defense called *stateful inspection*.

3 Another line of defense is an outbound-blocking firewall. An outbound-blocking firewall stops any program from making a connection from a PC to the Internet, unless the PC owner explicitly says the connection can be made. In this way, even if a PC is infected, zombies or Trojans will not be able to work because they will be blocked from making a connection out to the Internet.

Outbound firewall

31338 1338

4 One more line of defense is to shut down common ports used by Trojans and zombies. This is only partially useful, though, because they can always switch the ports they use.

Trojans

CHAPTER

8

The Security Dangers in Browsers

ONE of the greatest security threats on the Internet attacks a piece of software you most likely use more than any other—your web browser, such as Internet Explorer or Firefox.

Increasingly, web browsers have become a primary way that hackers invade people's PCs. Hackers use browsers as a way to get into people's systems or install malware such as spyware or Trojans when someone visits a website that contains this type of attack.

Browser-based attacks have become more common over the last several years for a number of reasons. One is that computers have become more secure over time. Today it is standard for people to run antivirus software, and sometimes antispyware as well. In addition, people run firewalls that protect them from attacks. Hackers have been looking for new methods of attack—and browser-based attacks are a convenient one.

A second reason is how ubiquitous web use has become. Virtually anyone with a computer connects to the Internet and browses the Web, so there is a huge potential number of readymade targets.

Internet Explorer is the target of far more attacks than any other browser—in fact, far more than all other browsers combined. It's a primary target due to the sheer ubiquity of the browser, which is used by the vast majority of people who use the Internet. But it's also a target because it has more security holes than other browsers, such as the use of a technology called ActiveX, which is used to download and run software inside a browser.

Additionally, unlike other browsers, Internet Explorer is directly tied into Windows. If you can successfully attack Internet Explorer, you can use it to attack Windows and an entire computer. Other browsers, such as Firefox, are not tied directly to the operating system.

There are many ways to attack a computer via the browser. In one common exploit, malware such as spyware or a Trojan is downloaded via the browser without a user's knowledge. In a similar attack, the user agrees to download a piece of malware, thinking that it is a useful piece of software.

One thing all browser-based attacks have in common is that they start with a visit to a website. In some cases, the website is run by a hacker who uses the website to launch attacks. In other instances, a hacker has been able to invade a website and plant malicious software that attacks browsers that visit the site.

How Hackers Exploit Browsers

1 Browser attacks target specific browsers, such as Internet Explorer or Firefox. Internet Explorer is the target of most attacks because it is the most common browser and because it tends to have more security holes than other browsers.

2 One of the most common kinds of attacks is called a *buffer overflow attack*. A *buffer* is an area of memory allocated for a certain function. In a buffer overflow attack, the hacker writes code that downloads from a website and floods a specific area of memory with so much data that it overflows into a nearby area of memory.

3 The data that flows into the nearby area of memory contains malicious code, and that code can bypass normal security functions because of a flaw in the browser.

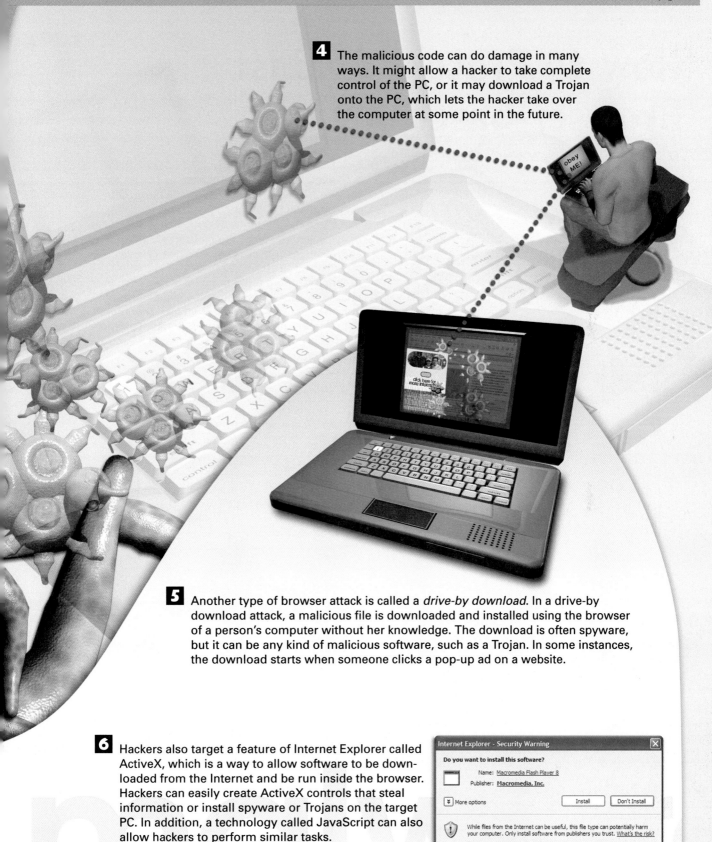

4 The malicious code can do damage in many ways. It might allow a hacker to take complete control of the PC, or it may download a Trojan onto the PC, which lets the hacker take over the computer at some point in the future.

5 Another type of browser attack is called a *drive-by download*. In a drive-by download attack, a malicious file is downloaded and installed using the browser of a person's computer without her knowledge. The download is often spyware, but it can be any kind of malicious software, such as a Trojan. In some instances, the download starts when someone clicks a pop-up ad on a website.

6 Hackers also target a feature of Internet Explorer called ActiveX, which is a way to allow software to be downloaded from the Internet and be run inside the browser. Hackers can easily create ActiveX controls that steal information or install spyware or Trojans on the target PC. In addition, a technology called JavaScript can also allow hackers to perform similar tasks.

How to Protect Against Browser-based Attacks

1 One simple way to avoid browser-based attacks is to avoid visiting sites that may be run by hackers or others who might want to do harm. Often, phishing attacks send people to sites that contain attacks. A *phishing attack* is one in which an email is sent appearing to be from a legitimate site, asking you to click a link. When you click the link, you're sent to a phony site that looks like the real thing but that might in fact host an attack. So, protecting yourself against phishing attacks is one way to prevent attacks. (For more details about phishing, refer to Chapter 6, "How Phishing Attacks Can Steal Your Identity—and How to Protect Against Them.")

2 Because Internet Explorer is subject to so many attacks, switching to another, safer browser such as Firefox cuts down on the possibility of being victimized.

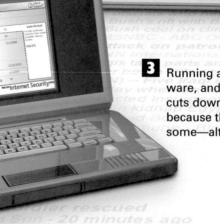

3 Running antivirus and anti-spyware software, and keeping them updated, also cuts down on the number of attacks because these programs can stop some—although not all—of the attacks.

4 Some browser-based attacks are launched when you visit a site with pop-up ads and you click the ad, which then downloads malware to your PC without your knowledge. So, never clicking pop-up ads can cut down on browser-based attacks.

5 Disabling several settings in Internet Explorer helps stop browser attacks. For example, disabling ActiveX controls and JavaScript and setting higher overall security settings for your computer can thwart many attacks.

C H A P T E R

9

How Worms and Viruses Do Their Damage—and How to Protect Against Them

IF you use the Internet, at one time or another your computer will most likely be attacked by a virus or worm. These pieces of malware are practically ubiquitous, and there's no escaping them.

The term *virus* is a somewhat generic term applied to a wide variety of programs. Viruses are written for specific kinds of computers, such as PCs or Macintoshes, because the files they infect run on only one kind of computer or operating system.

Viruses generally are malicious programs that invade your computer. They can cause many kinds of damage, such as deleting data files, erasing programs, or destroying everything they find on your hard disk. Not every virus causes damage; some simply flash annoying messages.

Although you can get a virus from the Internet by downloading files to your computer, the Internet is not the only place where viruses can be picked up. If you've received files via email or on your company's internal network, you can get viruses that way as well.

Traditional viruses attach themselves to programs or data files; infect your computer; replicate themselves on your hard disk; and then damage your data, hard disk, or files. Viruses usually attack four parts of your computer: its executable program files, its file directory system that tracks the locations of all your computer's files (and without which your computer won't work), its boot and system areas that are needed to start your computer, and its data files. At one time it was believed that data files could not be infected by viruses, but that is not the case—viruses have been written that infect data files, too. For example, some viruses attach themselves to Microsoft Word macros and are launched whenever a particular macro is run.

Worms are programs designed to infect networks such as the Internet, and they're another common danger. They travel from networked computer to networked computer and replicate themselves along the way. The most infamous worm of all was released on November 2, 1988. The worm copied itself to many Internet host computers and eventually brought the Internet to its knees.

The best way to protect your computer against viruses is to use antivirus software. There are several kinds of antivirus software from which to choose. A *scanner* checks to see whether your computer has any files that have been infected, whereas an *eradication program* wipes the virus from your hard disk. Sometimes eradication programs can kill the virus without having to delete the infected program or data file, but other times those infected files must be deleted. Antivirus software commonly includes both a scanner and an eradication component.

How Viruses Work

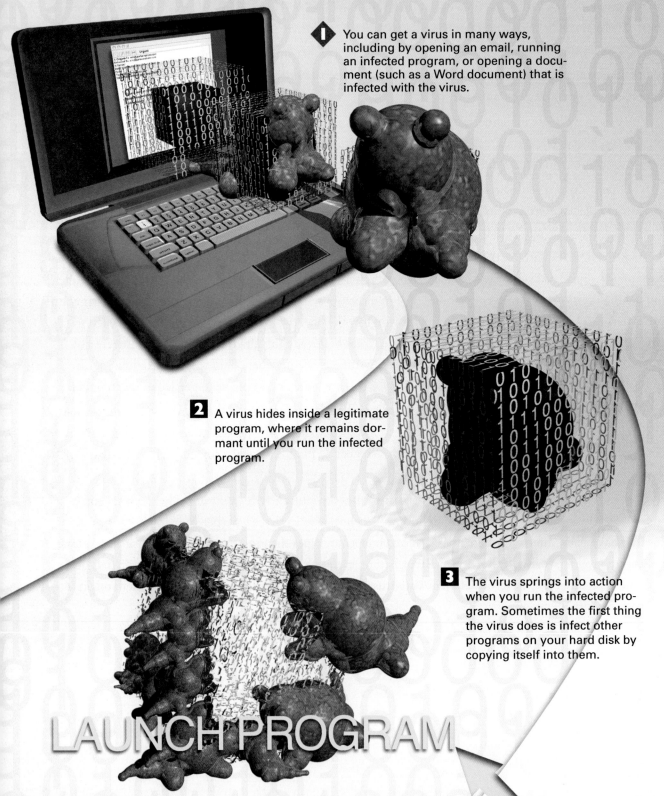

1 You can get a virus in many ways, including by opening an email, running an infected program, or opening a document (such as a Word document) that is infected with the virus.

2 A virus hides inside a legitimate program, where it remains dormant until you run the infected program.

3 The virus springs into action when you run the infected program. Sometimes the first thing the virus does is infect other programs on your hard disk by copying itself into them.

LAUNCH PROGRAM

4 Some viruses place messages called *virus markers* (*v-markers*) inside programs that they infect, and these messages help manage the viruses' activities. Each virus has a specific v-marker associated with it. If a virus encounters one of these markers in another program, it knows that the program is already infected so it doesn't replicate itself there. When a virus cannot find more unmarked files on a computer, that signals to the virus that there are no more files to be infected. At this point, the virus might begin to damage the computer and its data.

5 Viruses can corrupt program or data files so that they work oddly or not at all, or cause damage when they do run. They can destroy all the files on your computer, change the system files your computer needs when it is turned on, and cause other types of damage.

How Worms Work

① A *worm* is a generic term for a program that spreads over a network, such as the Internet or a corporate local area network. Worms spread and do damage in many ways. This illustration shows how a worm that spreads via email works.

2 The worm arrives in people's email inboxes—disguised as a normal email message—with a Microsoft Word file as an attachment. The subject line of the email reads, "important message from," followed by a person's name; that name might be the name of a friend, an acquaintance, or a co-worker of the person receiving the message. The body of the email reads, "Here is that document you asked for…don't show anyone else."

3 When the recipient opens the attached Word file, the worm springs to work. If the file isn't opened, the worm does no damage. The attached file appears to be a normal Word file that contains a list of pornographic sites. However, when the file is opened, a *macro* runs without the user knowing it. A macro is a set of automated commands, much like a program.

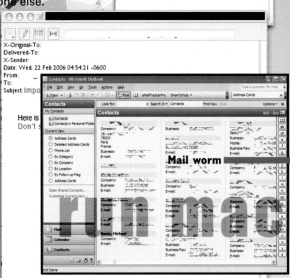

4 The macro checks to see whether the person has Outlook on his computer (Outlook is a Microsoft email program). If Outlook isn't present, the macro can't do any damage. (Note: Worms can spread via other email programs, but because Outlook is so popular, many are written specifically for Outlook.) If Outlook is present, the worm looks at the first 50 names in Outlook's address book and then makes a copy of itself and mails itself to all 50 of those names without the person knowing this is happening. The email sent to each of those people looks exactly like the email the first person received: The subject line of the email reads, "important message from," followed by the name of the previous person who had been infected by the Melissa worm. It appears that the infected person is sending a personal message.

Send worm

Send worm

Send worm

Send worm

Send worm

Send worm

Send worm

Send worm

Send worm

5 Each of these 50 people, in turn, receive the infected email and attached Word document. When each one opens the attached file, the worm does the same thing to her—it automatically sends itself to 50 more people.

6 The volume of email being sent quickly becomes so great that Internet and corporate email servers are unable to keep up with the demand for sending and receiving messages, and many of them crash. Many Internet and corporate mail servers are overwhelmed by the huge demand for sending and receiving email, so normal mail—not just worm-related mail—can't be sent or received. The problem is finally resolved when antivirus software is updated to include features that can detect and kill the worm.

How Antivirus Software Works

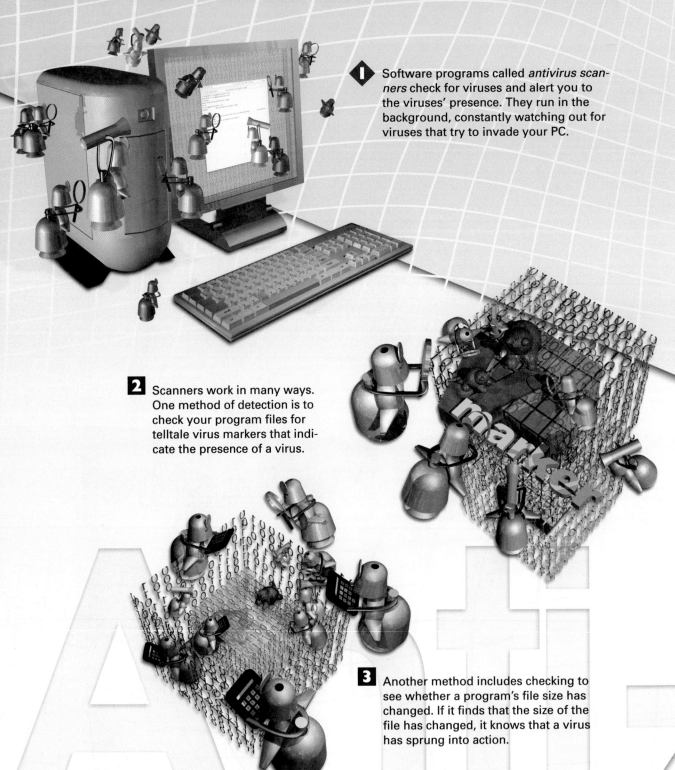

1 Software programs called *antivirus scanners* check for viruses and alert you to the viruses' presence. They run in the background, constantly watching out for viruses that try to invade your PC.

2 Scanners work in many ways. One method of detection is to check your program files for telltale virus markers that indicate the presence of a virus.

3 Another method includes checking to see whether a program's file size has changed. If it finds that the size of the file has changed, it knows that a virus has sprung into action.

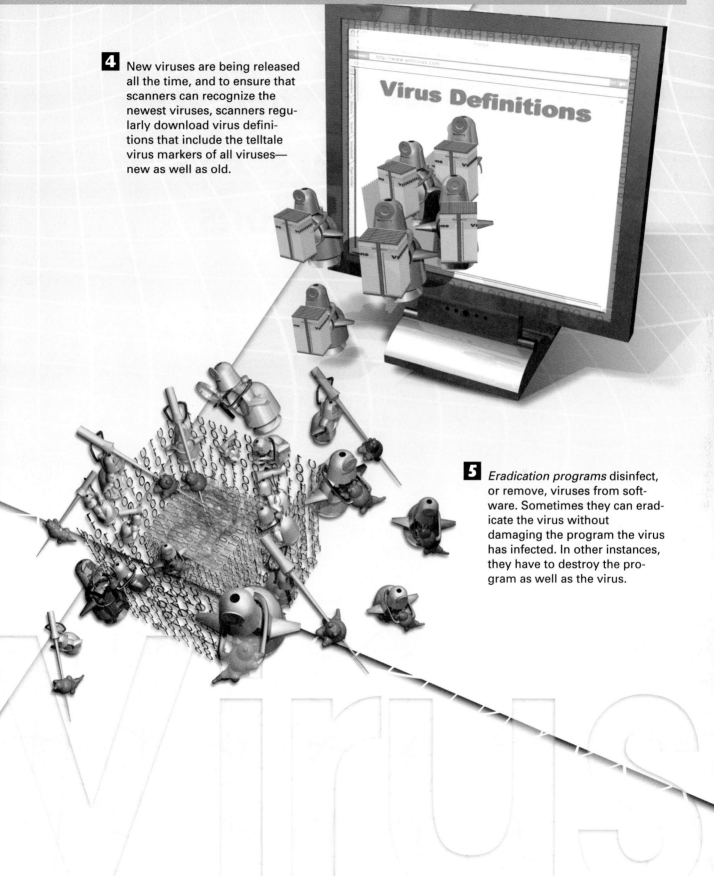

4 New viruses are being released all the time, and to ensure that scanners can recognize the newest viruses, scanners regularly download virus definitions that include the telltale virus markers of all viruses—new as well as old.

5 *Eradication programs* disinfect, or remove, viruses from software. Sometimes they can eradicate the virus without damaging the program the virus has infected. In other instances, they have to destroy the program as well as the virus.

Virus Definitions

C H A P T E R

10

Wi-Fi Security Dangers and Protections

MORE and more, when people connect to the Internet, they're not connecting via wires. Instead, they're connecting wirelessly. A transceiver in their laptop or desktop computer communicates with a wireless device called an *access point* or *router*, which gives them access to the Internet.

Home networks are mainly wireless rather than wired. In fact, it's difficult these days to even find a router for your home that is wired rather than wireless. Wireless home routers commonly include ports for connecting PCs with wires as well as wirelessly, so there's no need to buy a wired-only router.

In addition to connecting at home, more and more corporations are setting up wireless networks. They do it because it's much cheaper to set up a wireless network than a wired one, and it's more convenient for users because they can connect to the Internet and corporate network anywhere in the building, not just when they're next to an Ethernet port.

People also connect to the Internet when they travel, by using hotspots at cafes, airports, and other locations.

This wireless technology is called *Wi-Fi*. It is not a single standard. It refers to an entire family of standards based on the 802.11 networking protocol. There are multiple 802.11 standards: the now little-used 802.11a; 802.11b; the higher-speed 802.11g; and the highest-speed (as of this writing) 802.11n. As this book went to press, the final 802.11n standard had not been formally adopted, but some "pre-n" Wi-Fi equipment was being sold.

With all of Wi-Fi's convenience comes dangers. The same technology that lets you browse the Web from your back porch can let invaders hop onto your network from outside your house or apartment.

By its very nature, Wi-Fi is an open technology. A wireless router broadcasts its presence to any device with a Wi-Fi adapter within its range, and if the router is unprotected, anyone who wants to can connect to it and use the network. That makes it easy for intruders to get in.

A common kind of intruder is called a *war driver*. This person drives through areas of cities and suburbs known for having Wi-Fi networks and searches for unprotected networks he can break in to. He uses software that makes it easy to find unprotected networks. Some war drivers use high-power antennas so they can find as many networks as possible. But, in fact, they don't even need this kind of equipment to get into networks. Software built directly in to Windows XP, for example, lets anyone easily find and connect to an unprotected network.

When war drivers target a business network, they may be looking for proprietary business information or be looking to do malicious damage. When they target a home network, they might look for personal information, such as credit card numbers, or be looking to damage computers.

But Wi-Fi intruders can cause other problems—and these may be even more serious than stealing information or damaging computers. They can use the network for illegal activities, and if those activities are uncovered, it will look as if the owner of the network is guilty because the war driver will be long gone.

How Wi-Fi Works

1 A key component of a Wi-Fi network is an *access point (AP)* or a router. The access point consists of a radio transmitter and receiver as well as an interface to a wired network, such as an Ethernet network, or directly to the Internet. At home, for example, the access point connects to a cable modem or DSL modem to provide Internet access and allows PCs on the network to access the Internet. The access point serves as a base station and a bridge/router between the wireless network and a larger Ethernet network or the Internet.

server

Access point

Ethernet

Probe Request Frame

2 For a computer to become part of the network, it must be equipped with a Wi-Fi adapter so it can communicate with the access point. Each computer that's part of the network usually is referred to as a *station*. Many stations can communicate with a single access point. An access point and all the stations communicating with it are collectively referred to as a *basic service set (BSS)*.

4 Stations communicate with the access point using a method called *Carrier Sense Multiple Access with Collision Avoidance (CSMA/CA)*. It checks to see whether other stations are communicating with the access point; if they are, it waits a random amount of time before transmitting information. Waiting a random amount of time ensures that the reattempts at transmission don't continuously collide with one another.

Can I talk? (RTS)

Go ahead. (CTS)

Here's the data.

Got it! (ACK)

3 When a station is first turned on or enters an area near the access point, it scans the area to look for an access point by sending out packets of information called *probe request frames* and waiting to see whether there is an answering probe response from a nearby access point. If the station finds more than one access point, it chooses one based on signal strength and error rates.

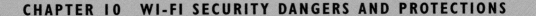

Ethernet

Access point

Access point

7 The station sends the packet to the access point. After the packet is received, the access point sends an ACK (acknowledgment) packet confirming that the data was received. If an ACK packet isn't sent, the station resends the data until it receives an ACK packet.

8 A Wi-Fi network can have many access points and many stations, and stations can move from access point to access point. Taken together, all the access points and stations are called an *extended service set (ESS)*.

5 Before a station transmits information or a request, it sends a short packet of information called a *request to send (RTS)*, which includes information about the request or data to come, such as its source, its destination, and how long the transmission will take.

6 If the access point is free, it responds with a short packet of information called a *clear to send (CTS)*, telling the station that the access point is ready to receive information or requests.

9 The Wi-Fi standard also allows stations to communicate directly with one another, without a connection to an access point, a network, or the Internet. When stations communicate directly with one another, it's called a *peer-to-peer network* or an *ad hoc network*. This enables the stations to do things such as share files and communicate directly with one another.

Extended service set

How Hackers Invade Wi-Fi Networks

1 A hacker first looks for a network he wants to break in to. He can do this by *war driving*—driving through a city or suburb using special equipment to find Wi-Fi networks. (For details, see the illustration later in this chapter, "How War Drivers Invade Your Network.") He can also do it by walking through a building or an office park, carrying a handheld device that finds wireless networks. Or he may just park his car in the parking lot of a targeted large business because many businesses these days have wireless networks.

2 Sometimes, the hacker needs to do nothing more than turn on his PC and make an automatic connection to the wireless network using Windows XP. Windows XP automatically finds and connects to nearby wireless networks. Many businesses don't bother to put protections on their Wi-Fi networks, so he might simply be able to log in.

3 Some networks are protected by Wi-Fi encryption technologies. (See the illustration later in this chapter, "How Wi-Fi Encryption Works," for details.) But some forms of encryption, such as the Wireless Encryption Protocol (WEP) are weak and can be cracked. By capturing many wireless packets and analyzing them, the hacker might be able to crack the encryption scheme by finding the encryption key. After he does that, he can get onto the network, even if it's protected by encryption.

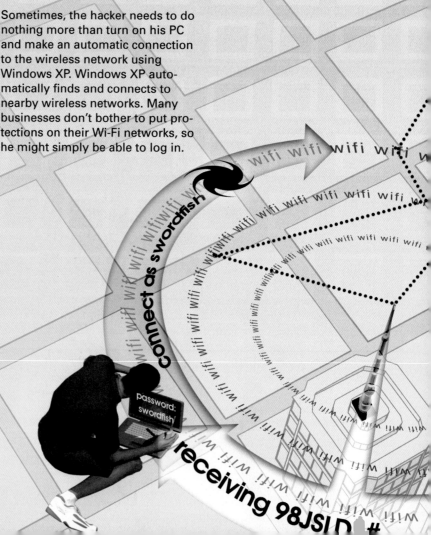

4 After he's on the network, he can access the person's or corporation's files, just as if he were an authorized network user. He can steal personal and corporate information, logons, and similar information; damage the network and computers; and do other malicious harm.

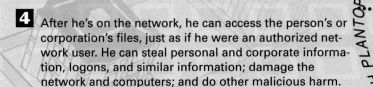

account: 8729-
password: mach...
bank statement:
July: $2,789.00
August: $9,638.00
Withdrawal Amount
$5,463.89

5 In some instances, the hacker doesn't actually break in to the network. Instead, he uses a piece of software called a *sniffer* to capture all the data going into and out of the network. In this way, he can capture logons and personal and financial information but does not actually have to be on the network itself, so he is less likely to be caught.

6 The hacker might not be after corporate information, but instead data the business has about its customers. For example, a hacker may break into the wireless network of a retail store and steal credit card information about its customers. For example, in August 2004, three men were found guilty of hacking into the wireless network of a Lowe's store in suburban Detroit. They had hacked in from a car in the Lowe's parking lot.

7 A hacker may use the network as a launching point for criminal activity—and it can then look like someone on the network was guilty, not the hacker. For example, in September 2004, a Los Angeles man pleaded guilty to using other people's Wi-Fi connections to send spam and pornography. And in 2003, a Toronto man was arrested for using someone's home Wi-Fi network to download child pornography. He was parked in a car outside the person's home at the time.

How Hotspots Work

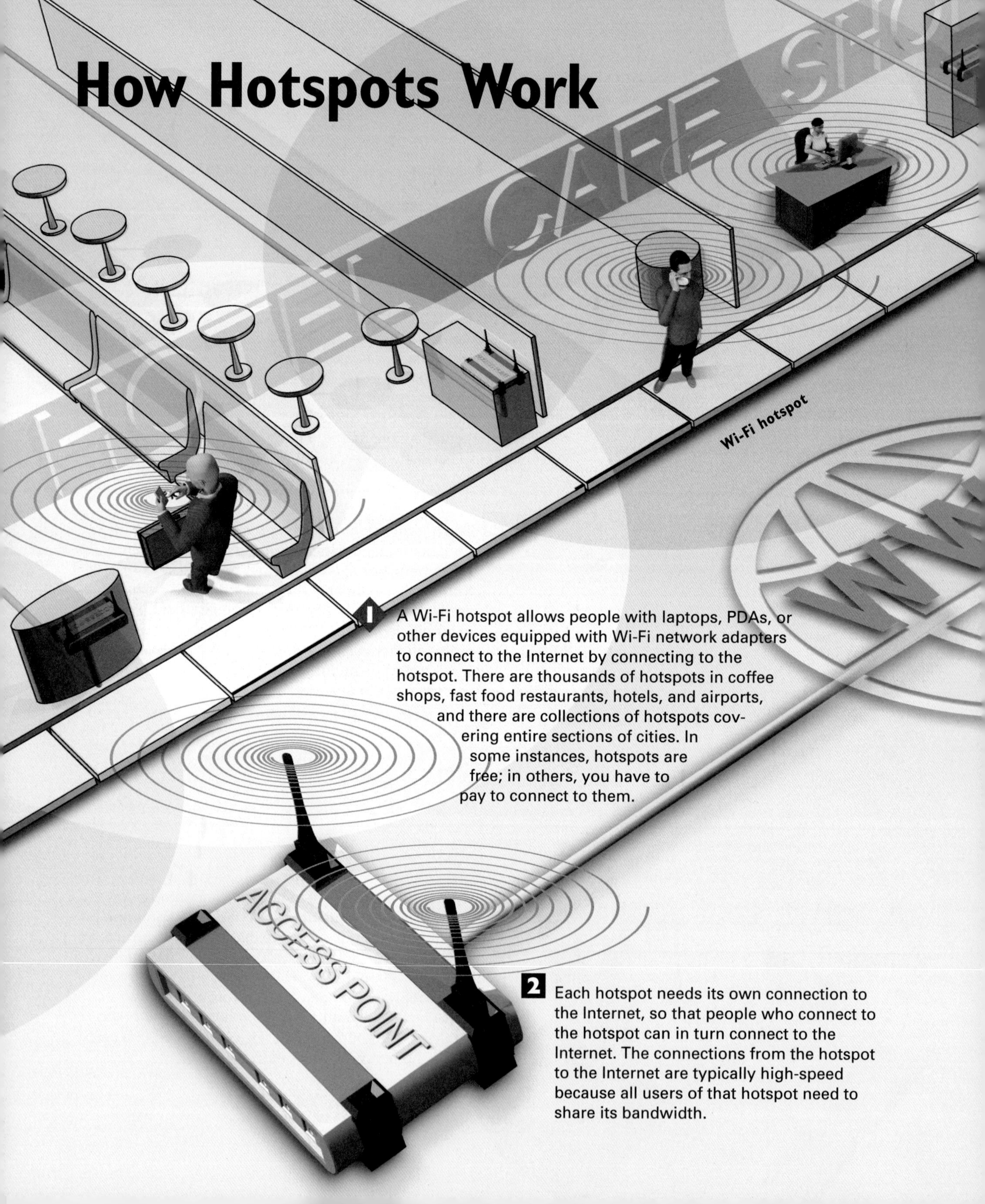

Wi-Fi hotspot

1 A Wi-Fi hotspot allows people with laptops, PDAs, or other devices equipped with Wi-Fi network adapters to connect to the Internet by connecting to the hotspot. There are thousands of hotspots in coffee shops, fast food restaurants, hotels, and airports, and there are collections of hotspots covering entire sections of cities. In some instances, hotspots are free; in others, you have to pay to connect to them.

ACCESS POINT

2 Each hotspot needs its own connection to the Internet, so that people who connect to the hotspot can in turn connect to the Internet. The connections from the hotspot to the Internet are typically high-speed because all users of that hotspot need to share its bandwidth.

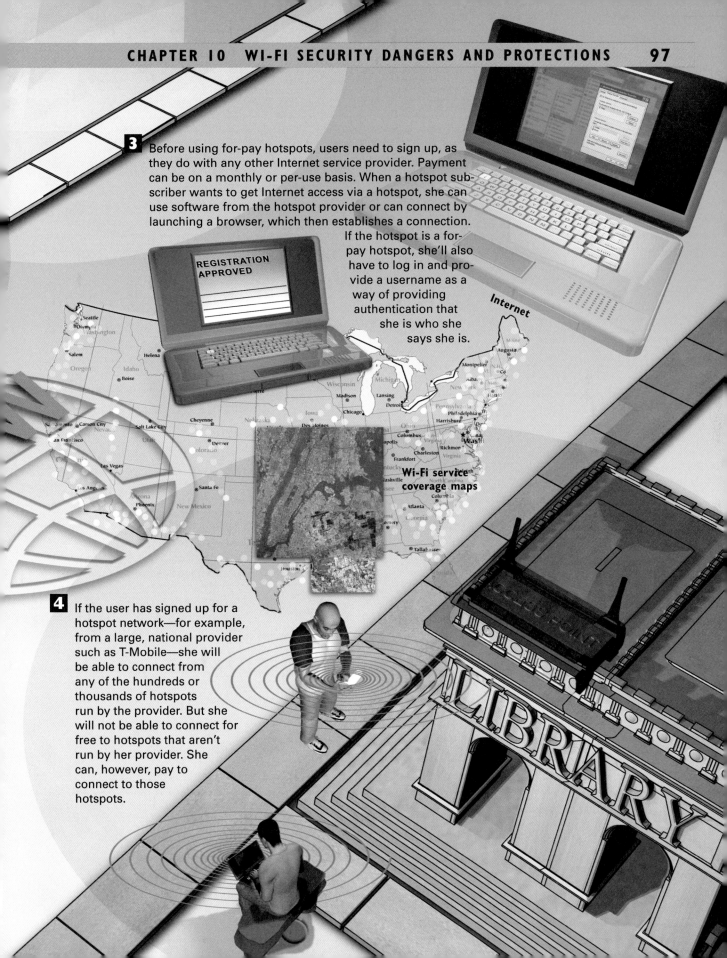

3 Before using for-pay hotspots, users need to sign up, as they do with any other Internet service provider. Payment can be on a monthly or per-use basis. When a hotspot subscriber wants to get Internet access via a hotspot, she can use software from the hotspot provider or can connect by launching a browser, which then establishes a connection. If the hotspot is a for-pay hotspot, she'll also have to log in and provide a username as a way of providing authentication that she is who she says she is.

REGISTRATION APPROVED

Internet

Wi-Fi service coverage maps

4 If the user has signed up for a hotspot network—for example, from a large, national provider such as T-Mobile—she will be able to connect from any of the hundreds or thousands of hotspots run by the provider. But she will not be able to connect for free to hotspots that aren't run by her provider. She can, however, pay to connect to those hotspots.

LIBRARY

How Hotspot Hacking Works

1 When you are on a hotspot, such as at a cafe or in an airport, you are connected to a network and are therefore vulnerable to other people who are on the same hotspot because you are all on the same network. In some instances—if you've turned on file sharing on your laptop, for example—they may be able to connect to your PC without your knowledge and steal the contents of your hard disk or delete files.

HACKED
budget.xls
personal expences $284.98
car expences: $657.45
food: $728.78............3/8.07
clothing: 276.84

2 A hacker at a hotspot can plant spyware and Trojans on other people's PCs. He might plant software that will turn the PC into a *zombie* or *bot*, allowing the hacker to later take control of the computer and use it to send spam or attack websites.

sniffing for passwords

3 Someone at a hotspot can use a sniffer to capture the packets of everyone else on the hotspot. Doing that, he can capture usernames, passwords, and credit card information and read personal emails. He could then use the credit cards to order goods and services or steal people's identities.

4 In some cases, no technology is needed to steal personal information. A hacker can surreptitiously stand behind someone when she is logging in to a website or entering credit card information, copy down her username, password, and credit card information, and then later use that information.

5 In some instances, a hacker can break in to your PC without your knowledge when you are not near a Wi-Fi network. In Windows XP, if you use a Wi-Fi adapter or Wi-Fi is built in to your laptop, and you turn on your PC and are not near a Wi-Fi network, your PC makes itself available as an ad hoc network. A nearby hacker could identify the name of the ad hoc network without your knowledge, connect to your PC, and steal information or do damage to it.

DELETE ALL FILES

How "Evil Twin" Hacks Work

1 In an *evil twin* hack, a hacker creates a twin of an existing hotspot to lure people into logging in to his hotspot rather than the real thing. First, a hacker finds a popular hotspot and finds its SSID (its network name). Next, he sets up a duplicate hotspot that has the same SSID as the real thing. He may use a small, hidden portable travel router to do this.

2 He might also use special software, such as one called Hot Spotter, that can turn an ordinary PC into a hotspot.

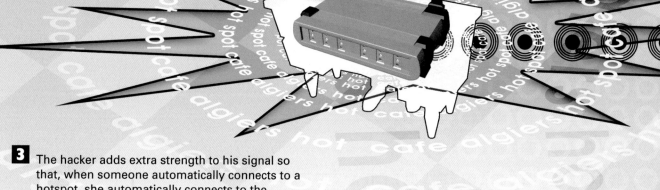

3 The hacker adds extra strength to his signal so that, when someone automatically connects to a hotspot, she automatically connects to the hacker's hotspot because it has the strongest signal. The hacker may also jam the signals of the real hotspot, ensuring that someone will connect to his hotspot instead of to the real thing.

4 The hacker can set up a phony login screen that asks for credit card information. Or, if it is a for-pay hotspot, he might mimic the login screen of the real hotspot. That way, he can steal credit card information.

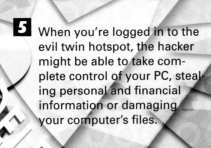

5 When you're logged in to the evil twin hotspot, the hacker might be able to take complete control of your PC, stealing personal and financial information or damaging your computer's files.

DELETE ALL FILES

MONEY

9786 3642 7618 8431
Windy Wright

cafe algiers hot spot cafe algiers hot spot cafe algiers hot spot cafe algiers hot spot cafe algiers hot spot cafe algiers hot spot cafe algiers hot spot cafe algiers hot spot cafe algiers

How War Drivers Invade Your Network

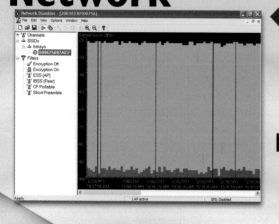

1 To go war driving, you need special software that can detect and report on any nearby Wi-Fi networks within range of the computer. A particularly popular one, pictured here, is the free program NetStumbler, available from www.netstumbler.com. The software can work with only certain brands and models of Wi-Fi cards.

2 Someone takes a Wi-Fi–equipped laptop with NetStumbler and drives around with it in a car, looking for Wi-Fi networks to tap into. To increase the distance from which the networks can be detected, an antenna can be attached to the laptop's Wi-Fi card. Often, a homemade *cantenna* is used— an antenna built using a tin can and copper wire.

3 One person drives, while the other watches NetStumbler for signs of nearby networks. When NetStumbler detects a wireless network, it reports the network ID, the channel over which the network is broadcasting, whether encryption is being used, and similar information.

4 Based on the information NetStumbler provides, the war driver can connect to the Wi-Fi network using software built in to the computer's operating system or that was provided along with the Wi-Fi card, if the network isn't protected by encryption and security. (Many Wi-Fi networks are left unprotected in businesses as well as homes.)

5 After the war driver connects to the network, he has the same access rights as any other user, so he can use all the network's resources and data. If he is a hacker, he can also try to take control of the network or damage it.

6 NetStumbler can save the information about all the networks it finds during a day of war driving. That information can be shared with others and be uploaded to a website, where it can be collated and published as a public map on the Internet. This lets anyone see where Wi-Fi networks are located. Many people use these maps not for nefarious purposes, but so they can connect to the Internet using these networks when they are away from home.

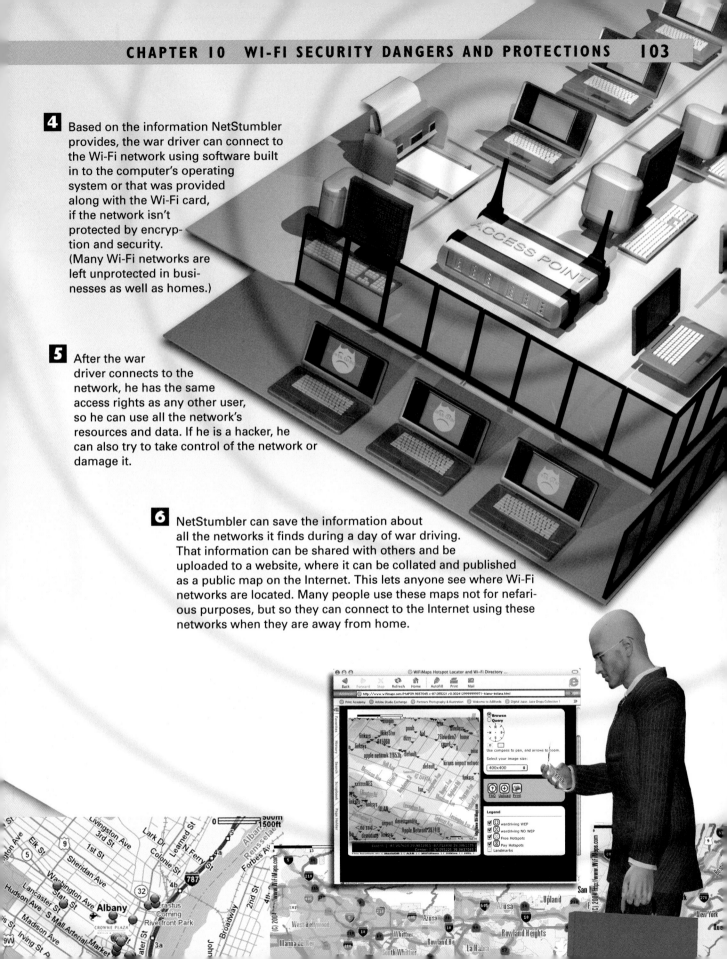

How Wireless Network Protection Works

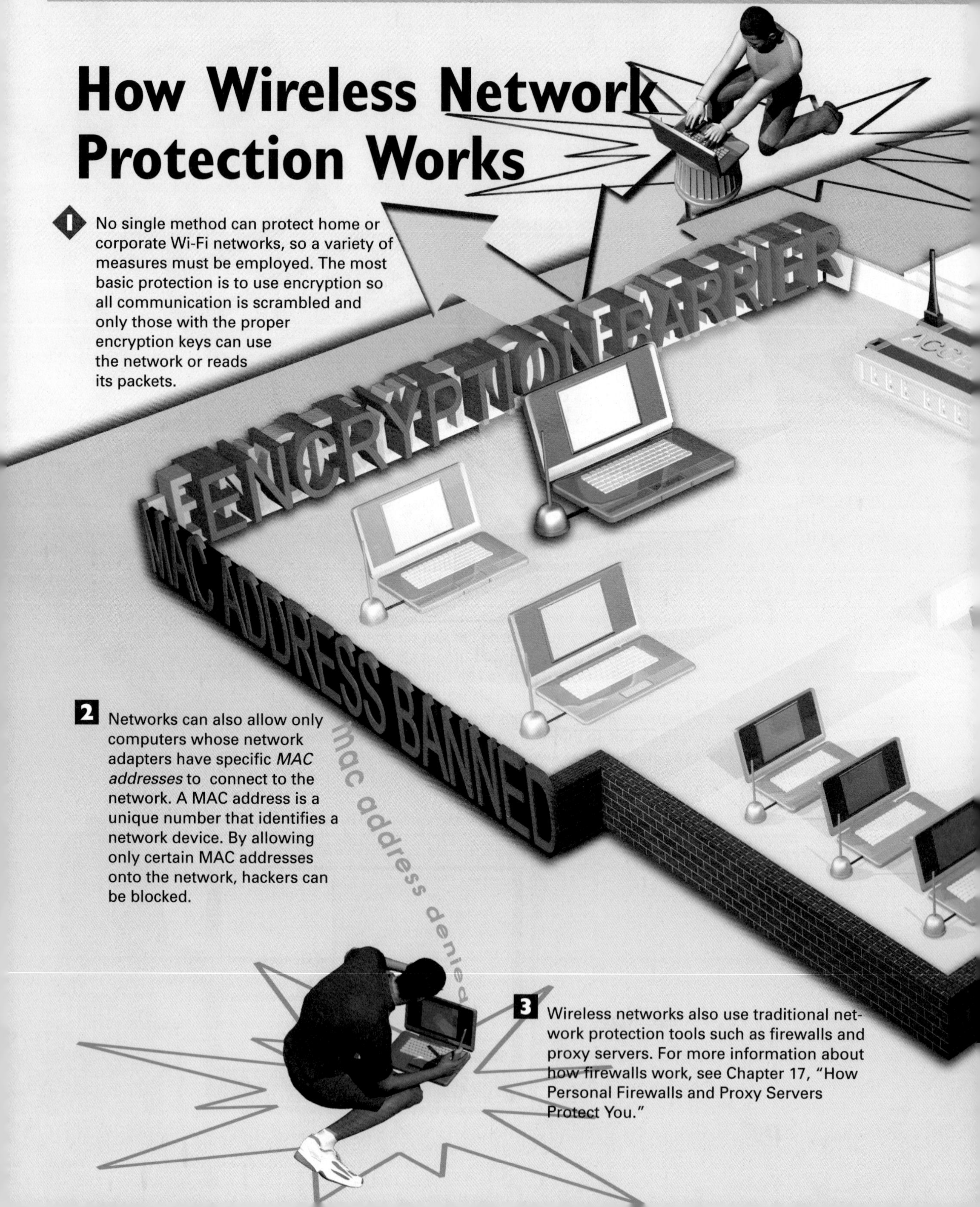

1 No single method can protect home or corporate Wi-Fi networks, so a variety of measures must be employed. The most basic protection is to use encryption so all communication is scrambled and only those with the proper encryption keys can use the network or reads its packets.

ENCRYPTION BARRIER

MAC ADDRESS BANNED

mac address denied

2 Networks can also allow only computers whose network adapters have specific *MAC addresses* to connect to the network. A MAC address is a unique number that identifies a network device. By allowing only certain MAC addresses onto the network, hackers can be blocked.

3 Wireless networks also use traditional network protection tools such as firewalls and proxy servers. For more information about how firewalls work, see Chapter 17, "How Personal Firewalls and Proxy Servers Protect You."

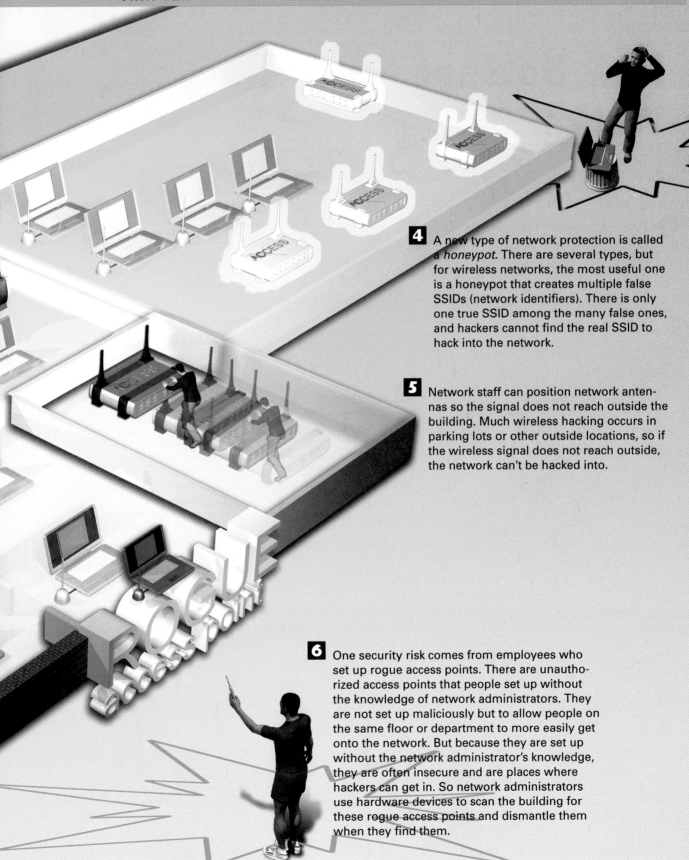

4 A new type of network protection is called a *honeypot*. There are several types, but for wireless networks, the most useful one is a honeypot that creates multiple false SSIDs (network identifiers). There is only one true SSID among the many false ones, and hackers cannot find the real SSID to hack into the network.

5 Network staff can position network antennas so the signal does not reach outside the building. Much wireless hacking occurs in parking lots or other outside locations, so if the wireless signal does not reach outside, the network can't be hacked into.

6 One security risk comes from employees who set up rogue access points. There are unauthorized access points that people set up without the knowledge of network administrators. They are not set up maliciously but to allow people on the same floor or department to more easily get onto the network. But because they are set up without the network administrator's knowledge, they are often insecure and are places where hackers can get in. So network administrators use hardware devices to scan the building for these rogue access points and dismantle them when they find them.

How Hotspot Protection Works

Firewall

1 When you are at a public hotspot, you are a potential hacking victim because you are on a network with many other people whom you don't know. The most basic form of protection is a personal firewall—preferably one that blocks unwanted outbound as well as inbound connections. For details, see Chapter 17, "How Personal Firewalls and Proxy Servers Protect You."

Virtual private network

2 The use of a virtual private network (VPN) can also provide protection against hackers at a hotspot. A VPN uses encryption and a technology that tunnels through the Internet to create a private network that encrypts all your communications while you are at a hotspot. Some business provide VPNs for their employees, but individuals can also subscribe to for-pay VPNs.

3 Many people turn on file sharing on all the PCs on their home networks so their computers can share information with each other. But if file sharing is left on at a hotspot, it can allow hackers to gain access to all a person's files. So, for hotspot protection, people should turn off file sharing.

4 For-pay hotspots, such as those run by T-Mobile, require that people pay on an hourly, a daily, a monthly, or an annual basis with a credit card. Using a credit card at a hotspot, though, is dangerous. So, for maximum security, people should pay with their credit card ahead of time; at the hotspot they can log in without actually entering credit card information.

5 Some people make sure that no sensitive data is kept on their laptop's hard disk. Instead, they store sensitive data on a portable USB drive about the size of a keychain. They use the USB drive with the sensitive data when at home, but when they go to a hotspot, they remove it, so that if their computer is hacked into, the hacker will not be able to find personal information or sensitive data.

How Wi-Fi Encryption Works

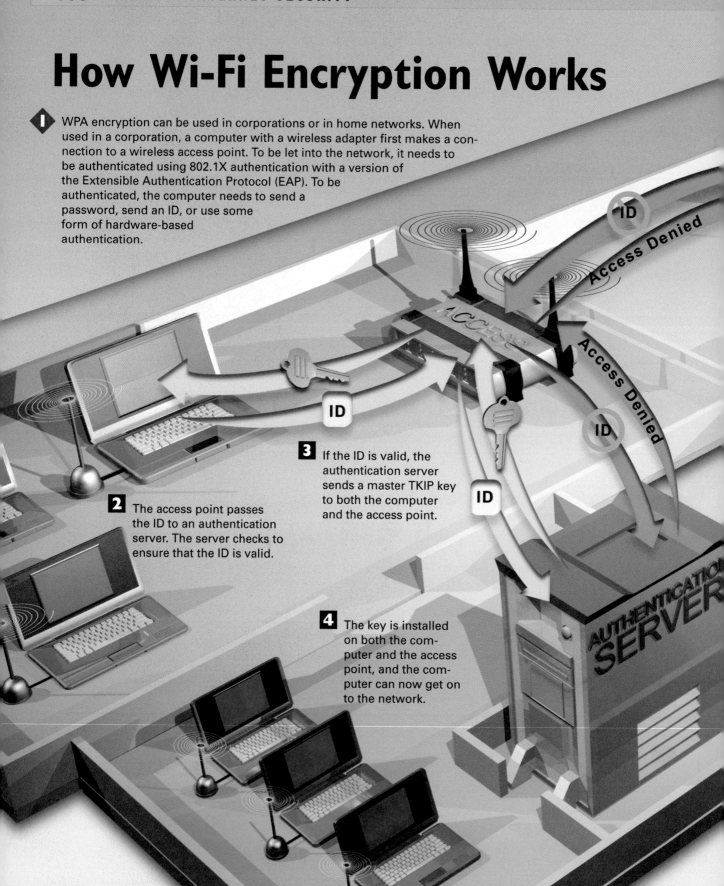

1 WPA encryption can be used in corporations or in home networks. When used in a corporation, a computer with a wireless adapter first makes a connection to a wireless access point. To be let into the network, it needs to be authenticated using 802.1X authentication with a version of the Extensible Authentication Protocol (EAP). To be authenticated, the computer needs to send a password, send an ID, or use some form of hardware-based authentication.

Access Denied

Access Denied

2 The access point passes the ID to an authentication server. The server checks to ensure that the ID is valid.

3 If the ID is valid, the authentication server sends a master TKIP key to both the computer and the access point.

4 The key is installed on both the computer and the access point, and the computer can now get on to the network.

AUTHENTICATION SERVER

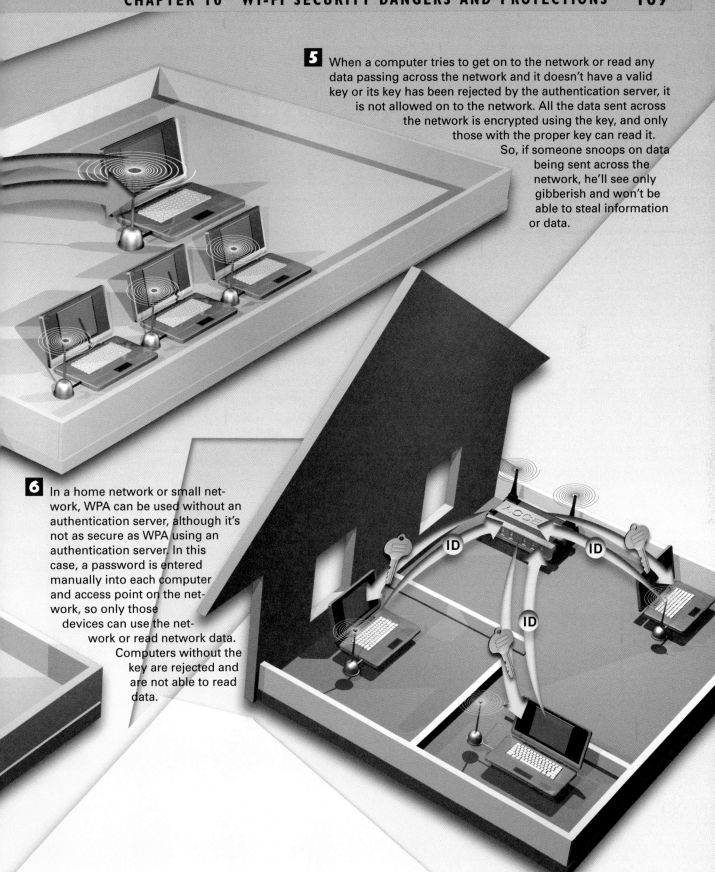

5 When a computer tries to get on to the network or read any data passing across the network and it doesn't have a valid key or its key has been rejected by the authentication server, it is not allowed on to the network. All the data sent across the network is encrypted using the key, and only those with the proper key can read it. So, if someone snoops on data being sent across the network, he'll see only gibberish and won't be able to steal information or data.

6 In a home network or small network, WPA can be used without an authentication server, although it's not as secure as WPA using an authentication server. In this case, a password is entered manually into each computer and access point on the network, so only those devices can use the network or read network data. Computers without the key are rejected and are not able to read data.

CHAPTER 11

Bluetooth Security Dangers

WI-FI (also known as 802.11b/g) is the most popular type of wireless technology for connecting computers, but there's another kind of wireless technology that has become widely used—Bluetooth. It is used primarily for cell phones and personal digital assistants (PDAs), although it can also be used for wireless keyboards, mice, and headphones and for connecting computers to one another.

Bluetooth was designed so that you do not need to do anything to connect devices to one another. Simply turn on the device, and it automatically looks for another Bluetooth device. If it finds one or more such devices, they set up wireless communications between the two of them (also known as *bonding*).

Bluetooth is an ad hoc network, which means that not only do the devices find each other on their own, but they also can communicate directly with each other without having to go through a central device, such as a server or network access point. This kind of network, in which devices connect directly to one another, is known as a *peer-to-peer network*.

The most common use of Bluetooth is for cell phones. Bluetooth headsets are becoming increasingly common for cell phone users. But Bluetooth connections are frequently used to connect phones to one another, so they can exchange files, for example. And Bluetooth is also used to connect cell phones to computers for doing things such as synchronizing address books.

Because cell phones have become so common, there is a growing worry that they will become the targets of hackers, notably hacking them using Bluetooth. For more information about cell phone hacking, including a variety of Bluetooth dangers, see Chapter 22, "How Cell Phones Can Be Hacked."

The illustrations in this chapter show how Bluetooth works and how Bluetooth can be hacked. Note that any kind of Bluetooth device can be hacked in the way described in this chapter, not just cell phones. So, for example, if two people are connecting their PCs to one another via a Bluetooth connection, they can be hacked in the same way as if two people were connecting their cell phones to one another.

How Bluetooth Works

1 Each Bluetooth device has a microchip embedded in it that can send and receive radio signals. It can send both data and voice. The radio signals are sent and received in the 2.4GHz radio band, in the Industrial, Scientific, and Medical (ISM) band. Inside the chip is software called a *link controller* that does the actual work of identifying other Bluetooth devices and sending and receiving data.

2 The Bluetooth device constantly sends out a message looking for other Bluetooth devices within its range.

3 When a Bluetooth device finds one or more other devices within its range, they go through a series of communications that establish whether they should communicate with one another. Not all devices will communicate—for example, a stereo might not communicate with a telephone. Devices determine whether they should communicate with one another by examining each other's Bluetooth profile, which is coded into each device's hardware by the hardware manufacturer. Profiles contain information about the device itself, what it is used for, and with which devices it can communicate. If devices determine they should communicate with one another, they establish a connection. The connection of two or more Bluetooth devices is called a *piconet*.

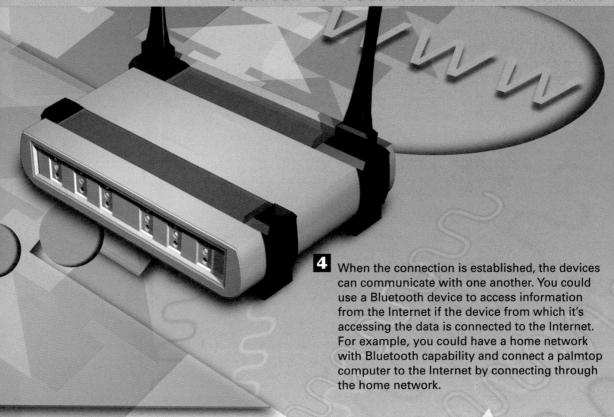

4 When the connection is established, the devices can communicate with one another. You could use a Bluetooth device to access information from the Internet if the device from which it's accessing the data is connected to the Internet. For example, you could have a home network with Bluetooth capability and connect a palmtop computer to the Internet by connecting through the home network.

5 If there are many Bluetooth devices or piconets near each other, their radio signals could conceivably interfere with one another. To ensure that doesn't happen, Bluetooth uses spread-spectrum frequency hopping. In this technique, the transmitters change their frequency constantly—1,600 times per second. In this way, the chance of interference is very small, and if there is interference, it happens for only a tiny fraction of a second. When two or more devices are connected in a piconet, one device is the master and determines the frequencies to switch among. It instructs all the other devices on which frequencies to switch to and when.

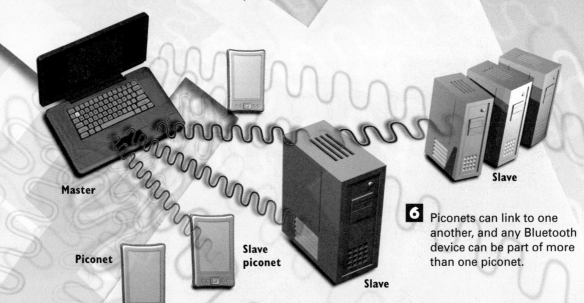

Master

Piconet

Slave piconet

Slave

Slave

6 Piconets can link to one another, and any Bluetooth device can be part of more than one piconet.

How Bluetooth Can Be Hacked

1 For Bluetooth devices to pair with each other, they must first establish a 128-bit key that is used to encrypt all communications. In this way, no one can snoop on the devices and steal data, and no outside device can pose as one of the devices because outside devices don't have the 128-bit encryption key. Both users of the devices that are to pair have to type in the same secret PIN, which is then used to create the 128-bit encryption key.

2 If a Bluetooth hacker is nearby during the pairing process, he can use a device called a *Bluetooth sniffer* that records the messages the pairing devices use to create the encryption key.

3 Those stolen communications are fed to a special piece of software that has information about Bluetooth algorithms. The software is able to go through all 10,000 PIN combinations and compare that PIN against the communications until it finds the right PIN. (Note: There are 10,000 PIN combinations because Bluetooth PINs use four characters. If it used more characters, there would be substantially more combinations to cycle through.)

4 After the hacker finds the right PIN, he can create the 128-bit encryption key. Using that encryption key, he is able to take control and hijack the Bluetooth device and can control it just as if it were in his hands. For example, he could steal files or make phone calls over someone else's Bluetooth telephone.

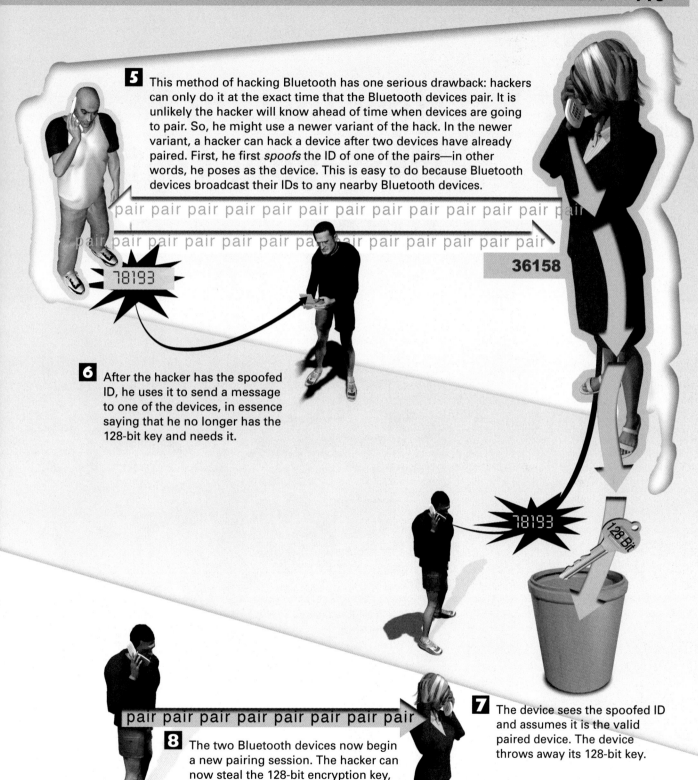

5 This method of hacking Bluetooth has one serious drawback: hackers can only do it at the exact time that the Bluetooth devices pair. It is unlikely the hacker will know ahead of time when devices are going to pair. So, he might use a newer variant of the hack. In the newer variant, a hacker can hack a device after two devices have already paired. First, he first *spoofs* the ID of one of the pairs—in other words, he poses as the device. This is easy to do because Bluetooth devices broadcast their IDs to any nearby Bluetooth devices.

pair pair pair pair pair pair pair pair pair pair pair pair pair
pair pair pair pair pair pair pair pair pair pair pair pair pair

78193

36158

6 After the hacker has the spoofed ID, he uses it to send a message to one of the devices, in essence saying that he no longer has the 128-bit key and needs it.

78193

128-Bit

7 The device sees the spoofed ID and assumes it is the valid paired device. The device throws away its 128-bit key.

pair pair pair pair pair pair pair pair

8 The two Bluetooth devices now begin a new pairing session. The hacker can now steal the 128-bit encryption key, as outlined in the earlier steps in this illustration.

CHAPTER

12

How Instant Messaging Pests Work

INSTANT messaging has become a way of life—not just for teens and children, but for people of all ages and even those in the corporate world, who use it for communicating while at work. With instant messaging, you hold live keyboard conversations with other people on the Internet—that is, you type words on your computer and other people on the Internet can see those words on their computers immediately, and vice versa.

The first instant messaging used over the Internet was *Internet Relay Chat (IRC)*. The capability to hold IRC chats is built directly in to the Internet. At one time, thousands of people all over the world used it to communicate with one another. It has even facilitated communications during natural disasters, wars, and other crises. In 1993, for example, during the attempted Communist coup in Russia when Russian legislators barricaded themselves inside the Parliament building, an IRC "news channel" was set up for relaying real-time, first-person accounts of the events taking place.

IRC is not particularly easy to use and is not used very frequently today. But there are people who use IRC for nefarious purposes. In certain circumstances, the protocols that make IRC possible can also be used to take control of people's PCs. In addition, IRC is used by those who control so-called *zombie networks* to attack computers or send millions of pieces of spam. (For more details, refer to Chapter 7, "How Zombies and Trojan Horses Attack You— and How to Protect Against Them."

Today, most instant messaging takes place using special software, notably AOL Instant Messenger (AIM), MSN Messenger, Yahoo! Messenger, and similar programs. When you run the software, you can communicate only with others who use the same software—the programs do not talk to one another.

It should come as no surprise that because instant messaging has become so popular, hackers and pests have followed. The security firm IMlogic reports that AOL Instant Messenger, MSN Messenger, and Yahoo! Messenger each send more than one billion messages per day. The firm says that instant messaging traffic will exceed email traffic by the end of 2006.

That's too big a target to ignore. So, even though instant messaging pests were unknown only a few years ago, they're common today. IMlog says that in 2005, instant messaging and similar threats increased by an astonishing 1,693% over 2004, with a total of more than 2,400 unique threats.

Despite this massive growth in instant messaging pests, many people do not realize that they are vulnerable, which is one of the reasons so many of the threats succeed. As you'll see in this chapter, although the pests are designed cleverly, there are also many ways that people can protect themselves.

How IRC Works

1 Internet Relay Chat (IRC) is a way for people all over the world to chat with one another using their keyboards. The typed words are instantly relayed to computers all over the world, where recipients can read them. This process occurs in real time, so everyone sees the words as people type them.

2 IRC runs on a client/server model; therefore, to use it, you need client software on your computer. Many IRC clients are available for PCs, Macintoshes, Unix workstations, and other kinds of computers.

Hi!

IRC server

3 When you want to chat, you make a connection to the Internet and then start your client software. Next, you must log on to an IRC server located on the Internet. Many IRC servers are located all over the world. They are connected together in a network so they can send messages to one another. The servers are connected in a spanning-tree fashion, in which each server is connected to several others, but all the servers are not directly connected to one another.

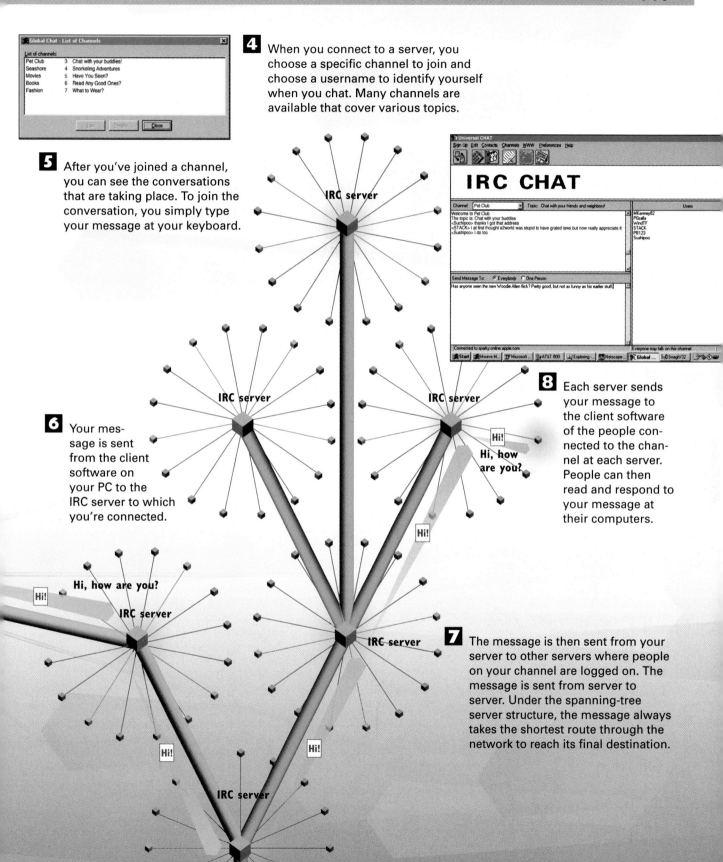

4 When you connect to a server, you choose a specific channel to join and choose a username to identify yourself when you chat. Many channels are available that cover various topics.

5 After you've joined a channel, you can see the conversations that are taking place. To join the conversation, you simply type your message at your keyboard.

6 Your message is sent from the client software on your PC to the IRC server to which you're connected.

8 Each server sends your message to the client software of the people connected to the channel at each server. People can then read and respond to your message at their computers.

7 The message is then sent from your server to other servers where people on your channel are logged on. The message is sent from server to server. Under the spanning-tree server structure, the message always takes the shortest route through the network to reach its final destination.

IRC CHAT

How Instant Messaging Works

1 The Internet version of America Online's Instant Messenger (AIM), one of the most popular instant messaging systems, runs as a piece of client software on your computer. To use it, you must be connected to the Internet. When you run the software, it opens a TCP connection to an Instant Messenger login server. The software sends your screen name and password over the connection to log you in to the server.

4 When you establish a connection with the AIM server, your client software sends a list of your buddies to the server. The server checks to see whether any of the buddies are online; it continues to do that for as long as you run the software on your computer. If you change the list of buddies during your session, that information is sent to the server as well so it can keep track of new buddies or ignore buddies you've deleted from your list.

3 Instant message software includes buddy list capabilities. That means you can keep a list of people to whom you want to send instant messages, and when they come online, you are notified so you can send instant messages to and receive instant messages from them. You create a buddy list in your AIM software by adding your buddies' screen names to it.

Cool Lizard is online.

"Hi, Mia. Are you interested in getting together next week?"

"Sure. Monday would be best for me. Let's chat later to confirm it."

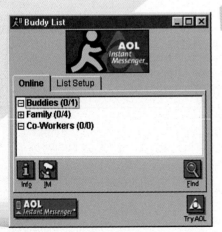

5 When any of your buddies runs AIM and logs in, your client software is told that he's online and you get a notice that he's online. You can now send messages to and receive instant messages from him.

2 The server checks the screen name and password. If they're correct, the login server instructs the Instant Messenger software to close the connection to the login server and to open a new connection to a different AIM server—the one that will handle your instant message session. This connection uses a special communications protocol that allows for AIM functionality, including instant messaging, chatting, transferring files, and video chatting.

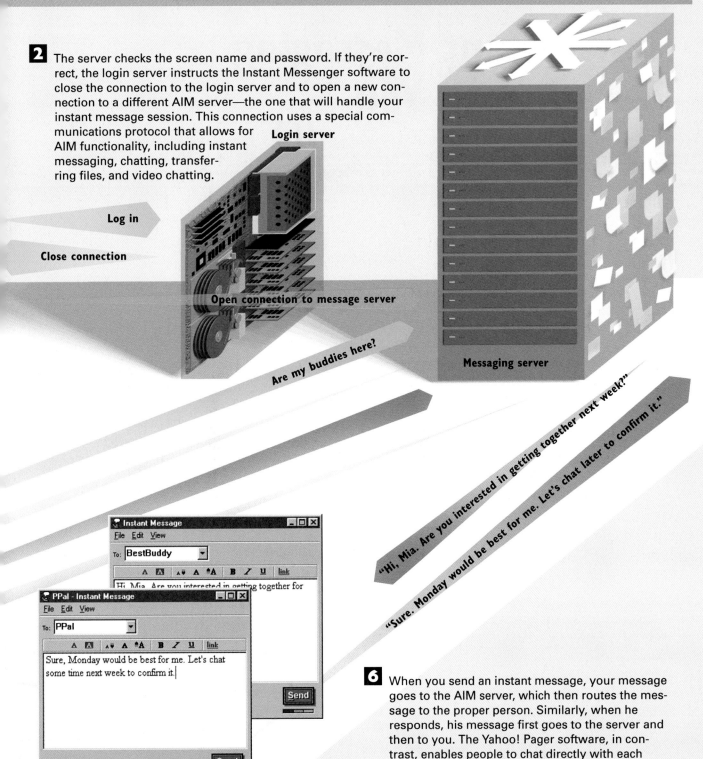

Login server

Log in

Close connection

Open connection to message server

Are my buddies here?

Messaging server

"Hi, Mia. Are you interested in getting together next week?"

"Sure. Monday would be best for me. Let's chat later to confirm it."

Instant Message
File Edit View
To: BestBuddy
A A A A A B I U link
Hi, Mia. Are you interested in getting together for

PPal - Instant Message
File Edit View
To: PPal
A A A A A B I U link
Sure, Monday would be best for me. Let's chat some time next week to confirm it.
Send
Send

6 When you send an instant message, your message goes to the AIM server, which then routes the message to the proper person. Similarly, when he responds, his message first goes to the server and then to you. The Yahoo! Pager software, in contrast, enables people to chat directly with each other without having to go through a server.

How Instant Messaging Pests Attack You

1 Instant messaging programs allow files to be sent from one computer directly to another, so a simple way of sending a virus, spyware, or other malware is to send it via instant messaging. Some instant messaging programs have settings that enable anyone to send you a file, even if you don't agree to receive it.

2 Some pests don't require a person to send them via file transfer; they can do it themselves. An example includes the W32.Funner worm. When a pest like the W32.Funner worm infects a PC, it first looks into the contact list of the person's instant messenger program.

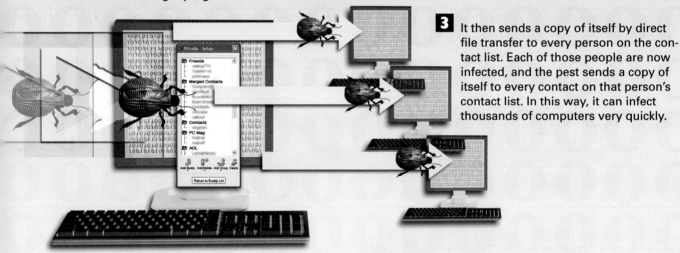

3 It then sends a copy of itself by direct file transfer to every person on the contact list. Each of those people are now infected, and the pest sends a copy of itself to every contact on that person's contact list. In this way, it can infect thousands of computers very quickly.

4 Some instant messaging pests spread via email—for example, the W32/Mytob-P worm. It infects a PC when someone opens an email attachment that contains it.

5 The worm then sets up an IRC backdoor on the infected computer, allowing remote intruders to take complete control of the PC. It also looks through the address book of the PC and sends itself to every person on the list, infecting many other PCs in this way.

6 Some instant messaging pests spread via the Web. When this kind of instant messaging pest invades a PC, it looks into the contact book and sends a message to everyone on the contact list, so the message appears to be from a friend. The message recommends that the person click a link to visit a website. When the person clicks a link, the site downloads the pest onto her PC.

7 Some types of instant messaging pests are capable of monitoring every key-stroke someone makes. This occurs not just when that person is using instant messaging, but when she's using any program on her PC. Those keystrokes are then sent to someone monitoring the PC, who can steal passwords and pose as the victim—for example, at online financial institutions.

How Instant Messaging Pest Protection Works

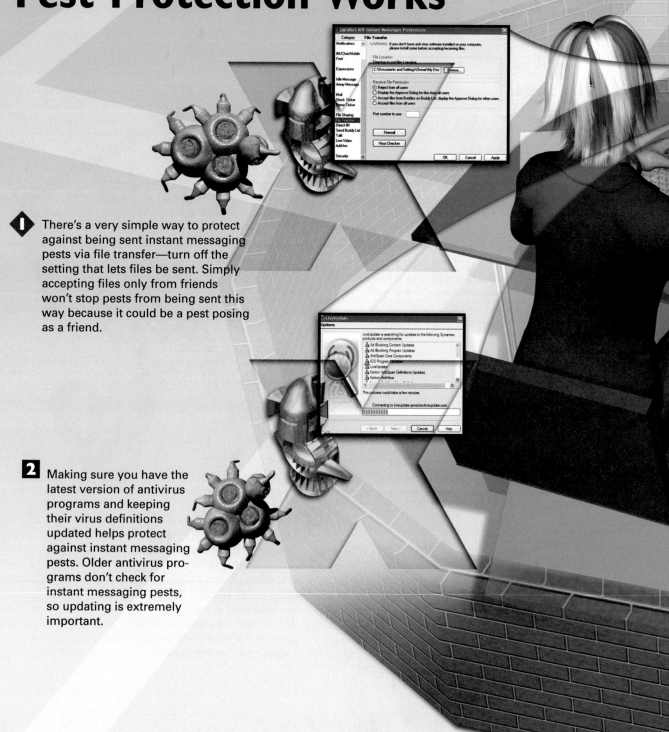

1 There's a very simple way to protect against being sent instant messaging pests via file transfer—turn off the setting that lets files be sent. Simply accepting files only from friends won't stop pests from being sent this way because it could be a pest posing as a friend.

2 Making sure you have the latest version of antivirus programs and keeping their virus definitions updated helps protect against instant messaging pests. Older antivirus programs don't check for instant messaging pests, so updating is extremely important.

3 Never clicking links without first checking that a person really sent them to you also protects against many pests. That way, if a pest sends a link to you, you won't click it because you'll have first checked to make sure a friend sent it.

http://www.partnersphoto.com
http://www.pestsite.com
http://www.artsupplies.com

DO NOT CLICK

Anti Spam   version 6.09   X

Anti Spam

Auto-Scan file

4 Using anti-spam software cuts down on instant messaging pests because it stops you from getting an instant messaging pest via email.

5 Corporations worried about instant messaging pests can purchase corporate-wide instant message protection from a company that specializes in it, such as IMlogic. IMlogic sells a solution called the Real-Time Threat Protection System (RTTPS) that monitors all instant messaging traffic and looks for telltale pest patterns. It then shuts down instant messaging sessions to close off access to the pest.

13

How Spam Works—and How to Fight It

WHAT is the most annoying thing that people face when they use the Internet? Spam.

Nothing else even comes close to being as annoying as spam. Unwanted email clogs all our inboxes, floods us with pornographic come-ons, and gets worse with each passing year.

The term *spam* comes from a *Monty Python* skit in which every item on a menu contains Spam luncheon meat. It was originally used to refer to unsolicited postings for commercial products or services on Usenet, especially when they were cross-posted to several newsgroups.

How bad is the problem? Postini, an email security and management company, claims that 88% of all email sent is spam. And security company MessageLabs claims that 69% of all email sent in 2005 was spam.

You might not get quite that much spam, but that's only because not all spam directed at you actually reaches you. Internet service providers (ISPs) and private businesses spend a significant amount of money every year filtering out spam before it reaches its intended recipients.

Spam has one purpose, and one purpose alone: to make money for spammers. Their emails are come-ons to click and get sent to a site, such as a get-rich-scheme or to buy phone pharmaceuticals. In some instances, such as in the infamous Nigerian 419 scam, millions of dollars have been lost to scammers who empty people's bank accounts.

Most people have never clicked a piece of spam or bought anything from a spammer. So one would think that spam is not cost-effective and would eventually go away. Unfortunately, though, spam is here to stay. That's because the cost of sending spam is miniscule—it's not as if spammers have to pay 39 cents for a stamp for every piece of spam they send.

In some ways, spam is not very different from traditional junk mail. A spammer buys or compiles massive lists of email addresses. The spammer then either uses special software to send the spam or hires a hacker to use his fleet of hijacked PCs, called *zombies* or *bots*, to send the spam.

Spam might seem like a minor annoyance, but it's much worse than an annoyance. It leads to scams, clogs the Internet, and floods mail servers with unnecessary messages. Some estimates hold that spam costs businesses an astonishing $20 billion a year in lost productivity, buying extra hardware and software, and troubleshooting costs.

A variety of methods have been devised to block spam, including having email filters on email software ignore any mail from known spammers. This doesn't always work, however, because spammers often change or forge their email addresses.

Congress stepped into the anti-spam wars in 2003 with the Can-Spam Act. But the law, by all accounts, has been so watered down that it has had no effect at all on spam. In fact, there are those who say that because it legalized certain forms of spam, it legitimized the practice. Since the law's passage, spam has skyrocketed.

Ultimately, the solution is more than legislative. It's in technology and changing people's behavior. If no one ever clicked a piece of spam, spam would disappear. And a variety of technological solutions are being called for, including a way of verifying the true sender of every piece of mail sent over the Internet. But those solutions may never come to fruition. Most likely, like it or not, spam is here to stay.

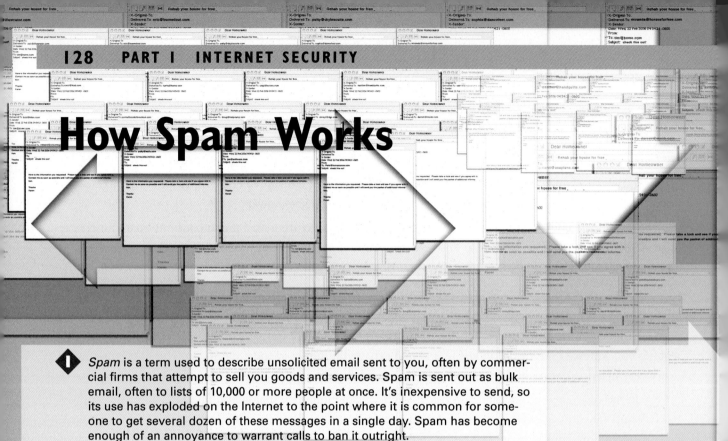

How Spam Works

1 *Spam* is a term used to describe unsolicited email sent to you, often by commercial firms that attempt to sell you goods and services. Spam is sent out as bulk email, often to lists of 10,000 or more people at once. It's inexpensive to send, so its use has exploded on the Internet to the point where it is common for someone to get several dozen of these messages in a single day. Spam has become enough of an annoyance to warrant calls to ban it outright.

patty@drybiscuit.com

2 To send unsolicited bulk email, a spammer first needs to get a list of email addresses. Often, spammers buy the lists from companies that compile them. These companies use automated software robots to get the email addresses, and the robots get the lists from a number of sources. One way is to go into Usenet newsgroups and harvest email addresses by looking inside every message, which usually has in it the email address of the person who posted it.

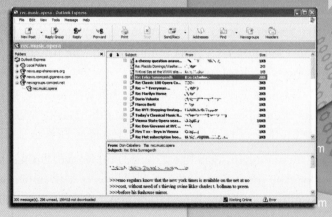

3 Email addresses also can be harvested from email directories on the websites that allow people to look up others' email addresses. Software robots can go into the directory and grab every address in the directory. Robots also can go into chat areas, such as those on America Online, and gather email addresses.

sophia@danear.com
.gov
.net
.com
@race.net
portia@goodfood.com
yours@56redhead
mark@globalview.com

4 Some spammers include in the email a return address to which someone who no longer wants to receive spam can send a message and be taken off the spam list. When the remove message is received, a robot automatically takes the person off the list. However, spammers rarely do this because most people would opt not to be on the spam lists.

If you would like to be removed from our mailing list please click the link below:

please remove me from your list

5 The spammer either buys the resulting email list or compiles one of her own. The spammer uses the list, along with bulk mailing software, and sends a spam message to every person on the list. In the message might be a return address, website, or phone number where the receiver can get more information about the goods and services being sold.

BULK emailer

click for more info

To:eric
From:Spam

6 Spammers realize that spam offends most people, so the spammers go to great lengths to hide their true email addresses. As one way of hiding their real email addresses, they forge parts of the message header in the email address, such as the From, Sender, and Reply fields, so it appears that the email has come from someone other than the spammer. Doing this is sometimes called *spamouflage*.

7 As a further way of hiding their true addresses, spammers relay their bulk spam to a server that is not associated with them and then have that server send the bulk spam. Sometimes spammers have the bulk spam relayed among several servers to make tracing who really sent the mail even more difficult.

SERVER

The Dangers of Spam

I A high percentage of spam is a scam of one kind or another, such as get-rich-quick schemes that only make the spammer rich or selling phony versions of drugs like Viagra. One of the most infamous spam scams, the Nigerian 419 scam, has led to people being bilked of millions of dollars. (For more details, see the illustration later in this chapter, "How Nigerian 419 Scams Work.")

2 Some spam includes attachments that, when opened, install spyware, viruses, Trojans, or other dangerous software on your PC.

attachment

3 Spam can overwhelm the mail servers of ISPs and private businesses. Companies are forced to spend unnecessary money to buy additional servers and more storage because of the volume of spam. They also need to buy anti-spam software to solve the problem and have their employees spend additional time fighting spam.

4 Spam can clog the networks of ISPs and private businesses. They may need to install higher-speed networks and purchase additional bandwidth so subscribers and employees can continue to use the network.

5 One of the most overlooked dangers of spam is the lost productivity it causes. Individuals spend hours a week deleting spam from their inboxes—time that could otherwise be spent on more productive work or leisure.

The research firm Basex says that spam costs corporations $20 billion a year and that spam can cost a corporation between $600 and $1,000 per user per year. These extra costs are due to lost productivity; the need to buy additional servers, storage, bandwidth, and anti-spam software; and the costs of troubleshooting spam problems.

How Nigerian 419 Scams Work

urgent attention needed   X

ASSISTANCE REQUIRED FOR ACQUISITION OF ESTATE
I write to inform you of my desire to acquire estates or landed properties in your country on behalf of the Director of Contracts and Finance Allocations of the Federal Ministry of Works and Housing in Nigeria.

1 Perhaps the most notorious spam scam of all time is the so-called Nigerian 419 scam, in which unwitting victims have been bilked out of millions of dollars. The scam originated in Nigeria, and many of the scammers are still from that country, although people in other countries now use the same scam. It is called the "419" scam because it violates that section of Nigeria's criminal code. These scams are often committed by gangs, not individuals.

2 A scammer goes to an Internet cafe and sends spam letters from a free mail service, such as Hotmail. He gets email addresses in the same way that any spammer does. (For details on how spammers get email addresses, see the illustration "How Spammers Find You," later in this chapter.)

There are many variants on the email that is sent, but most of them tell the intended victim that the sender of the email needs help transferring money from Nigeria to the United States—usually in amounts in the millions of dollars. The victim is told that he only needs to allow his bank account to be used to receive the money and in return he will get a portion of the transferred money, often 30%–40%. The scammers ask that the victim contact them and send them contact information, such as name, telephone number, and address.

Nigerian Commissioner
of Banking

Bank Transfer validation

3 When the victim gets in touch with the scammers, the scammers—to prove to the victim that the deal is real—send the victim a variety of official-looking documents by mail.

The scammers may also set up phony websites that appear to be government websites, fax numbers to which the victim can send faxes and from which faxes are sent, and phone numbers the victim can call. If the victim expresses doubt that the offer is real, the scammers tell him to get in touch via fax, phone, or the Web. It looks to the victim as if the arrangement is legitimate.

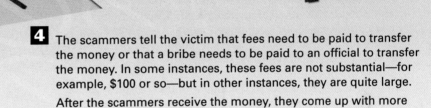

4 The scammers tell the victim that fees need to be paid to transfer the money or that a bribe needs to be paid to an official to transfer the money. In some instances, these fees are not substantial—for example, $100 or so—but in other instances, they are quite large.

After the scammers receive the money, they come up with more excuses for delays and ask for increasing amounts of money.

5 The scammers ask for information about the person's bank account and then transfer money out of the account.

Ransom Amount!!

send cash in the amount of $54,000.00 and we will release your sister imediately. Do not contact the officials.

6 In some instances, they tell the victim that to complete the transfer, he needs to fly to Nigeria to meet with officials. When he flies there, they demand more money from him. In some instances, people have been kidnapped and held for ransom.

At the end of the scam, the gang disappears without a trace. Because they used a free email address and a cyber cafe, there is no way to trace them.

How Spammers Hide Their Identity

1 One of the simplest ways in which spammers hide their real email addresses and identities is to use a free, web-based mail service like Hotmail or Yahoo! Mail. They sign up, send mail from the address, and then never use the address again.

2 *Open mail relays* have made it easy for spammers to hide their addresses. An open mail relay is a mail server designed to pass along email sent to it from any address, and it sends that email to any address. So, spammers need only send spam to an open mail relay—or a series of them—and the spam will be sent, hiding their true address. Open mail relays were designed in the days before spam when the Internet was open and were not regularly abused. Today, most mail servers are no longer designed to be open mail relays.

3 After open mail relays were shut down, spammers turned to *open proxies* to relay their mail. A proxy is a network service that can connect indirectly to other network services and request that they perform actions. A spammer can connect to an open proxy and then use that proxy to log in to a mail server and send mail. The mail appears to have come from the proxy, not the spammer. Increasingly, network managers are shutting down open proxies to cut down on their networks being used to send spam.

4 Most spammers *spoof* the return addresses on their spam messages. They go into their mail program and change the configuration settings so the return address on their messages isn't their true email address—it's someone else's. If you've ever received a piece of mail saying that a piece of mail you've sent was undeliverable—but you know that you never actually sent the mail—a spammer might have used your email address as the spoofed address.

5 Network administrators and ISPs have been increasingly vigilant about shutting off their email servers to spammers. Therefore, in the last several years, spammers have come up with a new technique—using zombies or bots to send spam. (For more information about zombies and bots, refer to Chapter 7, "How Zombies and Trojan Horses Attack You—and How to Protect Against Them.") A *zombie* or *bot* is a PC that can be controlled to perform actions by hackers who have planted software on it. Hackers control vast fleets of zombies—in some cases more than hundreds of thousands of them. A spammer pays a hacker to have the zombies send spam. In that way, the zombie PCs send the spam, so it cannot be traced to anyone except the sending PC.

How Spammers Find You

Public Sources for Spammers

1 Not all spammers compile their own spam lists. Many buy these lists from others, who use a variety of techniques to harvest email addresses or potential email addresses and then sell those lists to the highest bidder.

2 Spammers send automated spiders across the Internet that crawl across web pages looking for email addresses in **mail:to** links or posted on the page. The spiders send all the addresses back to the person compiling the spam list.

3 Spiders also look through Usenet newsgroups for email address, and when they find them, they send the addresses back to the spam list compiler.

4 Other kinds of spiders visit chat rooms and grab all the email addresses of those in the rooms.

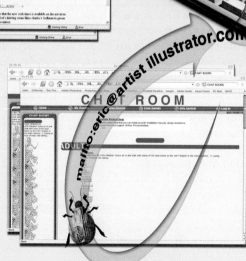

Harvesting from Email Directories

5 A *dictionary attack*, also called a *directory harvest attack*, is a common technique for harvesting email addresses. It is used to harvest email addresses from Internet service providers, mail services such as Hotmail, and private corporations. In the attack, software opens a connection to a mail server and sends millions of delivery attempt requests to email addresses on the server, such as **timsmith@hotmail.com**, **tomsmith@hotmail.com**, **tom1smith@hotmail.com**, and so on.

505 ERROR

505 ERROR

6 Because the software is only guessing at the addresses, most of the addresses are invalid and the server responds with a Simple Mail Transfer Protocol (SMTP) 550 error message, which means the address is not valid.

7 When the address being sent is real, the server responds with a message that the address is valid and real. The spammer compiles all these into a spam list. Even though a very low percentage of addresses is valid, if the spammer has sent millions of requests, he will get tens of thousands or more valid email addresses.

HARVESTED EMAIL
p35hj@hotmail.com
karenz43@hotmail.com
tom135555@hotmail.com

The Speed at Which Spam Spreads

How effective are spammers in harvesting email addresses from public locations? According to an investigation by the Federal Trade Commission and several law enforcement agencies, they are remarkably efficient. The commission and agencies posted 250 fresh, new email addresses in 175 locations on the Internet to see how much spam each received. The addresses were posted on web pages, dating services, chat rooms, message boards, Usenet newsgroups, and other locations. In the six weeks after posting, the addresses had received 3,349 pieces of spam. Eighty six percent of addresses posted to web pages drew spam, and an equal percent of addresses posted on newsgroups drew spam. Chat rooms were possibly the biggest spam magnets of all. One address used in a chat room received spam a mere 9 minutes after it was first posted.

How Anti-Spam Software Works

1 Spam can be stopped in a number of ways. The first way, and the least useful one, is to reply to the spammer and ask to be taken off the spam list. Because some spammers go to great lengths to hide their true email addresses, this isn't always possible. Often the email addresses they list to remove your name are dead addresses.

Please remove me from your list

Invalid address

SEN

SPAM FILTER
- BIG CASH NOW!!!
- Stop Smoking!!
- Earn Cash Today !

undeliverable spam

2 Some email software allows you to filter out messages from certain addresses; when email comes from that address, your email software won't allow it through. This feature is referred to as a *spam filter* or *spam blocker*. Whenever you receive spam, you can put that address into your spam filter and you'll never get email from that address again. Spam filters don't always work, however, because spammers often change their addresses and forge the From, Sender, and Reply fields in the email header. Online services such as America Online let you block email from any address you specify—in essence, it's a spam filter for those who use America Online. Additionally, some ISPs block spam.

BLOCKED

12.73.125.001	OK
124.5.65.0	OK
325.121.25.124	spam BLOCKED
635.31.125.124	spam BLOCKED

3 ISPs and online service such as America Online can block spammers from sending bulk mail to their subscribers. A router examines all incoming mail to the ISP or online service. The router has been told that when email comes from certain addresses, it should block mail from getting into the network. These addresses are put in a routing table that can be changed whenever new spammers are found. ISPs have a variety of other ways for detecting spam as well.

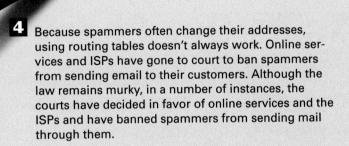

4 Because spammers often change their addresses, using routing tables doesn't always work. Online services and ISPs have gone to court to ban spammers from sending email to their customers. Although the law remains murky, in a number of instances, the courts have decided in favor of online services and the ISPs and have banned spammers from sending mail through them.

5 A number of laws and schemes have been proposed to regulate or outlaw spam. In one plan, every piece of spam would have to contain a specific piece of information in the message header, identifying it as unsolicited email. In this way, people could set their spam filters to block every piece of spam, filtering out that piece of information. Some laws have been proposed that would outlaw spam entirely, in the same way that junk faxes were banned.

6 One way to prevent being spammed is to ensure that your email address isn't added to spam lists. To do this, when posting to Usenet newsgroups, edit your header so it doesn't contain your email address. You should also notify email directories that you'd like to be taken off their lists. In this way, your email address won't be harvested by robots and you should get less spam.

How Anti-Spam Software Sniffs Out Phony Email

1 There are many types of anti-spam software. Some reside on a mail server and delete spam before it reaches people's PCs. Another common type runs inside a person's email program and routes suspected spam to a special spam folder, where the mail can be examined and deleted. Most ISPs include anti-spam software, but that in itself isn't enough to stop the deluge of spam from reaching people, so most people also run anti-spam software on their own PCs.

In Box

SPAM

BLACK LIST

hacker@scam.com

gio@mobster.com

2 Blacklists are a common way of fighting spam. A *blacklist* is a list of email addresses and Internet domains known to be spammers. When anti-spam software comes across an address on the blacklist, it flags it as spam.

Watch out AT&TΣ —**SPAM**

you,re about to get disconnected by
„iPhone2‰!

uy IPHN now, while it's under $1.00. Because
heir new technology will soon drive the stock
above $20!. —**SPAM**

SPAM

w about VoIP (Voice over Internet Protocol), that turns your computer into a telephone.

one2 (IPHN) is introducing the next generation. Not only does iPhone2's advanced new technology let you place
where in the world on your computer, but these amazing video/voice calls are free

Company:
iPhone2, Inc.
Stock Symbol:
OTC Pink Sheets: IPHN
Recommendation:

Buy IPHN today

false positive

positive

positive

Incredible broadband growth launches IPHN

WHITE LIST
email
KAREN@WIFE.COM

---

3 Anti-spam software also uses content filtering, in which the software examines the body and subject line of an email message and looks for specific words that indicate spam. The software contains a database of terms and phrases spammers often use, such as *Viagra*. So, if the software comes across a subject line such as *Herbal Viagra!*, it would consider that message spam.

4 A Bayesian filter might be the most powerful anti-spam technique of all. A Bayesian filter analyzes the actual content of a message, compares the content to a database of spam characteristics, and calculates the probability that the message is spam. All messages above a certain threshold are considered spam, and messages below that threshold are not considered spam. You can tune the filter to change the threshold level, depending on whether you want to be more aggressive or less aggressive in flagging spam. Being more aggressive means you'll get less spam, but also more *false positives*—messages that are not actually spam. Being less aggressive means that more spam will get through, but you'll get fewer false positive.

When you use a Bayesian filter, as you get mail, you flag certain messages as spam and as not being spam. So the more you use a Bayesian filter, the more effective it becomes because as you tell it what is spam and what isn't, it adds that information to its database. Bayesian filters are more effective than content filters that only block email with certain words or phrases because spammers can easily alter the spellings of words.

What Is Spammerwocky?
Some spam includes random words and lines of gibberish, such as "inexorable lie stone liver conclude grandma trickster." This technique, called *spammerwocky*, tries to fool spam filters into believing the message is not spam. The spammer hopes that the inclusion of random words will not be construed as spam by Bayesian filters. But spam-killing software has caught on and includes methods for detecting spammerwocky.

5 Whitelists can be used to tell anti-spam software that certain addresses are valid, and so should always be let through by anti-spam software. For example, some anti-spam software examines a person's contact list and automatically adds all those addresses to a whitelist. Additionally, you can add addresses to a white list, telling the anti-spam software to let certain addresses through.

6 Some software uses peer-to-peer technology to fight spam. Everyone who uses the anti-spam software flags certain messages as spam. This information is sent to a central server, which compiles blacklists and whitelists. The software on each person's computer is then updated by the central server.

KAREN@WIFE.COM   KAREN@WIFE.COM

14

How Denial-of-Service Attacks Bring Down Websites

AMONG the most publicized of Internet dangers are denial-of-service (DoS) attacks. In a DoS attack, a hacker floods a website or an Internet service provider (ISP) with so much malicious, junk traffic that the site is no longer able to function or functions at a very low level. Visitors are not able to get to the site.

DoS attacks often make the headlines because their targets are often high-visibility websites and ISPs. Through the years, sites such as Amazon, CNN.com, eBay, and many others have been victimized by these attacks.

But it isn't only these high-visibility sites that are targets. Plenty of smaller sites and ISPs have been targeted as well. In fact, according to researchers at the University of California, San Diego, in 2003 there were nearly 4,000 DoS attacks launched per week.

There are several ways that a hacker can launch a DoS attack. One of the most popular ways is also called a *smurf attack*, or *smurfing*. In a smurf attack, a hacker floods the target with so many garbage packets that all the target's available bandwidth is used up. If the target is an ISP, the ISP's customers can't send or receive data and can't use email, browse the Web, or use any other Internet service.

In a smurf attack, a hacker exploits a commonly used Internet service—ping (Packet Internet Groper). People normally use *ping* to see whether a particular computer or server is currently attached to the Internet and working. When a computer or server is sent a ping packet, it sends a return packet to the person who sent the ping, which in essence says, "Yes, I'm alive and attached to the Internet." In a smurf attack, a hacker forges the return addresses on ping requests so that, instead of going back to them, the return packets go to the hacker's target. The hacker is able to use networks attached to the Internet as a way of relaying her ping requests and magnifying each ping request many times. In this way, a hacker can use networks attached to the Internet to flood the target with so many return ping packets that the target's customers can't use the website or services. A hacker can use multiple networks attached to the Internet in a single smurf attack.

Sites have difficulty fighting smurf attacks because the ping answering packets come from legitimate networks and not from the hacker. The site has to track down where the ping answering packets are coming from and then contact each of those networks to ask them to turn off the ping answering packets. Making this more difficult is that, when an ISP goes down, its customers often send ping requests to it to see whether it is alive and connected to the Internet. The ISP has a difficult time separating the legitimate ping packets from the smurf attack packets.

Until several years ago, DoS attacks were launched for purely malicious purposes. Today, though, that has changed. Today, cyberextortionists have gotten into the act. The extortionists send blackmail notes to websites or ISPs, warning them that if they don't pay extortion money, the extortionists will launch a DoS attack to bring down the site. This can have severe economic consequences that can range into the millions of dollars. Some sites pay up; others report the extortion to authorities or hire experts who can protect them against DoS attacks and hunt down the perpetrators.

How Denial-of-Service Attacks Target Websites

1 In a *denial-of-service (DoS)* attack (also called a *smurf attack* or *smurfing*), a hacker targets an ISP or a website and floods it with so much garbage traffic that none of the ISP's customers are able to use the service or no one can reach the website. DoS attacks have become one of the most popular kinds of hacker attacks on the Internet. The attack starts when a hacker sends a series of *ping* (Packet Internet Groper) packets to a network attached to the Internet. Ping uses the *Internet Control Message Protocol*—a widely used protocol for, among other things, determining whether a particular computer is attached to the Internet and working properly. The network being pinged is not the target of the attack. Instead, it is used as a way to attack the ISP.

2 The hacker forges the return address on the ping packets. Instead of having his address, it has the address of the ISP the hacker will be attacking. This serves two purposes: It attacks the ISP or website, and it shields the hacker from being caught because his address is not on the ping requests.

3 The ping requests are sent in a constant stream to the network's *directed broadcast* address. This address, in turn, sends the ping requests to every computer attached to the network, which can be several hundred or more computers.

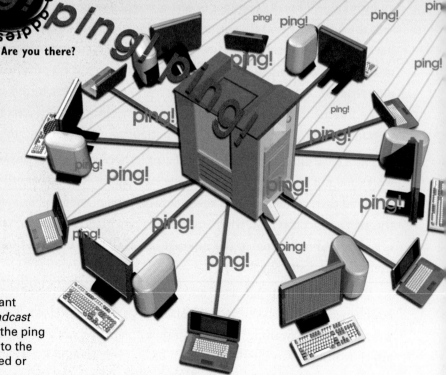

Are you there?

forged return address

Are you there?

ping! ping! ping! ping! pin

Network server 1

4 Each one of those several hundred or more computers responds with answer packets to each ping request. The computers send the answer packets to the target ISP or website whose address is on the ping request. The answer packets aren't sent to the hacker because he has forged the return address on the ping request.

5 The target ISP or website is flooded with tens of thousands of ping answer packets per second—easily more than 5 megabytes (MB) of data per second from a single network.

6 To make the attack even more devastating, the hacker can send similar forged ping requests to other networks, each of which can flood the target ISP or website with more than 5MB of packets per second.

Network server 2

7 The ISP or website is flooded with so much data streaming into it every second that the ISP's users can't send or receive data because the ping packets take up all the ISP's bandwidth. They aren't able to send or receive email, browse the Web, or use any other Internet service. If a website is targeted, visitors are not able to visit it because the bandwidth is taken up and the servers are flooded with traffic.

How Hackers Invade Websites

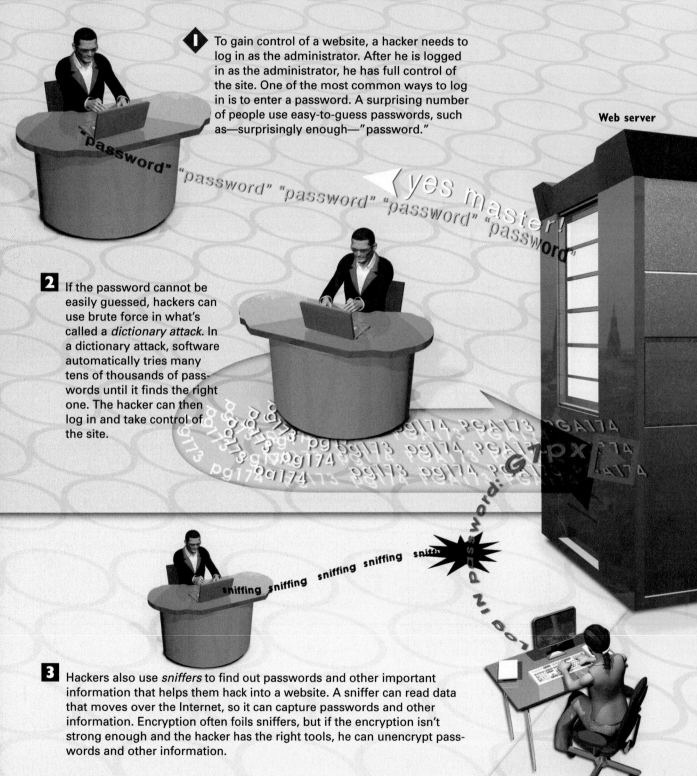

1 To gain control of a website, a hacker needs to log in as the administrator. After he is logged in as the administrator, he has full control of the site. One of the most common ways to log in is to enter a password. A surprising number of people use easy-to-guess passwords, such as—surprisingly enough—"password."

Web server

2 If the password cannot be easily guessed, hackers can use brute force in what's called a *dictionary attack*. In a dictionary attack, software automatically tries many tens of thousands of passwords until it finds the right one. The hacker can then log in and take control of the site.

3 Hackers also use *sniffers* to find out passwords and other important information that helps them hack into a website. A sniffer can read data that moves over the Internet, so it can capture passwords and other information. Encryption often foils sniffers, but if the encryption isn't strong enough and the hacker has the right tools, he can unencrypt passwords and other information.

4 The web server software may have security holes in it that can be exploited to allow the hacker to take control of the site. For example, a hacker might be able to exploit a *buffer overflow* in which a particular portion of a server's memory is flooded with so much data that the hacker can gain access to other portions of memory and then take control of the server or damage it in some way.

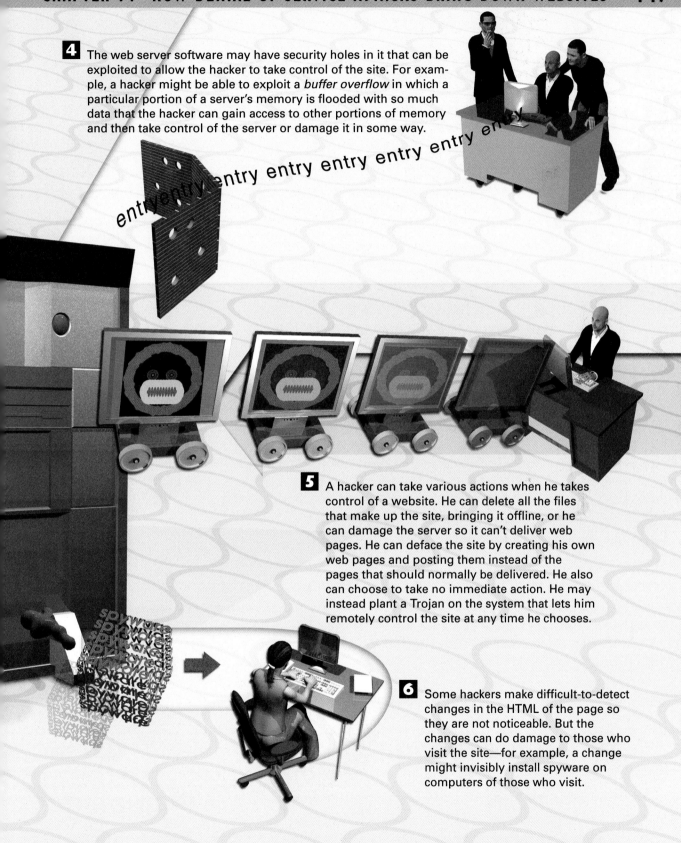

5 A hacker can take various actions when he takes control of a website. He can delete all the files that make up the site, bringing it offline, or he can damage the server so it can't deliver web pages. He can deface the site by creating his own web pages and posting them instead of the pages that should normally be delivered. He also can choose to take no immediate action. He may instead plant a Trojan on the system that lets him remotely control the site at any time he chooses.

6 Some hackers make difficult-to-detect changes in the HTML of the page so they are not noticeable. But the changes can do damage to those who visit the site—for example, a change might invisibly install spyware on computers of those who visit.

How to Protect Against Denial-of-Service Attacks

1 Hardware has been designed to protect websites from denial-of-service attacks. The hardware filters out data packets that appear to be *redundance*—that is, are duplicate, junk data designed to bring down a site. It lets valid packets through and filters out the attack packets.

2 The hardware might not be powerful enough to protect against massive attacks. To protect against larger attacks, a company can use, or hire, massive data hubs that each contains powerful hardware to protect against the attacks. The hubs in essence act as a holding pen for data and only allow through valid data while filtering out the attack packets.

Data hub

3 Hardware solutions and data hubs alone may not be able to protect against the attacks. For maximum safety, an organization needs to employ a holistic approach by putting together a comprehensive anti-DoS plan. Servers and other hardware should be kept up to date with the latest security patches, firewalls. In addition, other security software and hardware should be used and all hardware, including desktop PCs and servers, should be scanned for the presence of Trojans. A comprehensive rapid response plan should be in place for when an attack does occur.

DoS Checklist
- √ Firewall
- √ Security
- √ Patch
- √ Virus Scan
- √ Rapid Response Team

Website

Send the money or else!

4 Large sites that have been the target of cyberextortion or worry that they may become targets can hire security firms that specialize in protecting against DoS attacks. For example, the firm Prolexic, founded in 2003, operates DoS-preventing hubs, works to track down the source of attacks, and helps protect against attacks in other ways as well.

ping!ping!ping!ping!
ping!

5 To a great extent, attacks can be decreased not by actions of the site being attacked, but by other sites and users. DoS attacks are launched when unwitting PCs and networks are used as launching pads. If those networks and PCs take simple, basic security precautions, they can't be used to launch attacks. Anti-spyware should be installed on all PCs, for example. And network managers can alter network settings that prevent their networks from being used to attack websites. For example, they can turn off the forwarding of IP-directed broadcast packets and block certain kinds of traffic being sent to broadcast addresses. And they can turn off Internet Control Message Protocol for sending ping requests.

CHAPTER

15

How Virtual Private Networks and Encryption Keep You Safe

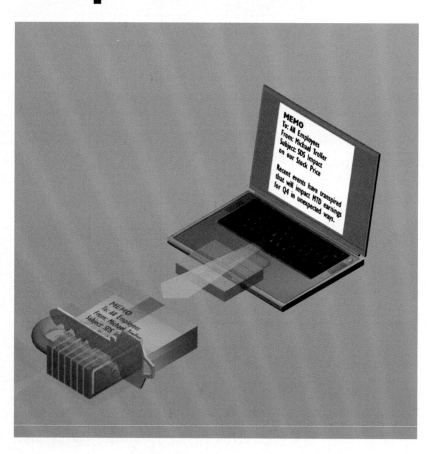

THE Internet is notoriously insecure. Whatever you send out across it can be potentially read—corporate information, your credit card numbers, and more.

There is a related problem as well. How can a site know whether the person sending the information across the Internet, such as credit card information, is really who she says she is? There are ways for people to forge identities and steal credit card numbers, and websites, financial institutions, and other businesses require ways to verify people's identities.

Several ways have been developed to solve these problems. At the heart of them is *encryption*—a way of altering information so that to anyone other than the intended recipient it looks like meaningless garble. When the recipient gets the information, it needs to be *decrypted*—that is, turned back into the original message by the recipient, and *only* by the recipient. Many complex cryptosystems have been created to enable this type of encryption and decryption.

Cryptosystems use what are called *keys*—secret values computers use in concert with complex mathematical formulas called *algorithms* to encrypt and decrypt messages. If someone encrypts a message with a key, only someone else with a matching key can decrypt the message.

There are two kinds of common encryption systems: *secret-key cryptography* and *public-key cryptography*, also called *asymmetric cryptography*. Public key cryptography is commonly used on the Internet.

In public-key cryptography, two keys are involved: a public key and a private key. Every person has both a public key and a private key. The *public key* is made freely available, whereas the *private key* is kept secret on the person's computer. The public key can encrypt messages, but only the private key can decrypt messages the public key has encrypted. If someone wants to send a message to you, for example, she would encrypt it with your public key. But only you, with your private key, would be able to decrypt the message and read it. Your public key could not decrypt it.

Digital certificates use encryption to verify that the person sending information, such as a credit card number, a message, or anything else over the Internet, really is who she says she is. The certificates place information on a person's hard disk and use encryption technology to create a unique digital certificate for each person. When someone with a digital certificate goes to a site, that certificate is presented to the site and it verifies that the user is who she claims to be.

Digital certificates are issued by certificate authorities. These certificate authorities are private companies who charge either users or companies for the issuance of the certificates. You might be familiar with one such certificate authority, called VeriSign. Digital certificates contain information such as your name, the name of the certificate authority, the certificate's serial number, and similar information. The information has been encrypted in a way that makes it unique to you.

Also important for security are virtual private networks (VPNs), which let company employees connect securely to a company network no matter where they are—at home, on the road, or anywhere else. They use a kind of tunneling technology to let people use the public Internet to connect to the company intranet, while keeping all communications secure and encrypted.

How Virtual Private Networks Work

1 This example shows a remote PC sending a file to someone inside a corporate network, using a VPN to tunnel through the Internet. To connect to the VPN, client software must be running on the PC on one end of the tunnel. The client first encrypts each of the document's packets.

VPN Client Software

Michael's Private Key

2 After the packets are encrypted, each of them is encapsulated inside a normal IP packet. The IP packets have a destination address of the PC or router at the other end of the tunnel. This ensures that as the packets travel across the Internet, the true destination IP addresses can't be read by snoopers. Only the tunnel IP address is read.

3 The packets travel across the Internet as they do normally. Routers looking at the packets see only the IP headers with the address of the VPN tunnel, not the headers inside the encapsulated packets.

To: 197.1.3.4

Router

The Internet

To: 197.1.3.4

To: 197.1.3.4   To: 197.1.3.4   To: 197.1.3.4   To: 197.1.3.4

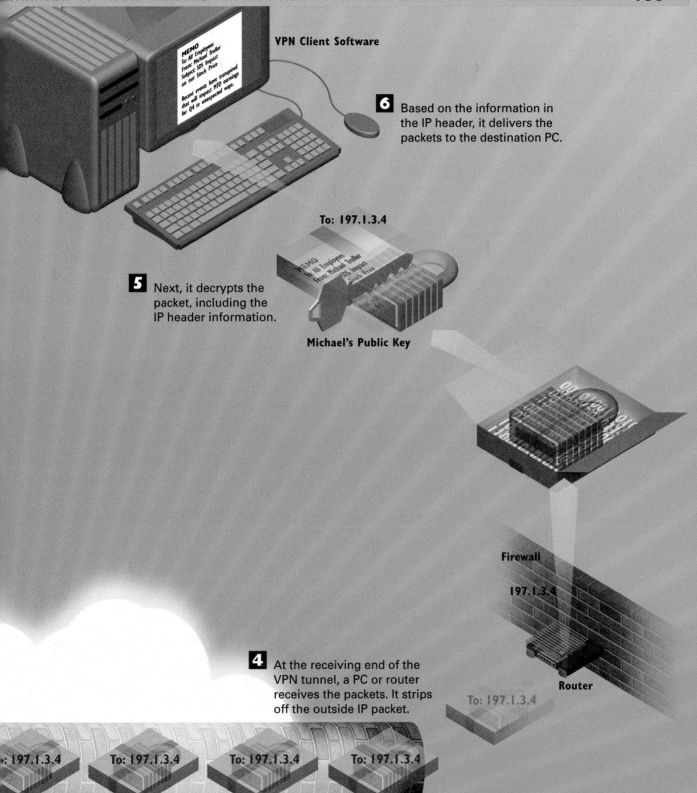

VPN Client Software

6 Based on the information in the IP header, it delivers the packets to the destination PC.

To: 197.1.3.4

5 Next, it decrypts the packet, including the IP header information.

Michael's Public Key

Firewall

197.1.3.4

Router

To: 197.1.3.4

4 At the receiving end of the VPN tunnel, a PC or router receives the packets. It strips off the outside IP packet.

: 197.1.3.4   To: 197.1.3.4   To: 197.1.3.4   To: 197.1.3.4

How Cryptosystems Work

1 Gabriel wants to send a confidential message over the Internet to Mia. Mia will need some way to decrypt the message as well as a way to guarantee that Gabriel—and not an imposter—has actually sent the message. First, Gabriel runs his message through an algorithm called a *hash function*. This produces a number known as the *message digest*. The message digest acts as a sort of "digital fingerprint" that Mia will use to ensure that no one has altered the message.

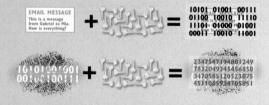

2 Gabriel now uses his private key to encrypt the message digest. This produces a unique digital signature that only he, with his private key, could have created.

3 Gabriel generates a new random key, which he uses to encrypt his original message and his digital signature. Mia will need a copy of this random key to decrypt Gabriel's message. This random key is the only key in the world that can decrypt the message—and at this point, only Gabriel has the key.

4 Gabriel encrypts this new random key with Mia's public key. This encrypted random key is referred to as the *digital envelope*. Only Mia will be able to decrypt the random key because it was encrypted with her public key, so only her private key can decrypt it.

5 Gabriel sends a message to Mia over the Internet that is composed of several parts: the encrypted confidential message, the encrypted digital signature, and the encrypted digital envelope.

Original Message

Hash function

Message digest

Gabriel's public key   **Gabriel's private key**   **Mia's public key**

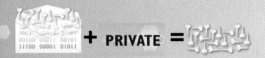 + PRIVATE =

6 Mia gets the message. She decrypts the digital envelope with her private key and out of it gets the random key Gabriel used to encrypt the message.

7 Mia uses the random key to decrypt Gabriel's message. She can now read the confidential message he sent to her. However, she can't yet be sure that the message hasn't been altered en route to her or that Gabriel was definitely the sender.

8 Mia now uses the random key *and* Gabriel's public key to decrypt his encrypted digital signature. When she does this, she gets his message digest, the message's digital fingerprint.

9 Mia uses this message digest to see whether Gabriel indeed sent the message and that it was not altered in any way. She takes the message she decrypted and runs it through the same algorithm—the *hash function*—that Gabriel ran the message through. This produces a new message digest.

10 Mia compares the message digest she calculated to the one she got out of Gabriel's digital signature. If the two match precisely, she can be sure that Gabriel signed the message and that it was not altered after he composed it. If they don't match, she knows that either he didn't compose the message or that someone altered the message after he wrote it.

identical

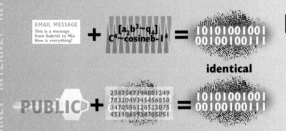

How Digital Certificates Ensure Internet Security

1 A digital certificate is used to guarantee that the person who sends information or email over the Internet or who makes a financial transaction really is who he says he is. Digital certificates are issued by certificate authorities (CAs). To get a digital certificate, you typically visit a CA site and request a certificate. You then provide information about yourself, such as your name and other identifying information.

CERTIFICATE

Name: Gabe Gralla

Authority: VeriPure

Serial #: 00518

Version #: 3

Expires: 11/09/2008

Key: 87162552

Digital Sig: 001 -1001110

2 You are issued a digital certificate, which has been digitally signed to guarantee its authenticity. The certificate is data unique to you and is put on your hard disk, along with a private key.

3 The digital certificate is composed of information such as your name, the name of the CA, the unique serial number of the certificate, the version number of the certificate, the expiration date of the certificate, your public key, and the digital signature of the CA. The exact format of the certificate is defined by a standard known as X.509.

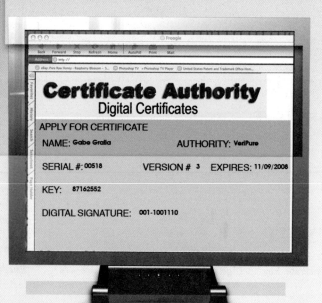

Certificate Authority
Digital Certificates

APPLY FOR CERTIFICATE

NAME: Gabe Gralla   AUTHORITY: VeriPure

SERIAL #: 00518   VERSION # 3   EXPIRES: 11/09/2008

KEY: 87162552

DIGITAL SIGNATURE: 001-1001110

4 When you want to send email to someone and have her know for certain that it is you and no one else who has sent the mail, you attach the digital certificate to your email message. One of the things the certificate does is sign the message with a private key you were given as part of the digital certificate.

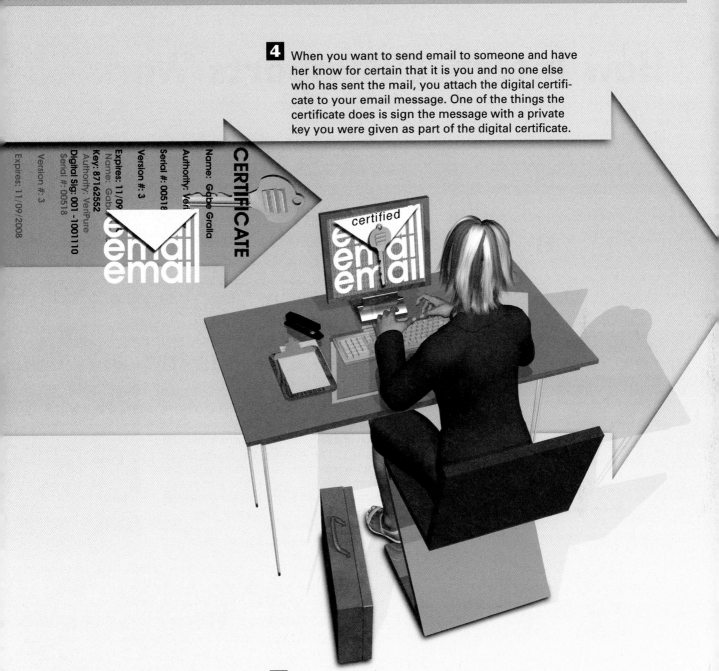

5 The person to whom you're sending email gets your digital certificate along with your email. The key is used to read the private key's signature. That signature matches information found in the digital certificate, so the receiver is assured that the message really came from you.

How Internet Passports Work

2 When the user visits a web-site, the information in the profile the person has put into his passport is sent to the site's web server.

Username: JonJohnson
Password: JIF

Welcome Jon Johnson

INTERNET PASSPORT

OK - News Sharing

NO - Buying Information

Name: Jon Johnson
Username: Jordan
Password: JIF

Passport

3 The server examines the information in the passport. In this instance, the profile includes a username and password, so the username and password are sent to the website, automatically logging the person in to a special portion of the site that allows only those who have already regis-tered at the site. The server might then send a welcome message to the person logging in.

Utah: 107
Chicago: 103

No Buying
Information

Reads sports scores

Web server

4 While on the site, the person reads news about the latest sports scores and then buys an electric razor and a book about sailing. The website puts into the person's profile that he has read sports scores but not that he has bought a razor and a book—because the person's profile said it would allow informa-tion about which news sto-ries he reads to be shared but not information about what he buys.

1 Internet *passports* are designed to let people decide what personal information they will allow to be released to websites. A variety of tech-nologies are involved with Internet passports, including the Platform for Privacy Preferences (P3P), the Internet Content and Exchange standard (ICE), and the Open Profiling Standard (OPS). The passport lives inside a web browser. A user fills out a profile in the browser, determining which information can be made available to websites, such as name, address, occupation, username and password, and age. The user also decides which type of information about his surfing habits can be shared among websites—and which can't. In this instance, the person has decided that information about which news stories he reads can be shared but not information about which products he buys.

5 The person visits another website. The information in the profile the person has put into his passport is sent to the site's web server. The server sees that the person has recently read a story about sports scores, so it sends him a daily digest of the latest sports news. Because the profile doesn't have any information about what the person has bought, it doesn't send any information about special sales on the site.

Reads sports scores

Daily
Sports
Digest

News site

6 The person now surfs to a different website. This site allows in only people who have agreed, in their profiles, to allow their online buying habits to be shared among sites. Because the person has said he doesn't want that information to be shared, the person is not allowed onto the site.

No buying
information

Cannot
Visit
Site

Buying site

CHAPTER

16

How Web Blocking and Parental Controls Work

THE Internet allows for the free, unfettered flow of information among people—and this freedom poses problems for some people, as well as for some governments.

Some parents in particular are concerned about the kinds of material their children may come across on the Internet. It is extremely easy for children to come across pornographic pictures and material. And it's not just pornography that is a problem. There is a great deal of hate material, racist material, and violent material as well.

To try to solve this problem, Congress and other legislative bodies have tried to take steps to ban certain types of content from being available on the Internet and to ban libraries and other public facilities from allowing access to certain material. As a result of these efforts, controversial laws have been passed against online pornography. Sometimes the laws are overturned by the courts. For example, a law called the Communications Decency Act was ruled unconstitutional by the Supreme Court. But sometimes the laws stand.

A technology solution is available as well. Parental control software can stop children from viewing objectionable material. The software can be installed on a single computer or a network—for example, to block all computers at a library from viewing objectionable material.

Businesses are also concerned with the type of Internet material their workers are accessing over corporate networks. Displaying sexual material on computers in the workplace can be interpreted as sexual harassment and can lead to serious legal ramifications. Additionally, most companies simply don't want their workers accessing that material on company time. Some companies now lease filtering software. Instead of installing the software on individual computers, though, the software is installed on a server and checks all incoming Internet traffic to every computer in the company.

There is a dark side to blocking Internet content, though. Authoritarian and dictatorial governments such as China and Saudi Arabia block their citizens from reading material that the *government* finds objectionable but that citizens want to read—for example, news about democracy, religion, or dissent.

Many governments block websites, but the problem is particularly egregious in China. By some accounts, China has the world's second-largest number of Internet users, after the United States. China has the world's most sophisticated system for blocking Internet content, called "The Great Firewall of China" by some.

The government blocks an astonishing amount of content, sites, and even individual words. For example, researchers at Harvard Law School's Berkman Center for Internet & Society checked more than 204,000 websites and found that China blocked more than 19,000 of them at some point. For example, the top 10 Google results returned after searching for "Tibet," "Taiwan China," and "equality" were all blocked. So were 8 of the top 10 results using the terms "democracy China" and "dissident China."

The government also blocks access to news sites; sites about religion; and many other types of sites, including universities such as Columbia University and the Massachusetts Institute of Technology.

How Web Blocking Works

1 Many countries around the world block access to certain parts of the Internet or certain content on the Internet. They fear that unfettered access to information will lead to greater calls for democracy and freedom. The largest and most sophisticated blocking effort is undertaken by the Chinese government and is called "The Great Firewall of China" by those who oppose it. While no one is sure exactly how it works, many people have researched it and come up with some basic outlines of the plan, which are shown in this illustration.

www.epochtimes.com

2 One level of blocking takes place at the major backbones that provide Internet access into China. Routers or servers examine all information traveling over those backbones and look for URLs and IP addresses the Chinese government has banned, such as news sites, sites dedicated to democracy, and sites of the religious group the Falun Gong. When it finds one of those URLs or IP addresses, it does not let the site load.

3 Blocking also takes place at the local level, such as at Internet service providers (ISPs), universities, and other places that provide Internet access. This means that what is blocked varies from location to location in China. For example, hotels that cater to foreign tourists allow more sites through than do other places in China.

Note: In a controversial case involving China and the Internet, Yahoo! turned over to the Chinese government emails from a Yahoo! mail account used by a Chinese journalist. The journalist, Shi Tao, was jailed for 10 years for sharing a memo with foreigners, written by the Chinese authorities. The memo warned newspapers not to play up the 15th anniversary of the killings in Tiananmen Square.

4 China also uses a technique called *DNS hijacking* to block access to sites. The DNS system underpins the functioning of the Internet. Servers and routers can only understand IP addresses in numbers, such as 63.240.93.132, and not URLs, such as www.quepublishing.com. So every time you type in a URL, it is sent to a DNS server, which translates that URL into its proper numeric IP address; then you go to the site.

China blocks access to sites by changing their entries in the country's DNS servers. So, if the government wanted to block access to www.quepublishing.com, it would give that URL an incorrect IP address entry in the DNS server—for example, sending it to an IP address that doesn't exist and blocking access to the site.

5 The Chinese government also blocks search engines from showing results the government does not want displayed. In the case of Yahoo!, Yahoo! has agreed to block access to certain words and sites. Google has not agreed to that blocking, so the Chinese government uses filters to check all Google searches and blocks access to certain sites and search terms.

Blocking also takes place in discussion boards and chat rooms. Filters look for certain words and block those words from being displayed. In some cases, U.S. companies perform the blocking, not the Chinese government. For example, Microsoft blocks certain words from being used on its MSN site in China.

6 As a way around the Great Firewall, some Chinese Internet users connect to proxy servers located outside China. When they do that, the server contacts sites, rather than the individual inside China, and then forwards the information to the person inside China. This often lets people visit blocked sites. The government and surfers are involved in a cat-and-mouse game because when the government finds out about a proxy server, it blocks access to it. But new servers spring up all the time.

How Parental Controls Work

1 Parental control software is installed on a computer a parent wants to monitor to ensure that children can't get to objectionable material on the Internet. When a child launches software to get onto the Internet, SurfWatch monitors the TCP/IP data stream coming from the Internet.

2 The parental control software examines the incoming URL of every address stack. It looks specifically for several types of URLs, including http, nntp, ftp, and IRCs, among others. It takes each of those types of URLs and puts it in its own separate "box." It allows the rest of the Internet information coming in to go through. Parental control software checks for these types of URLs because they are the ones that are the most likely to contain objectionable material.

SurfWatch

www.disney.com

irc.adultstuff ftp.nastystuff nntp.violence gopher.sex

TCP/IP stack

HTTP   NNTP   FTP   Gopher   IRC

3 Every URL in each of the boxes is checked against a database of the URLs of objectionable sites. If SurfWatch finds that any of the URLs are from objectionable sites, it doesn't allow that information to be passed to the computer, blocking the site and preventing information from being viewed. It alerts the child that the site has been blocked. The parental control software checks thousands of sites and lists in its database the ones that are found to be objectionable.

4 If the URL is not in the database, parental control software does another check of the URL. This is called *pattern matching*, and it looks at the words in the URL and checks them against a database of words to see whether any of them indicates a request for objectionable material. Often, people creating objectionable material put representative words in the URL to draw attention to the site. If SurfWatch finds a matching pattern, it doesn't allow that information to be passed on to the computer, blocking the site and preventing information from being viewed. It also alerts the child that the site has been blocked.

5 Parental control software also uses a rating system called Platform for Internet Content Selection (PICS) that embeds information about the site's content in its documents—saying, for example, whether objectionable material can be found there. If parental control software finds that the URL is of a site containing objectionable material, it doesn't allow that information to be passed on to the computer, blocking the site and information from being viewed. It also alerts the child that the site has been blocked.

6 If the URL is not found to be of an objectionable site after the checks have been completed, the URL is passed to the computer and then to the Internet software, where the child can view it and interact with it. Parental control software does all the checking practically instantly, so there is no apparent delay in getting material from the Internet.

SurfWatch

Kid Sites 101
KIDSEARCH
TEENSTREETS
DISNEY.FUN

www.disney.com
www.familyfun.com
www.safekids.com

updates updates upd
updates updates updates
updates updates

TCP/IP
stack

7 Because the Internet is growing so quickly and so many new sites are being created every month, the parental control database of objectionable sites could become outdated. To solve the problem, the database is constantly updated. That way, the list of sites is always kept current.

8 Parents aren't the only people who want to filter out objectionable sites. Many businesses also might want to ensure that their workers aren't accessing objectionable sites over their corporate networks. Instead of having a copy of the control software installed on every user's computer, the software is installed on a network server through which all Internet traffic must travel. At the server, the software checks for objectionable sites in the same way it does at individual machines. However, when software is on a server, the software filters all Internet traffic for the entire company.

CHAPTER

17

How Personal Firewalls and Proxy Servers Protect You

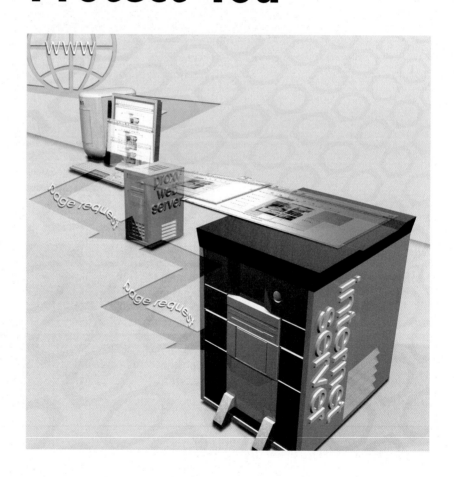

TO connect to the Internet is to be under attack. Whether you're connected via a corporate network, via your home network, or via an ISP, hackers and others are constantly probing your system for vulnerabilities.

The most vulnerable are corporate networks and individuals who connect via high-speed connections such as with cable or DSL modems. Corporate networks have vast amounts of data and resources and are therefore big targets. They also have lots of bandwidth, which hackers can use to launch attacks against others. Cable modem and DSL users are targets because they have a lot of bandwidth as well.

Corporations and individuals can protect themselves in a number of ways, however. One of the most common ways is by using firewalls. There are two primary kinds of firewalls: personal firewalls and corporate firewalls. A *personal firewall* is an inexpensive or free piece of software, such as ZoneAlarm or Norton Personal Firewall, that protects computers from attack. Windows includes a free firewall as well. It's less effective than other personal firewalls, although the firewall built in to the newest version of Windows—Vista—is effective.

Corporate firewalls are much more sophisticated than personal firewalls. There are hardware and software combinations that are built using routers, servers, and a variety of software. They sit at the most vulnerable point between a corporate network and the Internet and can be as simple or as complex as system administrators want to build them.

One of the simplest kinds of firewalls utilizes packet filtering. In *packet filtering*, a screening router examines the header of every packet of data traveling between the Internet and the corporate network. Packet headers have information in them, such as the IP address of the sender and receiver, the protocol being used to send the packet, and other similar information. Based on that information, the router knows what kind of Internet service—such as FTP or rlogin—is being used to send the data, as well as the identities of the sender and receiver of the data. (The command rlogin is similar to Telnet, which enables someone to log in to a computer. It can be dangerous because it enables users to bypass having to type in a password.) After this information is determined, the router can bar certain packets from being sent between the Internet and the corporate network. For example, the router could block any traffic except for email. Additionally, it could block traffic to and from suspicious destinations or from certain users.

Proxy servers are also commonly used in firewalls. A *proxy server* is server software that runs on a host in a firewall, such as a bastion host. Because only the single proxy server (instead of the many individual computers on the network) interacts with the Internet, security can be maintained. That single server can be kept more secure than can hundreds of individual computers on a network.

Even more powerful than firewalls are *intrusion protection systems*, which constantly monitor network traffic, look for telltale signs of an attack, and then either take action on their own or alert administrators that an attack is underway.

How Personal Firewalls Protect PCs

1 People who use high-speed connections such as cable modems at home might be prone to hackers' attacks because computers connected to the Internet in this way are more vulnerable and more enticing to hackers. To protect home computers, many people have turned to *personal firewalls*—software that runs on the computer and protects the computer against Internet attacks. To understand how personal firewalls work, you first need to understand the concept of Internet ports. An *Internet port* isn't a physical device; rather it's a virtual entranceway between your computer and the Internet. When you make an Internet connection, many of these virtual connections are opened, and each has its own number and purpose. For example, email software usually uses port 110 on a mail server to get mail and uses port 25 on a mail server to send mail. FTP software usually connects to FTP servers using port 21.

2 Personal firewalls work by examining the data packets your computer receives. These data packets have a great deal of information in them, such as the sending computer's IP address, your computer's IP address, the port over which the packet will be transmitted, and other pieces of information. Firewalls can filter out packets being sent to certain ports. For example, a firewall can block all packets being transmitted to port 21 so that an FTP program can't be used to attack your PC. Firewalls can block every port to your PC, or they can block them selectively—for example, only blocking ports that are commonly used in hacker attacks, such as blocking port 31338, which is one of the ports often used by the infamous Back Orifice Trojan horse.

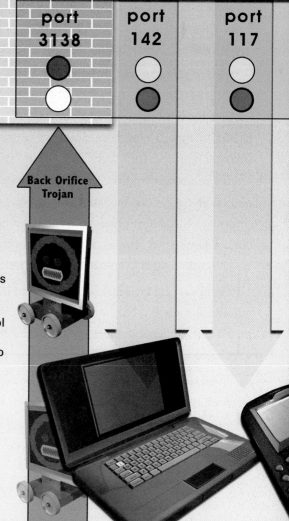

port 3138

port 142

port 117

Back Orifice Trojan

3 One way hackers can attack your computer is to plant a Trojan horse in it. That Trojan horse can then connect to a hacker on its own, which would give him complete control of your computer. Personal firewalls can tell you when programs from your PC attempt to connect to the Internet and then allow only programs you know are safe, such as your email software, to access the Internet.

4 Firewalls can also block specific IP addresses from contacting your computer. For example, if you know the IP of a hacker who has attacked you before, you can have your firewall block his address from getting through to your computer.

Banned IPs

23.54.12.0
37.23.122.
249. 07.8
 2.19

port 3138

port 21

NAT

5 Many home network routers include a hardware-based personal firewall that protects you from the Internet using a technique called *network address translation (NAT)*. With NAT, your true IP address is shielded from the Internet—it can't be seen by anyone or any application outside your home network. In essence, it's invisible and can't be reached by hackers.

Personal firewall

6 Many personal firewalls keep a running log of every attempt made to attack or probe your PC. These logs can be sent to your ISP, which can use them to try to track down the hackers and shut them down.

How Network Address Translation Protects Home Networks

1 Computers and devices on the Internet need to have a unique IP address to perform simple tasks such as browsing the Web. But the Internet has grown so substantially since it was invented that there are not enough IP addresses to go around. To solve the problem, network address translation (NAT) is used, and NAT has the added benefit of protecting PCs inside a network. In a home network, NAT is performed by a home router.

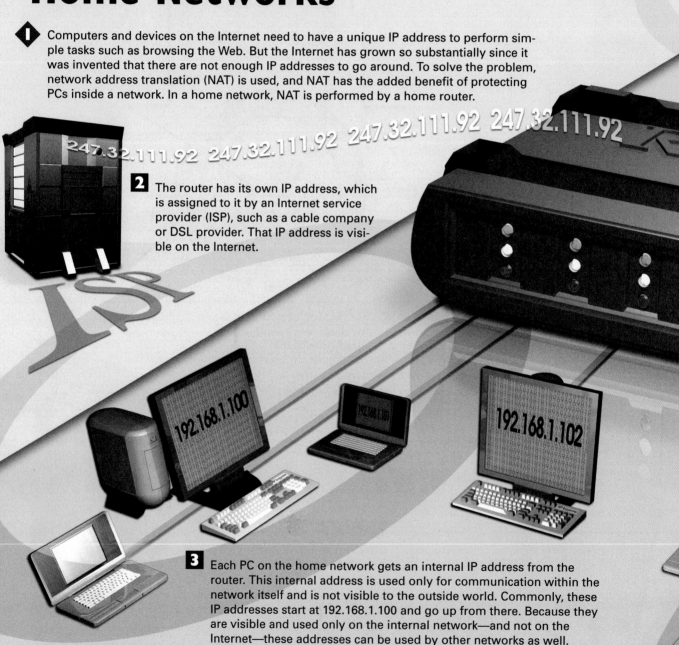

247.32.111.92 247.32.111.92 247.32.111.92 247.32.111.92

2 The router has its own IP address, which is assigned to it by an Internet service provider (ISP), such as a cable company or DSL provider. That IP address is visible on the Internet.

ISP

192.168.1.100

192.168.1.101

192.168.1.102

3 Each PC on the home network gets an internal IP address from the router. This internal address is used only for communication within the network itself and is not visible to the outside world. Commonly, these IP addresses start at 192.168.1.100 and go up from there. Because they are visible and used only on the internal network—and not on the Internet—these addresses can be used by other networks as well.

4 When a PC goes onto the Internet, it appears that it has the router's IP address, not the internal IP address. It can browse the Web and use the Internet normally.

5 All the PCs in a network have the same external IP address. But internally, they use the router-assigned IP addresses. So, when a PC browses the Web, for example, the router is capable of sending the data to the proper PC because it knows the PC's internal IP address.

6 NAT helps protect PCs against hackers and attacks because, to the Internet and hackers, the PC's IP address appears to be the router's IP address. Because of this, it is shielded from many kinds of attacks.

How Proxy Servers Work

1 System administrators can set up proxy servers to be used for many services, such as FTP, the Web, and Telnet. System administrators decide which Internet services must go through a proxy server. Specific proxy server software is required for each kind of Internet service.

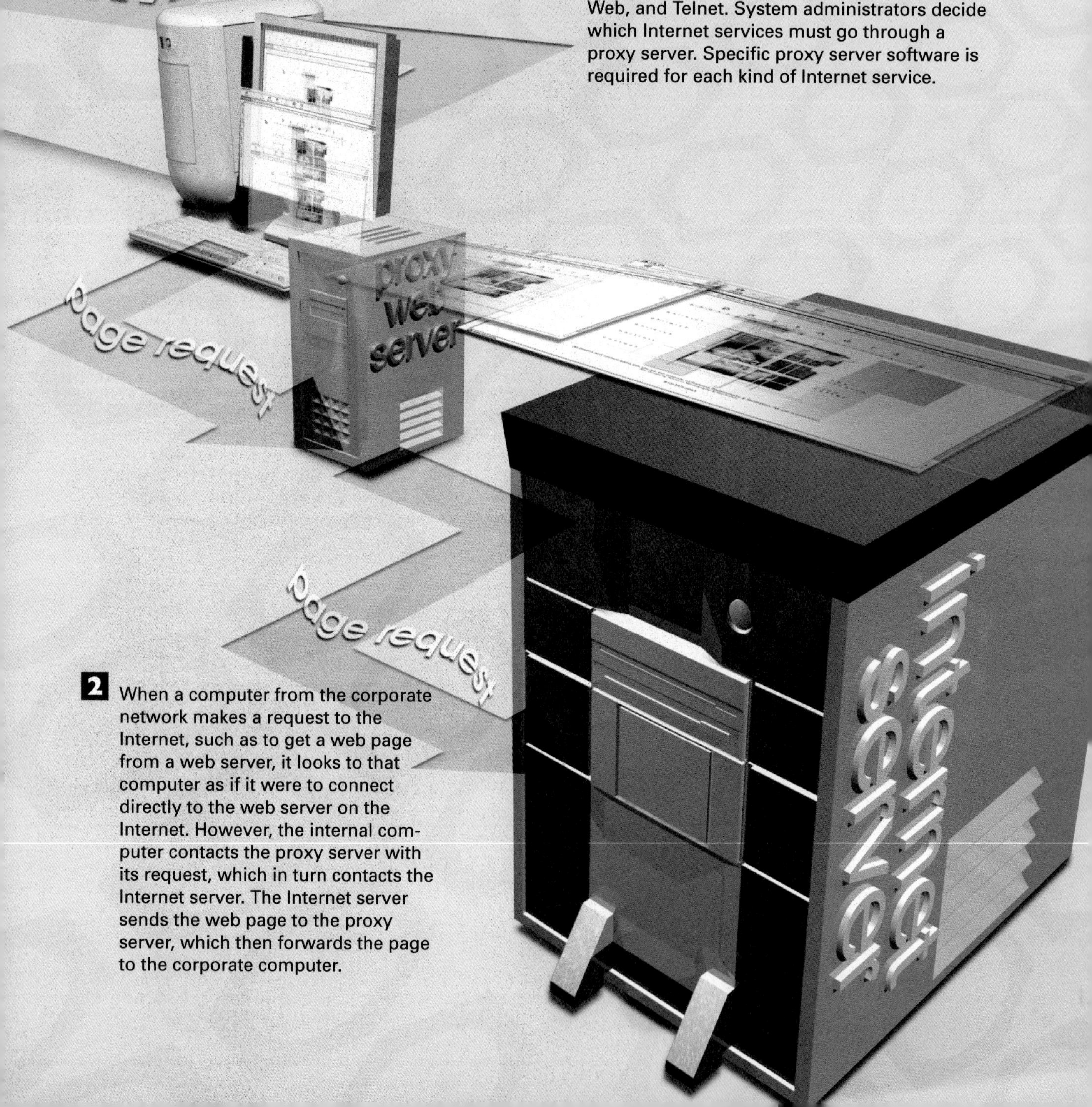

page request

proxy Web server

page request

internet server

2 When a computer from the corporate network makes a request to the Internet, such as to get a web page from a web server, it looks to that computer as if it were to connect directly to the web server on the Internet. However, the internal computer contacts the proxy server with its request, which in turn contacts the Internet server. The Internet server sends the web page to the proxy server, which then forwards the page to the corporate computer.

3 Proxy servers can be used as a way to log the Internet traffic between an internal corporate network and the Internet. For example, a Telnet proxy server could track every keystroke in every Telnet session, and it could track how the external server on the Internet reacted to those keystrokes. Proxy servers can log every IP address, the date and time of access, the URL, the number of bytes downloaded, and so on. This information can be used to analyze any attacks launched against the network.

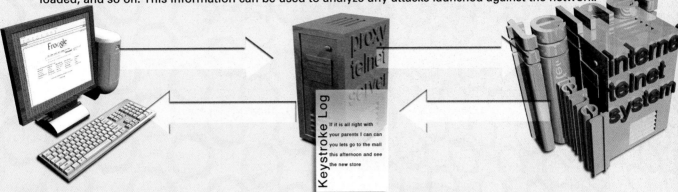

4 Proxy servers can do more than simply relay requests back and forth between a computer on a network and a server on the Internet. They can implement security schemes as well. For example, an FTP proxy server could enable files to be sent from the Internet to a computer on a corporate network but not enable files to be sent from the corporate network out to the Internet, or vice versa.

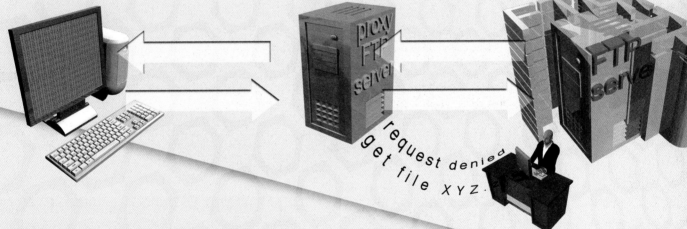

5 Proxy servers can also be used to speed up performance of some Internet services by *caching data*—keeping copies of the requested data. For example, a web proxy server could cache many web pages. Then, whenever someone from the internal corporate network wanted to get one of those web pages, that person could get it directly from the server at a high speed instead of having to go out across the Internet to get the page at a lower speed.

How Corporate Firewalls Protect the Workplace

Internet router (choke router)

1 The *firewall* shields the internal corporate network from the Internet. The internal network works as networks normally do—servers provide internal services such as email, access to corporate databases, and the capability to run programs from servers.

Finance

2 When someone on the corporate network inside the firewall wants to access the Internet, the request and data must go through an internal screening router (sometimes called a *choke router*). This router examines all the packets of data traveling in both directions between the corporate network and the Internet. Information in the packets' headers gives the router important data, such as the source and destination of the packet, the kind of protocol being used to send the packet, and other identifiers.

3 Based on the information in the headers, the screening router allows certain packets to be sent or received but blocks other packets. For example, it might not allow some services, such as rlogin, to be run. The router also might not allow packets to be sent to and from specific Internet locations because those locations have been found to be suspicious. Conceivably, a router could be set up to block every packet traveling between the Internet and the internal network, except for email. System administrators set the rules for determining which packets to allow in and which ones to block.

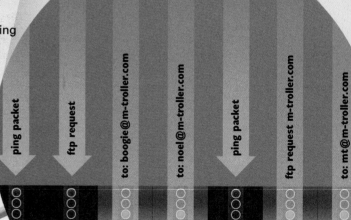

ping packet

ftp request

to: boogie@m-troller.com

to: noel@m-troller.com

ping packet

ftp request m-troller.com

to: mt@m-troller.com

To manufacturing

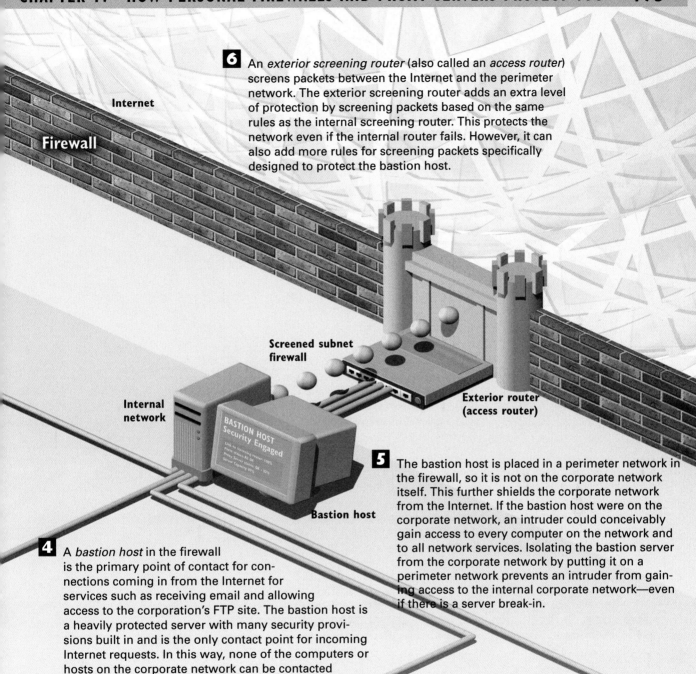

6 An *exterior screening router* (also called an *access router*) screens packets between the Internet and the perimeter network. The exterior screening router adds an extra level of protection by screening packets based on the same rules as the internal screening router. This protects the network even if the internal router fails. However, it can also add more rules for screening packets specifically designed to protect the bastion host.

Internet

Firewall

Screened subnet firewall

Internal network

BASTION HOST Security Engaged

Exterior router (access router)

Bastion host

5 The bastion host is placed in a perimeter network in the firewall, so it is not on the corporate network itself. This further shields the corporate network from the Internet. If the bastion host were on the corporate network, an intruder could conceivably gain access to every computer on the network and to all network services. Isolating the bastion server from the corporate network by putting it on a perimeter network prevents an intruder from gaining access to the internal corporate network—even if there is a server break-in.

4 A *bastion host* in the firewall is the primary point of contact for connections coming in from the Internet for services such as receiving email and allowing access to the corporation's FTP site. The bastion host is a heavily protected server with many security provisions built in and is the only contact point for incoming Internet requests. In this way, none of the computers or hosts on the corporate network can be contacted directly for requests from the Internet, which provides a level of security. Bastion hosts can also be set up as *proxy servers*—servers that process any requests from the internal corporate network to the Internet, such as browsing the Web or downloading files via FTP.

To marketing

To HR

How Intrusion Protection Systems Work

1 Intrusion protection systems use a variety of methods to protect networks. There is no single standard or method of detection, but this illustration shows many of the most common ones.

2 An intrusion protection system monitors all incoming and outgoing packets on all ports as a way to detect intrusions.

3 A signature-based intrusion detection system looks for attacks that fit known patterns of malicious behavior and hacking. These patterns of malicious behavior are called *signatures*. The system constantly watches network traffic and compares that to its database of signatures; when it find traffic that matches a signature, it knows that an attack is underway.

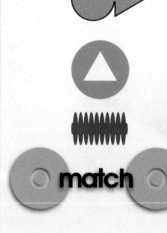

Signature Data

match

ALERT! WARNING!!

4 In a *zero day attack*, a hacker launches an attack that is so new or novel that it does not match any existing signatures. Some intrusion protection systems can guard against zero day attacks by looking for network anomalies—for example, a sudden surge in traffic on a certain port for no apparent reason.

5 Some intrusion protection systems are *passive*. They log information about the attack but take no action on their own; they only issue an alert that an attack has taken place. They may flash an alert on a monitor, send an email to network administrators, and include information about the attack, but they take no action on their own.

6 Other intrusion protect systems are *active*. In addition to logging information and issuing alerts, they also take immediate action, such as logging off a suspicious user and blocking her from getting back onto the Internet or reprogramming a firewall to block traffic to and from a specific port.

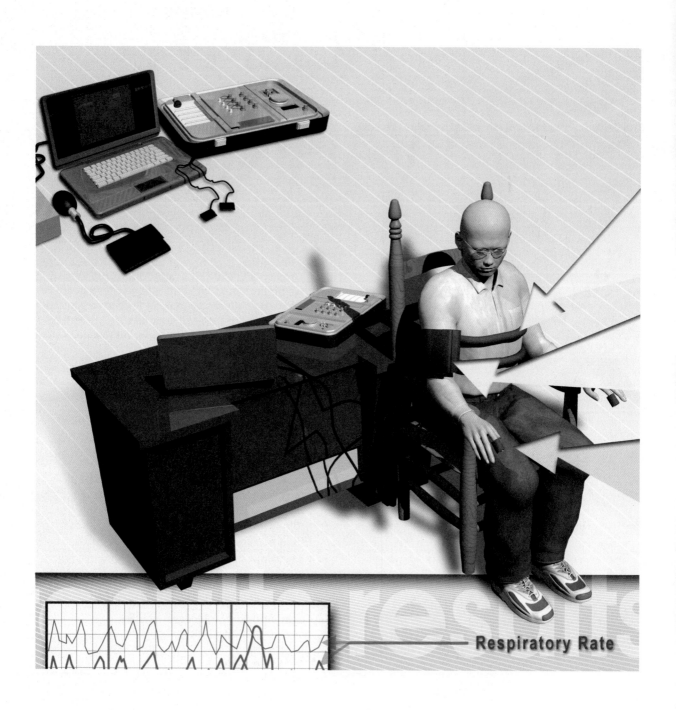

Respiratory Rate

P A R T

Personal Privacy and Security

THESE days, the entire world, not just the Internet, has become an insecure place. It's not just possible terrorist threats that make it so. Identity thieves and others bent on invading your privacy make it dangerous as well.

And to a certain extent, it's not only criminals who invade your privacy. As you'll see in this section, private businesses do as well. And the federal government may just be the most intrusive of all.

Chapter 18, "How Identity Theft Works," shows you how identity thieves can steal your identity, pose as you, and wreak havoc with your private life and finances. It also follows the money trail and shows how thieves can make money from stealing your identity. The chapter also details how you can protect yourself against identity theft.

In Chapter 19, "Credit Card Security," you'll learn the ins and outs of how your credit information is kept safe, but you'll also see how that doesn't always work and how it is often stolen. And you'll take a look inside the seamy black market that traffics in stolen credit cards.

Chapter 20, "The Dangers of Data Mining," examines this little-known way in which your privacy can be invaded. In data mining, companies or government agencies gather all the information they can about people and their habits and then use special techniques to build personal profiles, track people, and more.

Chapter 21, "The Dangers of Workplace Surveillance," details the ways in which people are tracked every moment of their workday. Tens of millions of people work in businesses that track their activities—everything from web surfing to email, telephone calls, and even surveillance cameras.

Chapter 22, "How Cell Phones Can Be Hacked," shows you that when you talk on your cell phone, your conversations may be open to the world. And it's not just your conversations that can be snooped upon. As cell phones have turned into small computers, your data can be stolen as well. The chapter also looks at how B-list celebrity Paris Hilton's cell phone was hacked and how a technique called *Bluesnarfing* works.

Chapter 23, "How Biometrics Works," covers an increasingly popular means of identifying people. Biometrics uses people's physical characteristics as a way of confirming their identity. For example, fingerprint scanners and iris scanners can be used to confirm that someone is who she says she is.

In Chapter 24, "How Radio Frequency ID Can Invade Your Privacy," we examine a technology just starting to make its way into retail stores. Radio frequency ID (RFID) uses small tags and radio waves to track goods such as clothing and pharmaceuticals; as you'll see, it can track your use of them as well. In the future, RFID may become frequently used, with an enormous potential for privacy invasion.

Chapter 25, "How Location Tracking Works," shows how your precise location can easily be tracked using common technologies such as the Global Positioning System (GPS). Unknown to most people is the fact that even your cell phone can track your location.

In Chapter 26, "How DNA Matching Works," you'll learn about the frontiers of technology: how your DNA can be tracked and matched. You'll also learn about the potential dangers of this technology and how it might help deny people jobs and health insurance, among other threats.

In Chapter 27, "How Airport Scanners and Security Cameras Work," you'll see how some of the technologies in the front line against terrorism work. We'll also take a closer look at terrorist tracking systems that try to make sure no terrorist can board airplanes.

Chapter 28, "The Federal Government, Privacy, and Electronic Surveillance," looks at the intelligence-gathering powers, and enormous potential for privacy invasion, posed by the federal government. It looks at some of the more controversial government programs, such as the National Security Agency's Echelon program that taps into global phone, data, and Internet communications and that has also been turned against U.S. citizens at home. The chapter also shows how the FBI's Carnivore program—an extremely controversial program that enabled the federal government to read people's email and follow their Internet activity without people knowing about it—worked.

Finally, Chapter 29, "How Wiretapping and Lie Detectors Work," shows you how these law-enforcement tools work, how they can be used to protect us, and also how they can be used to invade our privacy.

CHAPTER
18

How Identity Theft Works

ONE of the most well-publicized threats to personal security in recent years has been identity theft, in which someone's private financial information is stolen and then used illegally.

This information can be used in a variety of ways. In the simplest way, someone uses the stolen credit card or bank account. However, the information can also be used to open bank accounts, get new credit cards, and take out bank loans in the victim's name—and the criminal gets off scot-free, while the victim may have to spend years clearing his name.

Identity theft can also be used by terrorists or illegal aliens who want to establish a legal identity in the United States.

There's good reason that identity theft has gotten a lot of publicity—it's very big business. According to a study done by the Council of Better Business Bureaus and Javelin Strategy & Research, identity theft cost consumers a staggering $57 billion in 2005.

The survey shows that, despite the publicity surrounding the practice, identity theft continues to grow. It found that it cost U.S. consumers 4% more in 2005 than it did in 2004. And the average fraud also grew, from $5,885 to $6,383.

One of the more surprising results of the survey is that those with low incomes are more vulnerably to identity theft than those with higher incomes. And young people are more vulnerable than those who are older.

The survey did not explain why those who earn less money are more vulnerable to identity theft. One reason, though, might be that they could be more susceptible to some of the get-rich-quick or "credit repair" scams that lead to identity theft.

Most headlines in recent years about identity theft have focused on how the Internet is used to steal people's identity. For example, *phishing* scams, in which a phony email gets someone to log in to a phony website and submit personal information, have gotten a good deal of press. And many people know that it's dangerous to enter their credit cards into sites that do not appear reputable.

Surprisingly, though, the survey found that the Internet is not the primary method criminals use for stealing people's identities. It found that only 3% of identity theft results from phishing attempts. And overall, Internet fraud accounted for only 9% of identity theft cases.

By way of contrast, 30% of victims had their wallets, checkbooks, or credit cards stolen or lost. Fifteen percent were victimized by family, friends, or acquaintances. Another 15% were victimized by fellow employees, and 8% were victimized by stolen mail or misdirected mail.

How Thieves Can Steal Your Identity

1 The term *identity theft* is a very broad one and covers many criminal activities, from stealing credit cards, to posing as another individual, including that person's driver's license and Social Security number. This illustration covers some of the most common ways in which identities are stolen.

2 The most common type of identity theft is the theft of credit cards. Credit cards are stolen in many ways, including by hackers breaking into card systems and *dumpster divers* who look in dumpsters for credit card slips. For more information about credit card theft, see the illustration "How Credit Card Information Is Stolen" in Chapter 19, "Credit Card Security."

3 Various Internet scams can lead to identity theft. For example, in a phishing scam, you are lured via email to log in to a web page and then enter personal information. That information may include your Social Security number, credit card information, and your mother's maiden name, among other details. For more information about phishing, refer to Chapter 6, "How 'Phishing' Attacks Can Steal Your Identity—and How to Protect Against Them."

4 Spyware, keyloggers, and Trojans installed on people's computers can steal personal information and send it to hackers, or they can monitor every keystroke the user makes.

5 Some identity thieves can steal your identity the old-fashioned way—by physical theft. They steal wallets and purses and use the driver's licenses, credit cards, and other identifying information they find there.

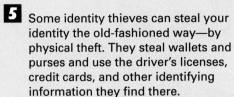

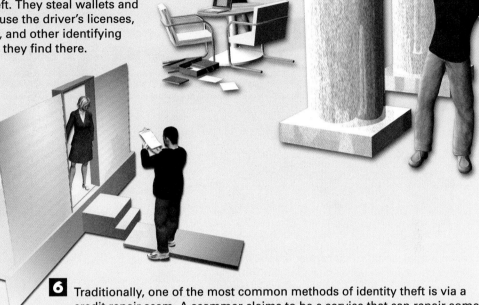

6 Traditionally, one of the most common methods of identity theft is via a credit repair scam. A scammer claims to be a service that can repair someone's bad credit. To repair the credit, they say, they need all personally identifying information, including your Social Security number, mother's maiden name, date of birth, credit card numbers, bank account numbers, and so on.

7 A significant number of identity thefts are committed by family, friends, acquaintances, and co-workers, who steal personal information.

8 Some identity thieves look for unprotected mailboxes. They then steal a person's mail and look for credit card and bank statements, utility bills, and so on. This information can be used in many ways. For example, many government agencies require utility bills to show proof of residence, so an identity thief can use those stolen bills to help get a new identity.

How Thieves Make Use of Stolen Identities

Transfer Funds Into Account 2367A2

1 When a thief steals credit card and bank information, he can empty the bank account and run up sizable credit card bills, shipping the goods he buys directly to himself. A thief can also open bank accounts, establish credit cards, get loans from financial institutions, and so on using the name of the person whose identity he has stolen. He then can write bad checks, make charges to credit cards he will not repay, and fail to repay the loans he has obtained because his real identity cannot be tracked.

2 There is a thriving black market for stolen identities. Many identity thieves don't use the information themselves; instead, they sell it to others. In some cases, they sell the identities directly to other people, but in other cases, they sell them to gangs, such as the Russian Mafia, who then resell the identities to others for a profit.

3 Stolen identities can be used for a variety of criminal activities, such as money laundering. In a money laundering scheme, someone uses a stolen identity, including Social Security number and other information, and sets up a bank account. Money is then laundered through that account.

deposit into laundry account

4 Stolen identities can also be used for illegal aliens or terrorists who want to hide their true identities and establish U.S. identities. An illegal alien or terrorist can be given someone's name, Social Security number, mother's maiden name, and other identifying information. Using that, he can get a legal driver's license, apply for employment, and establish a legal identity even though he is in the country illegally.

D and security #'s

How You Can Protect Against Identity Theft

1 Never respond to phishing attacks. Financial institutions rarely send emails asking that you log in to your account, so never click an email asking you to do so. Instead, call the institution or log in to your account on your own, not by following a link in an email.

Also, never give out your Social Security number unnecessarily. If a website asks for it, don't give it out unless it is a financial institution that requires it.

2 Shred sensitive documents before you throw them away. This includes credit card bills, bank account statements, and any paper that contains your Social Security number.

3 Don't carry your passport, Social Security card, or birth certificate in your wallet, purse, or any place where it can be easily stolen.

Credit card statement

4 Closely track your credit card statements and bank account statements every month, looking to see whether it contains any suspicious charges. If you can access your accounts online, check them weekly.

When using your credit card online, use it only on sites that are secure and use encryption.

5 Install and use anti-spyware and antivirus software. This protects against spyware, key-loggers, and Trojans.

Anti Virus software

scan
block
repair
support

CHAPTER

19

Credit Card Security

WHAT'S the most insecure thing about your life?

If you're like most people, it's your credit card—or to be more accurate, your credit cards because most people have multiple cards. Credit cards are stolen with astonishing regularity and account for substantial amounts of financial losses every year.

There is no single source of information about credit card theft, but the Federal Trade Commission reports that credit card and identity theft cost consumers more than $52 billion in 2004 alone.

Most people worry about their credit cards being taken when their wallet or purse is stolen or when they give out credit card information over the phone. But that does not account for most credit card theft. The vast majority of credit card theft is committed by hackers who break into financial sites and steal credit cards in bulk. In the most infamous of all credit card thefts, the payment processor CardSystems Solution had 40 million of its credit cards exposed to possible theft when a hacker broke into its system.

It's not only hackers who steal credit card information, though. People working at financial firms do it as well. Insiders stole tens of thousands of credit card numbers from Teledata Communications, Inc., which provides information to banks from the three commercial credit history bureaus.

Your credit card is vulnerable to hackers and insiders because many companies provide services to credit card companies, banks, and merchants. In fact, the companies that provide these services are, more often than not, the ones that are hacked into. The credit card companies and banks themselves tend to be more secure.

The Internet has become central to credit card theft and the sale of credit cards. Hackers use the Internet to connect to financial firms and hack into them, and scam artists have turned to the Internet to steal credit card information. So-called *phishing* schemes, in which emails lure you into providing your credit card information to hoaxers, are one of the primary ways in which credit cards are stolen.

Most of the time, those who steal credit cards don't use them for themselves. Rather, they sell them to gangs, often the Russian Mafia or gangs based in Southeast Asia. These gangs then sell the credit cards over the Internet, often for $50–$100 each.

How Credit Card Information Is Stolen

1 One of the most common ways in which credit card information is stolen is the simplest—physical theft. A thief steals a wallet or purse with the credit card inside, or she steals the credit card itself.

2 *Dumpster divers* look through dumpsters in search of canceled credit card transactions that have been thrown in the trash. In this instance, they don't have the physical credit card, but they do have the credit card number and the name of the owner, so they can use it in telephone and Internet transactions.

3 Those who work in service industries may steal credit card information when it is given to them over the telephone. For example, someone taking hotel reservations or waiting on you in a restaurant might copy your credit card information and use it.

4 The Internet has become one of the primary ways for stealing credit card information. A scammer might set up a phony retailing website, claiming to sell goods. When the credit card information is sent, the scammer then steals the information and makes use of it.

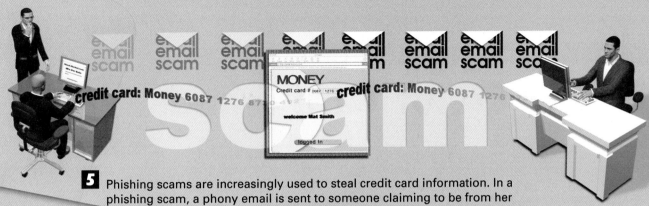

5 Phishing scams are increasingly used to steal credit card information. In a phishing scam, a phony email is sent to someone claiming to be from her financial institution or credit card company and asking her to log on to a website and enter her credit card number. The site is designed to look real but in fact is a fraud; the scammer then steals the credit card information. For more information about phishing attacks, refer to Chapter 6, "How 'Phishing' Attacks Can Steal Your Identity—and How to Protect Against Them."

6 The vast majority of credit card theft is not done by stealing individual cards, but instead by hackers breaking into systems that hold large numbers of credit cards. Break-ins have resulted in hundreds of thousands—and in some cases up to tens of millions—of credit cards being stolen. In some instances, people working inside the institution steal the information or are involved in the theft. For example, insiders stole tens of thousands of credit card numbers from Teledata Communications, Inc., which provides information to banks from the three commercial credit history bureaus, Equifax, Experian, and TransUnion. Therefore, Teledata workers had access to millions of credit card numbers. In the biggest incident in history, a hacker broke into a company called CardSystems Solutions, Inc., and stole 40 million credit card numbers.

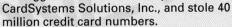

7 In some instances, credit card theft occurs because companies who have credit card information are extremely careless with that data. Some companies, for example, have lost CDs filled with the credit card numbers of individuals. The *Boston Globe* was guilty of one of the more incompetent handlings of credit card information. It printed credit card information of 240,000 of its subscribers and then used those printouts to wrap newspaper bundles distributed to retailers and newspaper carriers. The printouts with the credit card information went to 2,000 retailers and 390 carriers.

How Financial Firms Detect Credit Card Fraud

1 Credit card companies lose billions of dollars each year in fraud, so they've installed automated systems to detect potential fraud. The systems use artificial intelligence (AI) and run on powerful computers, often *neural networks*, which are large collections of powerful processors that work in tandem to process and solve problems.

Patty lee
Household
spending

Patty lee
apparel
spending

Patty lee
grocery
spending

Patty lee
travel
spending

Patty lee
restaurant
spending

2 Many types of AI systems detect potential fraud. They compare individual transactions to overall spending patterns, looking for transactions or patterns that seem anomalous or unusual. Some of the most sophisticated systems create spending profiles of each individual credit card user and compare new transactions against that profile.

Patty Lee Profile

Apparel: Saksz...Kohls
Judy Ray's

Furniture:Kittles...Ted's
****Prime Furniture??****

Travel: United...Holiday Inn
bernies....Hilton....

Dining: Friday's...Steak
House
Chuck's Sandwich Shop

BUY

Patty Lee

Forest Drive

Indianapolis IN 46287

Visa

2564 6826 8902 6424

Prime Furniture

$787.58

3 Every credit card transaction for every individual is automatically sent into the system. Each transaction is compared to the individual's profile and is given a numerical rating that measures the likelihood that the transaction is fraudulent.

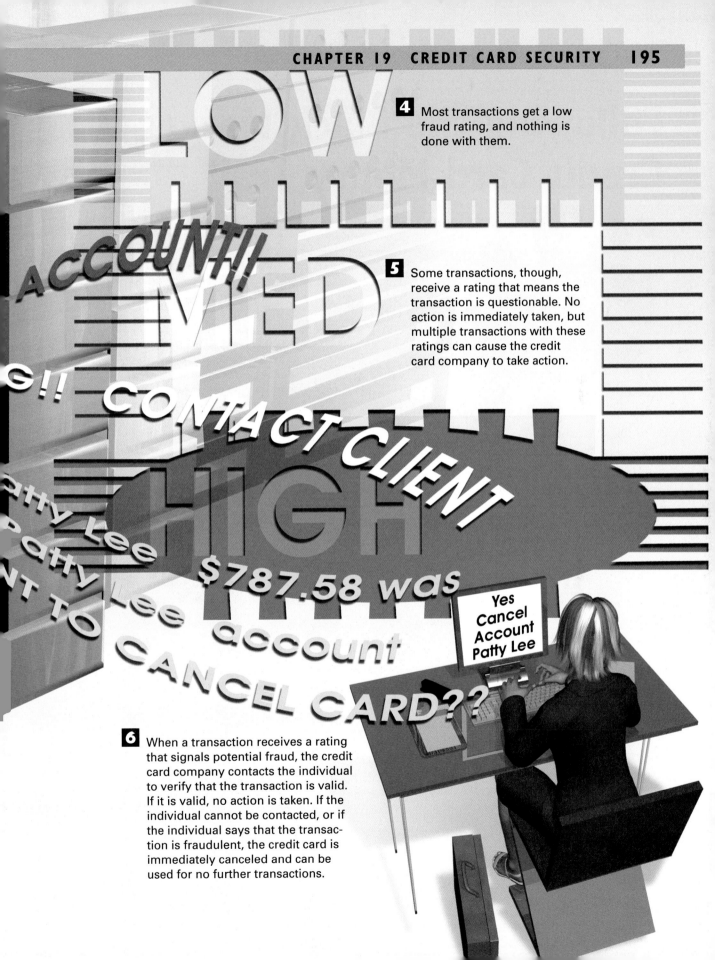

4 Most transactions get a low fraud rating, and nothing is done with them.

5 Some transactions, though, receive a rating that means the transaction is questionable. No action is immediately taken, but multiple transactions with these ratings can cause the credit card company to take action.

6 When a transaction receives a rating that signals potential fraud, the credit card company contacts the individual to verify that the transaction is valid. If it is valid, no action is taken. If the individual cannot be contacted, or if the individual says that the transaction is fraudulent, the credit card is immediately canceled and can be used for no further transactions.

Following the Black Market Credit Card Money Trail

1 Most stolen credit cards are not used by the thieves who steal them. Instead, they go onto the vast Internet black market for credit cards. The trail starts when a thief steals many credit card numbers, often by hacking into a financial site or via a phishing scam.

2 The cards are sold, in bulk, to gangs. The Russian Mafia is heavily involved in selling credit card numbers, as are gangs in Southeast Asia.

UCards4Us.com

3 The gangs create private, members-only websites on which they post credit card numbers. For some sites, a subscription fee must be paid.

UCards4Us

American Express "cob" $85	
American Express "cob" with social security number $215	
American Express "cob" $85	
American Express "cob" $85	
American Express "cob" $85	
Discover "cob" with social security number $115	
Discover "cob" with social security number $115	
Visa "cob" with social security number $165	
Visa "cob" with social security number $165	
Discover "cob" $50	

4 On the sites, thousands of cards are available for sale. Each card is priced according to its potential value. For example, a *cob* is among the most valuable of stolen cards because it is a freshly stolen card that also includes the PIN number that allows someone to change the billing address. At one site, Discover Card cobs were being sold for $50, while American Express cobs were sold for $85, most likely because American Express cards typically have no spending limit.

Discover Card "cob" $50

sold by Gio 57 ★★★★

For questions contact me at gio_____ouse.co

5 Some sites work like eBay, and individual sellers promote their cards for sale. They are even given seller ratings, just like eBay.

6 When someone wants to buy a card, the conversation usually moves to an instant messenger program—primarily ICQ because it allows people to register for it anonymously. Payment is frequently done via e-gold, which is an electronic currency issued by e-gold Ltd. (a company incorporated on the Caribbean island of Nevis). e-gold allows for absolute anonymity, so the identities of those in the transaction cannot be traced.

7 The person who bought the illegal credit card can now use it. In the case of a cob, the buyer changes the address to his own, so any goods he buys can be delivered to him. In some cases, he changes the address to a safe drop—for example, an empty apartment in a nearby building that he can watch to see when the goods are delivered. That way, his real address cannot be traced.

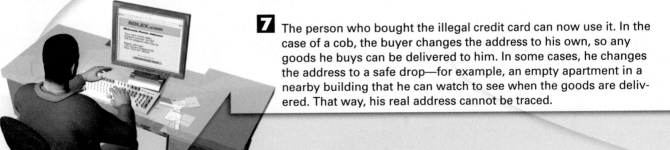

CHAPTER
20

The Dangers of
Data Mining

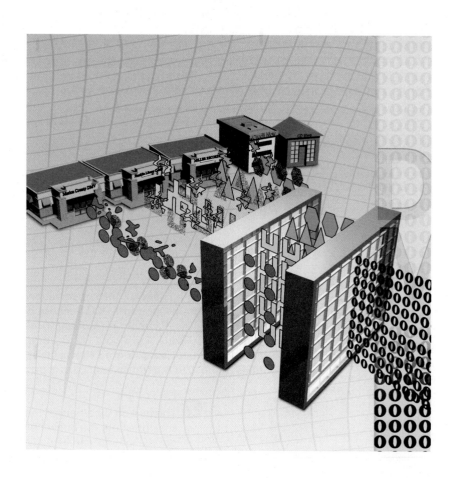

TO live in a modern society is to leave digital traces of yourself with almost every action you take. Buy a meal at a restaurant? You probably paid for it with your credit card. Take out a library book? There's a record of it in a database. Get born? That gets entered into a database as well. Whether you buy a car, visit a bank, make a phone call, or do any of many commonplace tasks, a record of that transaction exists somewhere.

Businesses see gold in that data about you and hundreds of millions of other Americans, and the government sees ways it believes it can better protect its citizens.

But the information is spread out across countless databases, so no one government agency or business has access to it all. And even if it could get access, how could it possibly make sense of it all, given that the databases are not connected to one another, run on different systems, and are in different formats?

Enter data mining. *Data mining* uses powerful data analysis tools to examine vast amounts of data and then discover unseen or previously unknown patterns and relationships in them. For example, a bank or credit card company may mine years of customer data and look for patterns that tell it which kind of customers are the best risk and which are the worst risk. It can then apply that knowledge to extending credit to good risks and denying it to poor risks. Medical researchers can mine data to try to uncover the relationship between lifestyle choices and diseases. A retailer might mine data to find out which of its sales, offers, coupons, and affinity programs works most effectively.

The government, to no one's surprise, uses data mining as well. For example, the Justice Department mines data about crime rates to find out where to best apply its money and help it decide where to make local grants. The Federal Aviation Administration uses data mining to examine plane crash data to help it find airplane defects and causes of crashes, so it can take action to prevent crashes in the future.

Since the terror attacks of September 11, 2001, the government has used data mining to try to track terrorists, prevent future attacks, and screen would-be terrorists from getting on airplanes.

But data mining has its dark side, as well. It can be used to peer into every aspect of a person's life and create extremely detailed profiles of a person's life—and practically track his every move. Data mining companies amass massive amounts of information about people, mine that data, and then sell it to the highest bidder. There have been security breaches at these companies, and detailed information about people, including their Social Security numbers, credit records, addresses, and more, has been stolen by criminals who can use it for identity theft.

In the hands of the government, people worry that data mining can be even more dangerous. The government already has enormous amounts of power, and combining this with the ability to create personal profiles of citizens is inherently dangerous, they warn. In addition, if a data mining program incorrectly labels a person as a "potential terrorist," that person's life has in essence been ruined.

Data mining is increasingly in the news. For example, it was at the center of a political storm when it was revealed that President Bush authorized the National Security Agency (NSA) to listen in on the conversations of possibly millions of Americans without a court warrant. The NSA tried to mine the data in the calls to find potential terrorists, but many warned that the action violated the law, and even the U.S. Constitution.

For better and for worse, data mining is here to stay. The issue is whether it can be controlled and put only to proper uses.

How Data Mining Works

1 The data miner first gathers the data to be mined. The data is found in many databases, and this step in data mining is extremely time-consuming and extremely important—if good data is not gathered, the exercise of mining data is pointless. The number of databases from which information is gathered can be relatively small if data is only mined from a single company. But it can also be enormous—for example, if the federal government is gathering information from multiple federal databases, the Internet, and numerous commercial databases.

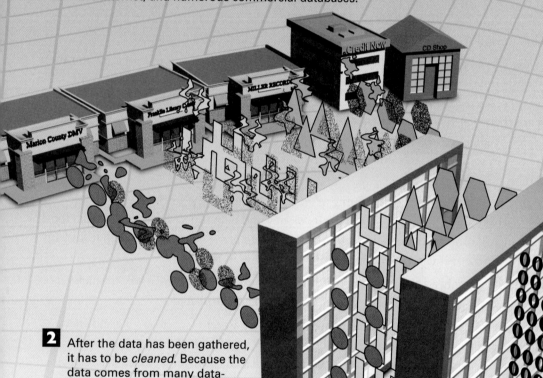

2 After the data has been gathered, it has to be *cleaned*. Because the data comes from many databases and sources, there may be duplicate information, information missing from some records, and incorrect information in them. Automated programs, guided by human intervention, clean the data.

3 The data now needs to be converted to a common format, so that software can search through it and mine it.

4 After the data is prepared and converted, software can begin to mine it. Powerful computers must be used to mine the data, and the more powerful the computer, the more data that can be examined. There are many types of data mining software and techniques, each best suited for particular purposes. Techniques called *regression* and *classification* are commonly used to find hidden relationship that otherwise might not be found. They are also used to find trends that are not obvious.

5 Neural networks can be used to help mine data. *Neural networks* are large networks of computers or processors that work together to solve a complex task. Each processor in the neural network can be assigned a particular variable to search through, and together the network is able to mine massive amounts of data.

6 Some data mining software uses three-dimensional visualization techniques to display relationships among data. A three-dimensional map is created of the information being examined. Peaks represent words that appear frequently, and when peaks are near one another, it means the words are related in some way. An analyst can click the peak and see the data that created the peak.

The Dangers of Data Mining

1 Large commercial data mining companies gather enormous amounts of information about people—everything from Social Security numbers to credit card information, spending and travel habits, personal financial information, and much more. They sell this information to private businesses, so people's private lives are up for sale.

2 Information can be stolen from data mining companies, either by hacking into their systems or by physically stealing disks. When this happens, millions of people are vulnerable to identity theft. For example, in 2005, information on 145,000 people was stolen from data mining giant ChoicePoint. The records stolen included Social Security numbers, addresses, and other personal information.

3 The federal government has many data mining projects, many of which were launched after the September 11, 2001 attacks on the World Trade Center and Pentagon. Critics worry that many of these projects invade people's privacy. The Total Information Awareness (TIA) project had to be cancelled because it intended to gather information from numerous government agencies, private sources, libraries, and other sources of data and could be used to create detailed profiles of many Americans.

ENEMIES LIST
Database

John Brown

Barbera Jones

4 There are concerns that large-scale use of private information will be mishandled by the government—for example, to mine data to look for critics of a current administration and then to take actions against those critics.

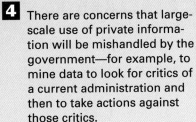

5 Another major concern is the issue of *false positives*, which are people whom data mining says are potential terrorists, even though they are not. For example, a system for screening passengers for terrorists in Florida flagged 120,000 people in that state alone who "had a statistical likelihood of being terrorists," clearly an overblown number. Once someone is tagged as being a potential terrorist, he may be pursued by law enforcement, not allowed to fly, and fired from his job, among other consequences.

CHAPTER

21

The Dangers of Workplace Surveillance

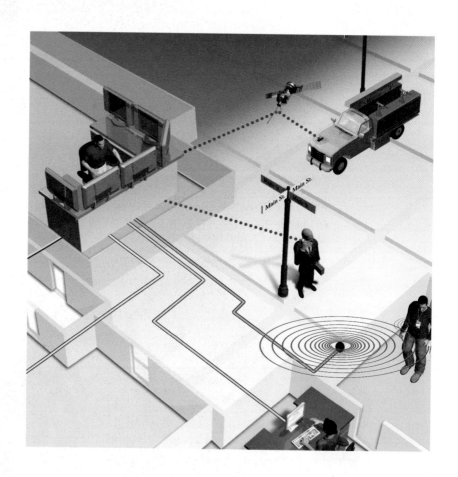

THE greatest danger to your privacy may not come from the Internet, from identity thieves, or from government agencies.

It may come from your boss.

Workplace surveillance has become extremely common in the United States, and it is becoming more common every day. In particular, employers monitor employee Internet and computer use, although new technologies help employers monitor employees in many other ways as well.

Monitoring employees in the workplace has become practically ubiquitous according to a recent study done by the American Management Association (AMA) and The ePolicy Institute. A 2005 study found the following:

- 76% of employers monitor their employees' web surfing activities.
- 66% of employers use software to block employees from accessing inappropriate websites.
- 55% of employers store and review employee email.
- 51% of employers monitor their employees using video cameras, primarily to counter theft, violence, and sabotage, they say. This number rose from 33% in 2001.
- 50% of employers store and review employee personal work files.
- 36% of employers track the content employees view as well as monitor their keystrokes and time spent at the keyboard.

There are a variety of reasons employers monitor employees. One is the fear of litigation. Some courts have ruled that if an employee visits inappropriate websites with sexual material and other employees come across him doing it, that it could be considered a form of workplace sexual harassment. Unless the employer finds a way to stop employees from visiting sexually explicit sites, the company could be sued.

Employers also worry that employees may spend too much time visiting websites that have nothing to do with work, such as eBay or retail websites.

When it comes to email, the law weighs in as well. Email frequently comes up as evidence in lawsuits, and employers are often required by law to keep employee email for a certain number of years.

Additionally, employers want to cut down on fraud, theft, and inappropriate behavior, and often workplace surveillance is the best way to do that.

But many people believe workplace surveillance has gone too far and unnecessarily invades people's privacy, is used to intimidate employees, and is used as a tactic to fight against unions being established. These people worry that Big Brother has come to the workplace and that employers are invading people's privacy in ways that might be illegal.

Whichever side of the debate you come down on, there's no doubt that workplace surveillance is here to stay and is becoming more common by the day. Internet surveillance, the use of video cameras, the use of phone tapping, and even the use of global positioning systems (GPS) will be used more and more in the future. People should recognize that, in their workplace, there most likely is no privacy.

How Workplace Surveillance Works

1 Some workplaces have instituted "continuous, systematic surveillance" according to a Privacy Foundation study written by Andrew Schulman. Companies that perform this kind of surveillance might have a central security office that contains equipment for all the workplace monitoring.

2 Closed-circuit cameras (often hidden) monitor employees as they work and enter and leave the workplace. The cameras often connect via a company network to a computer or other monitoring system, so that security staff can monitor many locations at once. Recordings are often kept, either on computer or on tape.

In some instances, small cameras focus on computer screens, so employers can keep track of computer use. However, because computers can be monitored more accurately in other ways, this is uncommon.

Can I help you?

3 Employers can legally wiretap employee phones and listen to all conversations. Wiretap laws normally forbid private individuals tapping conversations, but the Electronic Communication Privacy Act of 1986 lets employers listen in on "job-related" calls. As a practical matter, this includes all calls because it's argued that all calls in the workplace are work-related. The America Civil Liberties Union has estimated that approximately 400 million telephone calls are wiretapped by employers every year.

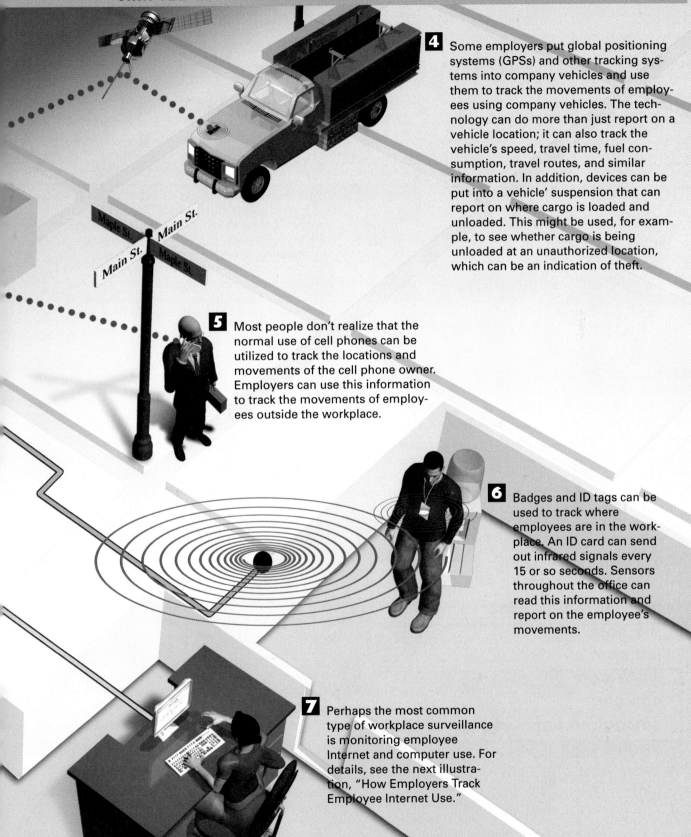

4 Some employers put global positioning systems (GPSs) and other tracking systems into company vehicles and use them to track the movements of employees using company vehicles. The technology can do more than just report on a vehicle location; it can also track the vehicle's speed, travel time, fuel consumption, travel routes, and similar information. In addition, devices can be put into a vehicle' suspension that can report on where cargo is loaded and unloaded. This might be used, for example, to see whether cargo is being unloaded at an unauthorized location, which can be an indication of theft.

5 Most people don't realize that the normal use of cell phones can be utilized to track the locations and movements of the cell phone owner. Employers can use this information to track the movements of employees outside the workplace.

6 Badges and ID tags can be used to track where employees are in the workplace. An ID card can send out infrared signals every 15 or so seconds. Sensors throughout the office can read this information and report on the employee's movements.

7 Perhaps the most common type of workplace surveillance is monitoring employee Internet and computer use. For details, see the next illustration, "How Employers Track Employee Internet Use."

How Employers Track Employee Internet Use

1 One of the most common ways in which companies track employee Internet behavior is through the use of packet sniffers. *Packet sniffers* are software that examines, or sniffs, every packet of data traveling across the network and stores it to a log file. An *unfiltered sniffer* captures every packet to the log, while a *filtered sniffer* captures only specified packets—for example, only packets that have passed into the network from specified websites.

This is John's final notice! Not Again!

He has a real PROBLEM!!

Internet Use Log
Thursday April 20

User: 451-John-9862

sex.com..s

tuff.com..

kinky.com

cnn.com

carsgalore.com

singles.com

2 After the packet sniffer saves the packets to a log file, technical support staff can use log software to examine the file and reconstruct employee Internet behavior, including websites visited, instant messages sent and received, and blogs the employee might have written.

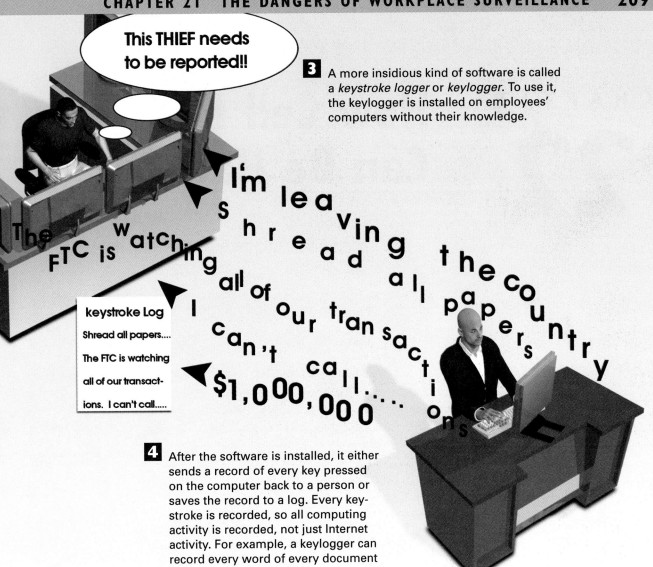

This THIEF needs to be reported!!

3 A more insidious kind of software is called a *keystroke logger* or *keylogger*. To use it, the keylogger is installed on employees' computers without their knowledge.

keystroke Log

Shread all papers....

The FTC is watching

all of our transact-

ions. I can't call.....

4 After the software is installed, it either sends a record of every key pressed on the computer back to a person or saves the record to a log. Every keystroke is recorded, so all computing activity is recorded, not just Internet activity. For example, a keylogger can record every word of every document created on the computer.

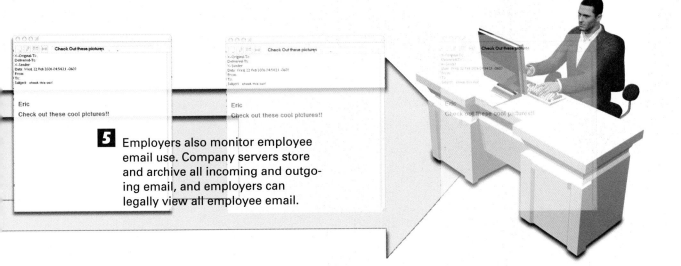

5 Employers also monitor employee email use. Company servers store and archive all incoming and outgoing email, and employers can legally view all employee email.

CHAPTER

22

How Cell Phones Can Be Hacked

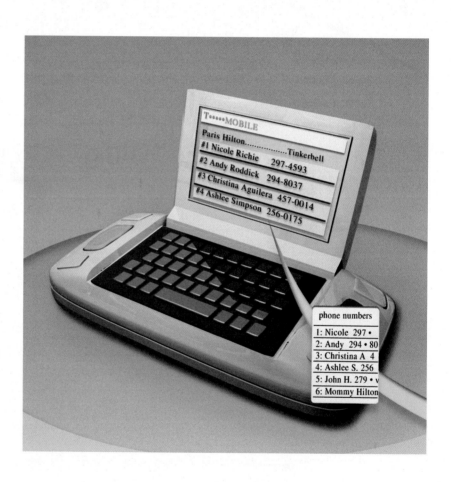

CELL phones these days do more than just let you talk to other people. They include digital cameras, the ability to record and play video, MP3 players, processors powerful enough to play games, and a great deal of memory. In fact, most cell phones are at heart computers—computers that are surprisingly powerful and that pack more power and memory than large computers of a dozen years ago.

And where there are computers, there are hackers. As cell phones become increasingly complex and powerful, they become more and more vulnerable to viruses and hackers. And as they get more powerful, they have more data that hackers want to use. For example, B-list celebrity Paris Hilton had her cell phone hacked and her personal address book and intimate photos on the phone were made available to the world when they were posted on the Internet.

Cell phones make inviting targets for several reasons. One is that they tend to have personal information available on them. Another is the always-on nature of cell phones. And because they were designed for communication, there are a variety of ways for intruders to try to get into the phones.

One of the primary ways in is via a technology called Bluetooth, which is designed to let devices easily connect to one another and establish ad-hoc networks so phones can communicate with one another without having to go through a central server.

This ease of communications leaves open security holes, and hackers have found ways to crawl in. To date, cell phone attacks and viruses have been sporadic, with nowhere near the ubiquity of attacks on computers. But that could well change in the future.

The danger goes beyond personal privacy and security. Cell phones are ubiquitous in corporations, and a surprising amount of corporate information can be found on them. In addition, some corporations have begun to develop ways for their employees to tap into corporate networks with cell phones or to synchronize information between a cell phone and corporate headquarters. That means a wily hacker could do more than just steal personal information by hacking into a cell phone—he could steal corporate secrets as well.

A Look at Cell Phone Hacking Dangers

1 Cell phone cloners can steal the identity of a cell phone and use that identity to make phone calls, leaving the owner of the cell phone holding the bill.

2 Cell phone snoopers can listen in on cell phone calls and invade people's and companies' privacy.

3 Viruses can be spread to cell phones in the same way they can spread to computers. Cell phones these days are in essence computers, so the viruses attack the phones just as they can attack computers. The viruses can also spread from cell phone to cell phone.

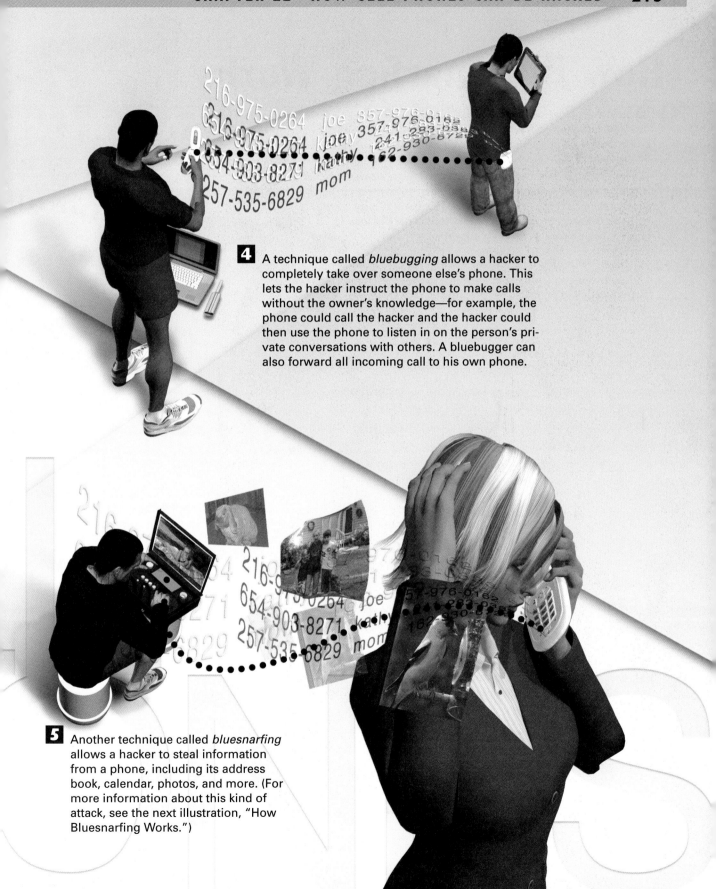

4 A technique called *bluebugging* allows a hacker to completely take over someone else's phone. This lets the hacker instruct the phone to make calls without the owner's knowledge—for example, the phone could call the hacker and the hacker could then use the phone to listen in on the person's private conversations with others. A bluebugger can also forward all incoming call to his own phone.

5 Another technique called *bluesnarfing* allows a hacker to steal information from a phone, including its address book, calendar, photos, and more. (For more information about this kind of attack, see the next illustration, "How Bluesnarfing Works.")

How Bluesnarfing Works

1 Bluesnarfing was one of the earliest attacks on Bluetooth-enabled cell phones. It will not work on newer phones, but it works against a number of old ones, including the Nokia 6310i, Nokia 7650, Nokia 8910i, Ericsson T39, and Ericsson R520m, among others.

A hacker first downloads a special piece of software to use in the attack, most commonly one called Bloover. (Bloover gets its name from a combination of *Bluetooth* and *Hoover*—Hoover because it can suck up information in the same way a Hoover vacuum sucks up dirt.) He installs the software on a laptop, although some versions can also be installed on cell phones.

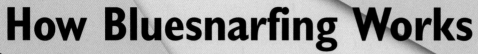

pb.vcf

Eric Lindley..457-387-8924

Joe Hill...426-175-0428

Seth Lower 537-685-2841

Miranda W. 416-263-9271

Sophia M. 537-172-0385

Patty Lindley.527-518-7284

2 The software scans the nearby area for any Bluetooth devices in discovery mode. When a Bluetooth device is in discovery mode, it allows nearby Bluetooth devices to connect to it, although in some instances a pairing must take place in which both parties agree to connect. (For more information about Bluetooth, refer to Chapter 11, "Bluetooth Security Dangers.")

3 The software uses Bluetooth's OBEX protocol, which is normally used to connect Bluetooth devices. It connects using the Push profile, which is typically used to send information. Using a security flaw in early versions of how the OBEX protocol was implemented on some phones, it instead uses a get request for files with commonly used names, such as the phonebook file (**telecom/pb.vcf**) or the calendar file (**telecom/cal.vcs**). In this way, the hacker can steal phonebook information, calendar information, and other files on the phone.

5 The hacker can also use the software to broadcast a corrupted message that crashes any phone within range.

4 He can also alter files without the knowledge of the phone user.

EDIT cal.vcf

EDIT>

EDIT

EDIT

How Paris Hilton's Cell Phone Was Hacked

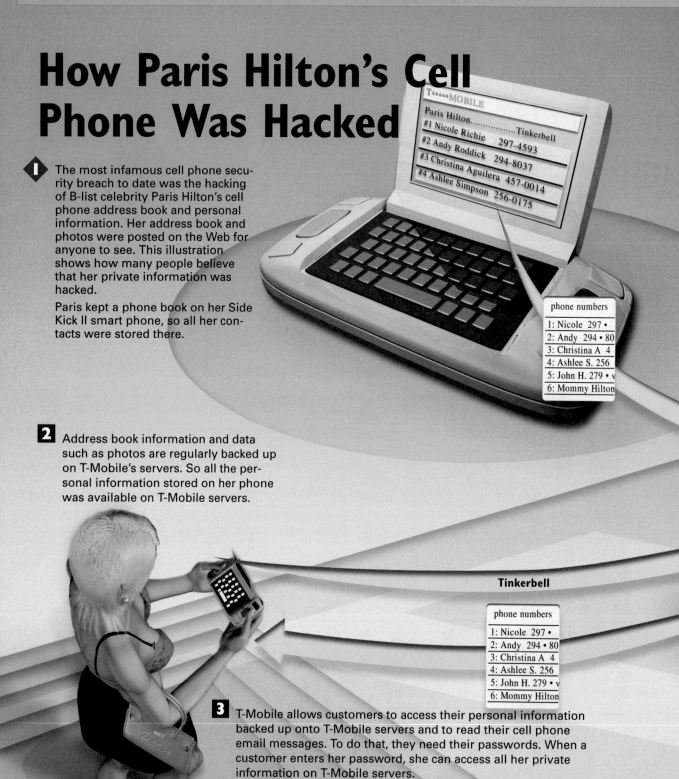

1 The most infamous cell phone security breach to date was the hacking of B-list celebrity Paris Hilton's cell phone address book and personal information. Her address book and photos were posted on the Web for anyone to see. This illustration shows how many people believe that her private information was hacked.

Paris kept a phone book on her Side Kick II smart phone, so all her contacts were stored there.

T······MOBILE

Paris Hilton........................Tinkerbell
#1 Nicole Richie   297-4593
#2 Andy Roddick   294-8037
#3 Christina Aguilera   457-0014
#4 Ashlee Simpson   256-0175

phone numbers
1: Nicole 297 •
2: Andy 294 • 80
3: Christina A 4
4: Ashlee S. 256
5: John H. 279 • v
6: Mommy Hilton

2 Address book information and data such as photos are regularly backed up on T-Mobile's servers. So all the personal information stored on her phone was available on T-Mobile servers.

Tinkerbell

phone numbers
1: Nicole 297 •
2: Andy 294 • 80
3: Christina A 4
4: Ashlee S. 256
5: John H. 279 • v
6: Mommy Hilton

3 T-Mobile allows customers to access their personal information backed up onto T-Mobile servers and to read their cell phone email messages. To do that, they need their passwords. When a customer enters her password, she can access all her private information on T-Mobile servers.

Customers sometimes forget their passwords. To allow a customer who has forgotten her password to access her account, sites ask a "secret question." If a customer answers the secret question, she is given her password and can access her account.

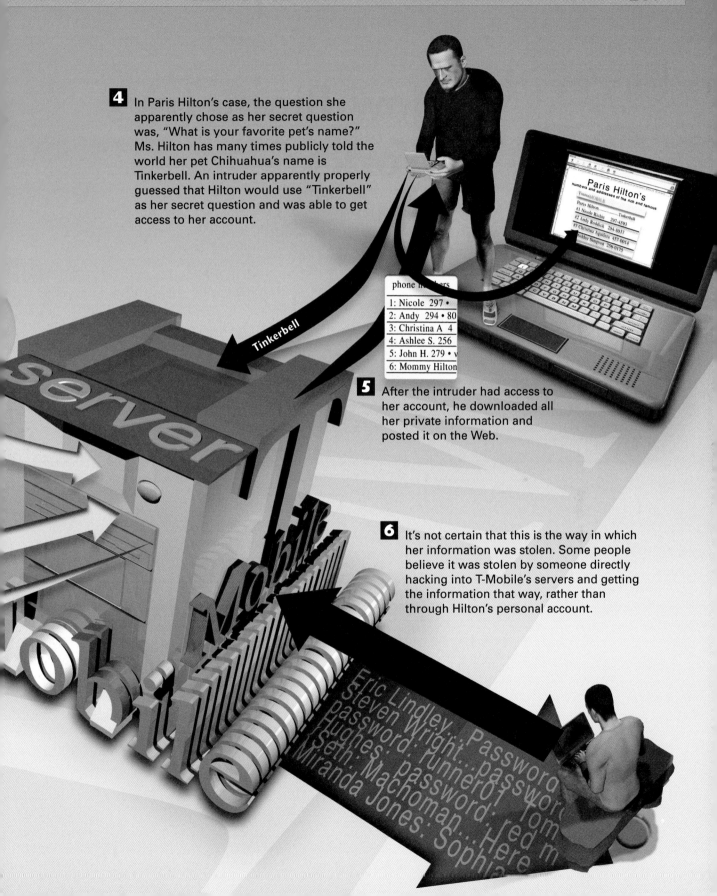

4 In Paris Hilton's case, the question she apparently chose as her secret question was, "What is your favorite pet's name?" Ms. Hilton has many times publicly told the world her pet Chihuahua's name is Tinkerbell. An intruder apparently properly guessed that Hilton would use "Tinkerbell" as her secret question and was able to get access to her account.

5 After the intruder had access to her account, he downloaded all her private information and posted it on the Web.

6 It's not certain that this is the way in which her information was stolen. Some people believe it was stolen by someone directly hacking into T-Mobile's servers and getting the information that way, rather than through Hilton's personal account.

CHAPTER

23

How Biometrics Works

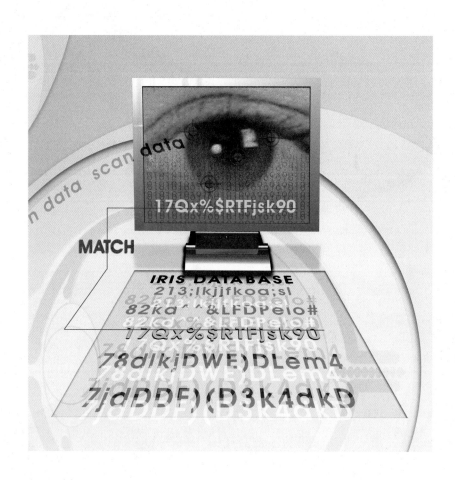

IN today's world, the ability to establish identity is more important than ever. Perhaps someone's identity must be verified before he is allowed into a place of work or a secure facility. Maybe a computer or network only allows certain people to use it, and the identities of those someones must be verified first.

For these and many other reasons, the ability to establish identity is vital. But traditional ways of establishing identity, such as looking at a photograph, simply are not accurate enough for high-security settings. And it is often not practical to compare photographs because that is too labor-intensive. Instead, a more cost-effective way needs to be found to establish identity.

This is where biometrics comes in. *Biometrics* establishes identity based on a person's unique physical characteristics, such as voice, fingerprint, iris, and even the structure of his veins.

A typical biometric system is made up of three components: a sensor that examines the physical characteristic being used to identify someone, a computer that stores the information, and special software that does the job of examining the information and determining identity.

These systems typically have three steps. First, someone enrolls in the system—for example, at a secure facility. When someone enrolls, his physical characteristic is scanned. Then the record is stored. Finally, when someone uses the system, his information is compared to the records, and if a match is found, his identity is verified and he is allowed admittance.

Biometrics is becoming increasingly common as hardware and software become less expensive and as the need for security increases. Not only is it used in secure facilities, but it is even used in typical workplaces as well, and the trend is likely to continue.

In fact, biometric systems can now be purchased for as little as $100 to protect a PC from being used except by authorized users. A small finger scanning device is connected to a computer via a USB port; and to use the computer, one needs to put a finger across the scanner.

Some people worry that biometrics could be used to invade people's privacy. For example, what if biometric information is sold in the same way that people's financial information or email information is sold? It would mean a great loss of privacy—for the first time, your actual characteristics would be on sale to the highest bidder.

At the moment, no laws cover the sale of such information. But, at the moment, there is no demand for such information, either. What's not clear is whether that might change in the future.

How Iris Scanning Works

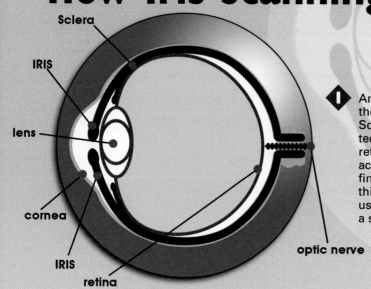

Sclera

IRIS

lens

cornea

IRIS

retina

optic nerve

1 An iris-scanning system takes a photograph of the iris as a way to verify someone's identity. Some people confuse iris scanning with an older technology called *retinal scanning*, in which the retina is scanned. But retinal scanning is not as accurate as iris scanning is, and some people find it more uncomfortable than iris scanning. In this illustration, you'll see how iris scanning is used to screen someone before letting him into a secure facility.

iris scanner

READY

scan data

3 A person stands from 3''–10'' from the front of the scanner. The camera then takes a photograph of the iris.

2 A charge-coupled device (CCD) digital camera is used to take a photo of the iris. The camera uses two kinds of light to take the photograph—visible light and near-infrared light. Near-infrared light is particularly well suited for taking photos of an iris because it makes the pupil look very black and therefore more easily shows the iris.

4 The camera sends the photo to a computer that analyzes several hundred reference points on the iris and, based on what it finds, creates a unique code that identifies the person.

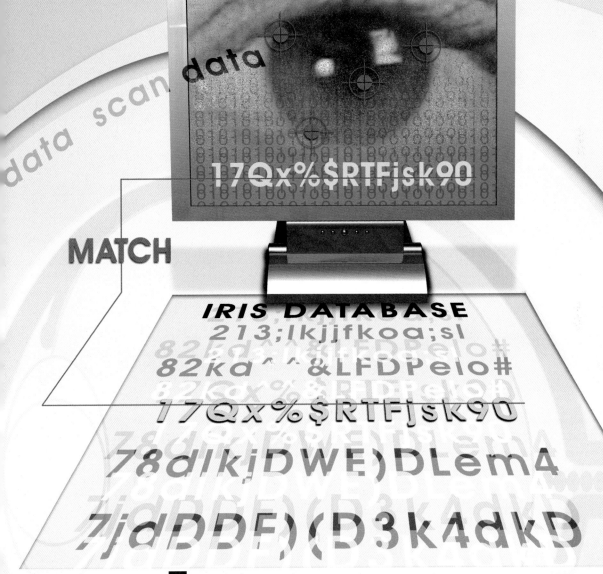

MATCH

17Qx%$RTFjsk90

IRIS DATABASE

213;lkjjfkoa;sl

82ka^^&LFDPeio#

17Qx%$RTFjsk90

78dlkjDWE)DLem4

7jdDDF)(D3k4dkD

5 The computer looks through a database for a unique code that matches the code of the person it just scanned. If it finds a match, it identifies the person and admits him. If no match is found, the person is not allowed in.

How Fingerprinting ID Works

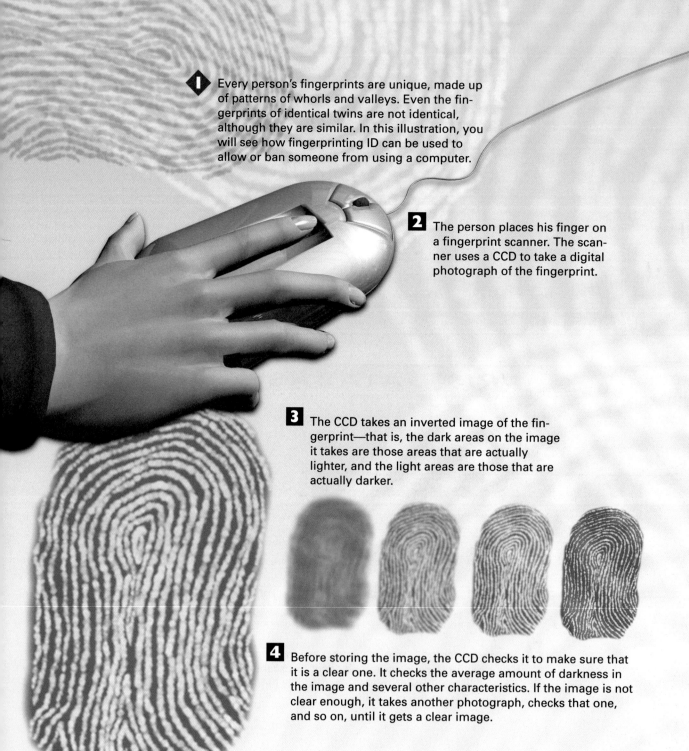

1 Every person's fingerprints are unique, made up of patterns of whorls and valleys. Even the fingerprints of identical twins are not identical, although they are similar. In this illustration, you will see how fingerprinting ID can be used to allow or ban someone from using a computer.

2 The person places his finger on a fingerprint scanner. The scanner uses a CCD to take a digital photograph of the fingerprint.

3 The CCD takes an inverted image of the fingerprint—that is, the dark areas on the image it takes are those areas that are actually lighter, and the light areas are those that are actually darker.

4 Before storing the image, the CCD checks it to make sure that it is a clear one. It checks the average amount of darkness in the image and several other characteristics. If the image is not clear enough, it takes another photograph, checks that one, and so on, until it gets a clear image.

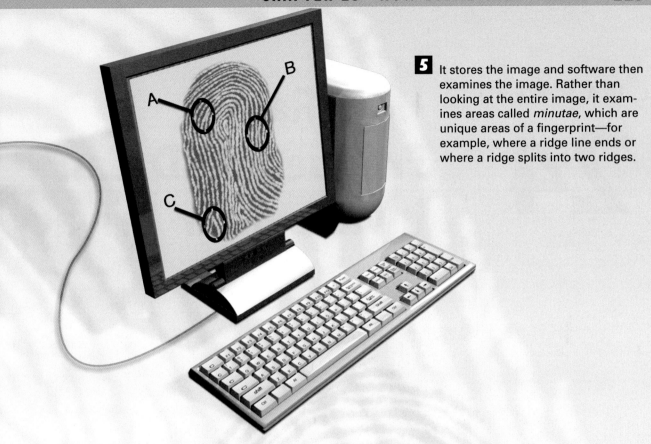

5 It stores the image and software then examines the image. Rather than looking at the entire image, it examines areas called *minutae*, which are unique areas of a fingerprint—for example, where a ridge line ends or where a ridge splits into two ridges.

6 Algorithms examine the minutae and compare them to records of other fingerprint minutae. If it finds a sufficient number of minutae matches, it determines that the fingerprints are identical. If it doesn't, it determines there is no match.

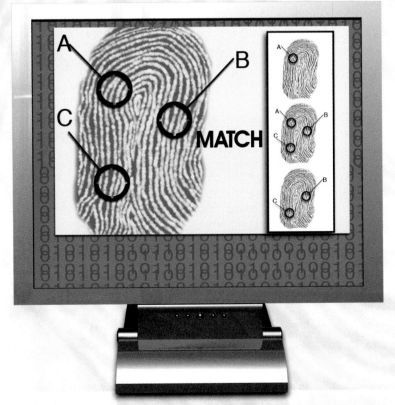

CHAPTER
24

How Radio Frequency ID Can Invade Your Privacy

MANUFACTURERS and retailers are always looking for ways to improve their efficiency, especially in tracking goods through the entire supply chain and retail cycle. Being able to track goods from warehouse to retailer has proven to be an exceedingly difficult task.

To solve these problems, manufacturers and retailers are turning to radio frequency identification (RFID) technology. RFID uses radio frequency communications as a way to track goods as they move through the supply chain. RFID tags are embedded into products, pallets, and cases, and the RFID readers read information from those tags. That information is relayed via a network or the Internet to a centralized database and application. That application collects all the information and gives manufacturers and retailers detailed information about the movement and sale of their goods. That information can also be used with other software to help manufacturers and retailers better gauge sales, for example.

RFID tags can be used for more than commerce, though—for example, there are calls to use them to track prescription medications. RFID tags have been implanted in animals, and there are worries that they may be used on humans in medical settings—the tags would contain information about the patient's condition, medication, and so on, helping to ensure that there are no errors in treatment.

While RFID tags have many uses, many privacy advocates worry that they can be used to invade people's privacy as well.

RFID tags might end up being embedded in the products themselves and might not merely be attached to them, much like UPC bar codes are embedded in many products. If RFID tags stay on products, the technology could be used not just to trace products from manufacturer through the supply chain and to the retailer, but also traced after you buy them. So, readers could conceivably track how you actually use those products, and that information could be collated into a comprehensive profile about you.

In addition, their use in government IDs such as passports and driver's licenses and for medical purposes could cause problems. One big issue is that any RFID reader might be able to read any RFID tag. So, as you traveled in public places and stores, people would be able to gather tremendous amounts of information about you.

As of this writing, the issue is still unsettled, with privacy advocates and RFID advocates still debating RFID use. However, it has moved forward in the supply chains of many companies due to mandates from Wal-Mart and the Department of Defense.

How RFID Works

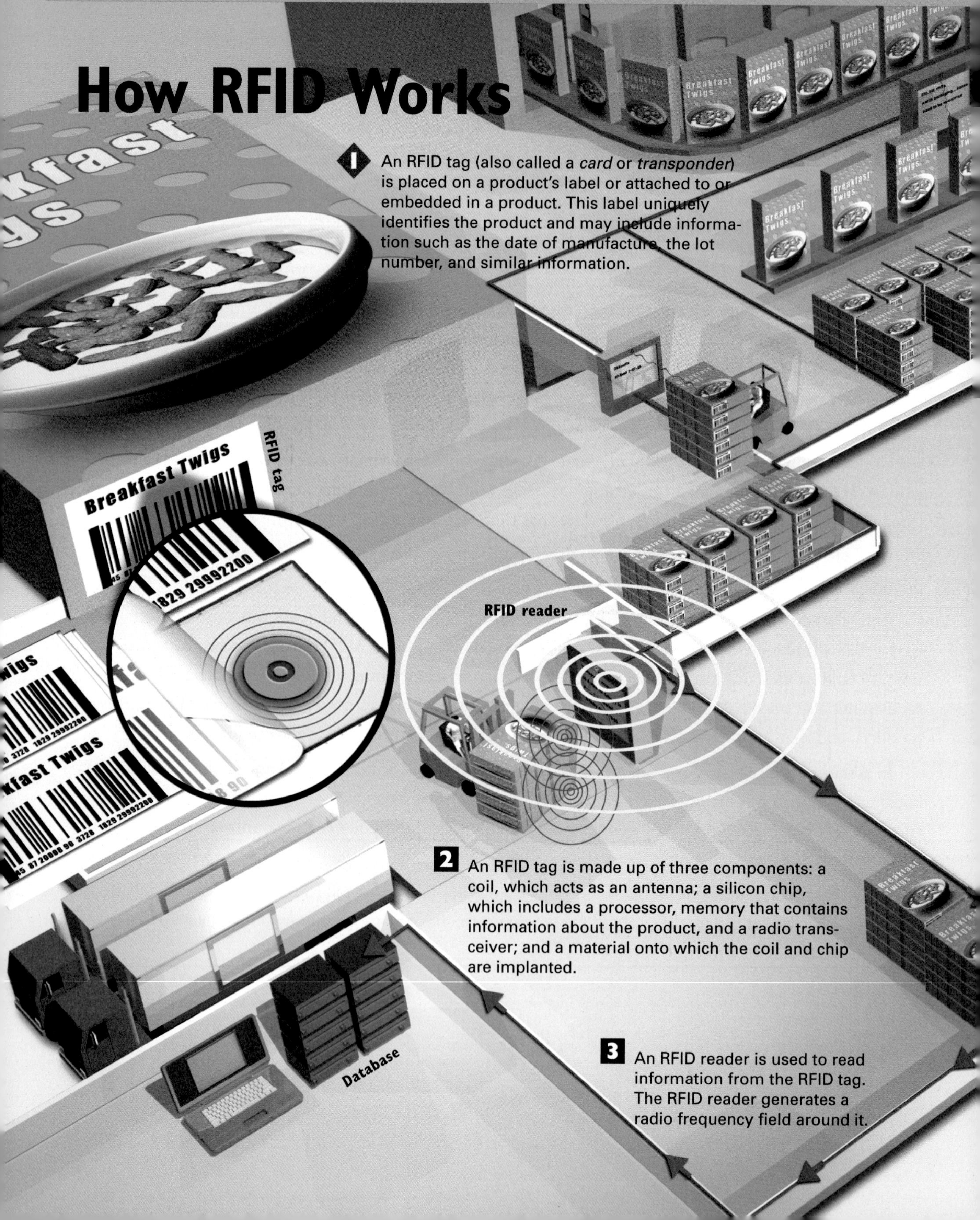

I An RFID tag (also called a *card* or *transponder*) is placed on a product's label or attached to or embedded in a product. This label uniquely identifies the product and may include information such as the date of manufacture, the lot number, and similar information.

RFID tag

Breakfast Twigs

RFID reader

2 An RFID tag is made up of three components: a coil, which acts as an antenna; a silicon chip, which includes a processor, memory that contains information about the product, and a radio transceiver; and a material onto which the coil and chip are implanted.

Database

3 An RFID reader is used to read information from the RFID tag. The RFID reader generates a radio frequency field around it.

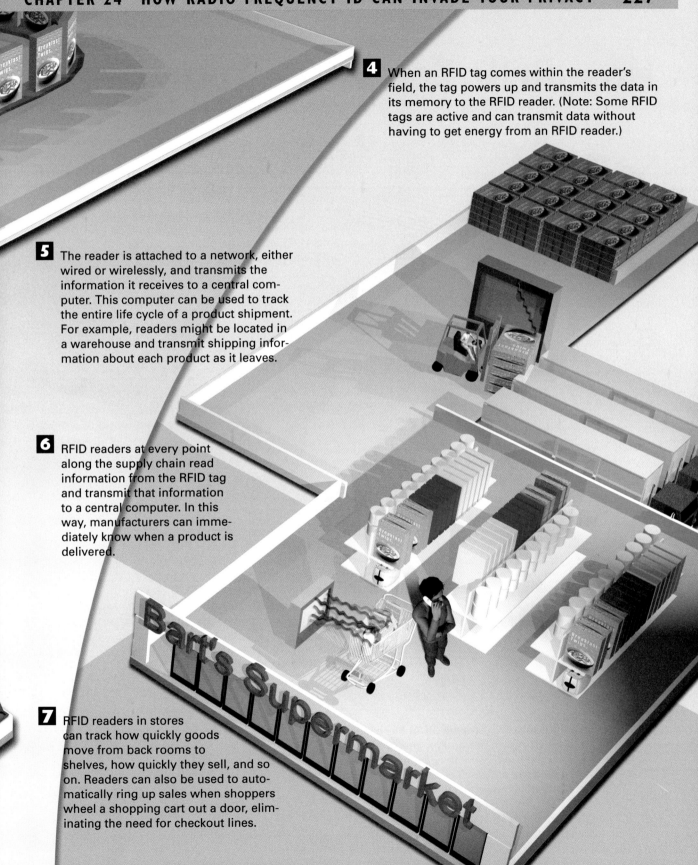

4 When an RFID tag comes within the reader's field, the tag powers up and transmits the data in its memory to the RFID reader. (Note: Some RFID tags are active and can transmit data without having to get energy from an RFID reader.)

5 The reader is attached to a network, either wired or wirelessly, and transmits the information it receives to a central computer. This computer can be used to track the entire life cycle of a product shipment. For example, readers might be located in a warehouse and transmit shipping information about each product as it leaves.

6 RFID readers at every point along the supply chain read information from the RFID tag and transmit that information to a central computer. In this way, manufacturers can immediately know when a product is delivered.

7 RFID readers in stores can track how quickly goods move from back rooms to shelves, how quickly they sell, and so on. Readers can also be used to automatically ring up sales when shoppers wheel a shopping cart out a door, eliminating the need for checkout lines.

Bart's Supermarket

How RFID Can Track Your Life

1 The key to understanding the privacy implications of RFID is recognizing that every RFID tag has a unique ID number that identifies the product to which it is affixed. Unlike bar codes, in which every item of the same type of goods (such as a can of Coke) has the same bar code, with RFID, every item of the same goods has a different RFID tag (meaning each one has an individual serial number). That makes it possible to trace that individual item anywhere it goes.

RFID reader

2 New advances in RFID technology worry privacy advocates. RFID chips can be embedded between layers of cardboard, molded into plastic, sewn into clothing seams, and integrated into packages. In addition, RFID chips can now be printed in ink and can use conductive ink rather than an antenna. That means it could be impossible for someone to know that she has bought goods or is carrying or wearing goods with RFID chips in them.

3 RFID tags can be read from a distance by readers, and anyone or any company with an RFID reader can read the tags—not just the company that sold or manufactured the item. So, as you move in public places and stores, those with RFID readers would theoretically be able to learn many details about your private life if you had items with RFID tags in them. Therefore, if your clothing, books, and other consumer items had RFID tags in them, someone or a store could easily find out intimate details of your private life.

4 The Food and Drug Administration (FDA) has called for the use of RFID tags in prescription medications as a way for consumers to be sure they are getting legitimate medications when they fill prescriptions. Privacy advocates worry that individual pills might be able to have tiny RFID tags printed on them, so privacy invaders with RFID readers could easily track what individual medications people are taking.

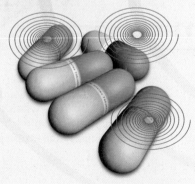

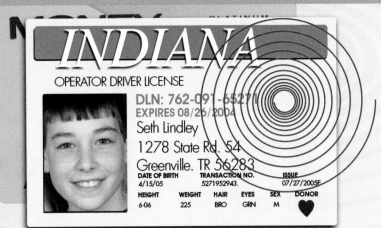

5 Some government agencies have proposed that ID cards, such as passports and driver's licenses, have RFID tags embedded in them. Privacy advocates warn that this would allow those with RFID readers to get a great deal of personal information about anyone passing by, including his name, date of birth, current address, and similar information.

6 Groups worry about the possible use of human RFID chip implantation—for example, in healthcare settings. RFID chips are now implanted in livestock as a way to track their movements, and even in endangered species to track their wanderings. But groups such as the Electronic Privacy Information Center (EPIC) say that there has been a movement to implant RFID chips in people in healthcare settings. The chips would contain a person's identification and health information, such as diseases, symptoms, medications being taken, and so on. Those with RFID readers would be able to gather this information about people.

RFID DATABASE

Seth Lindley: Born to parents Karen and Joe Lindl. Born at Marion County Memorial......Lives in Ohio and works at RagStudios as an animator........earns $ 167,000 annual income.....owns his own home.   Married with 5 children....travels monthly to both regional and international destinations. shops for movies at Blockdusters Movie House on 25th street Ohio.

7 Information from RFID readers could be compiled from multiple RFID sources and put into a database with information about individuals. So, a profile could be created about an individual, including the clothing she wears, the food she eats, the medications she takes, her medical conditions, and other information that is widely considered private.

CHAPTER

25

How Location Tracking Works

YOU *can run, but you can't hide.*

That might well be the motto of the modern age. Because these days it's easy to find out exactly where someone is at any given moment. If you use a cell phone, for example, there are ways for the cell phone company to know your general location. And global positioning systems (GPSs) can pinpoint your precise location with uncanny accuracy.

The GPS system is an especially revolutionary development. Originally developed by the military, GPS systems are now in widespread use. You can find them in cars for helping with directions and knowing exactly where you are and in handheld devices, which are increasingly used even by campers and hikers who don't want to become lost.

GPS systems use middle earth orbit (MEO) satellites, which orbit at an altitude of 5,000–15,000 kilometers above the earth. As you'll see in the illustration later in this chapter, GPS systems can pinpoint your location on Earth so you can know your current longitude and latitude. When combined with computer technology and a database of maps, they can provide navigation instructions. They also can be used to track your movements.

Cell phones will increasingly include built-in GPSs. These systems will be used for emergency purposes—call 911, and the GPS system on your phone will kick in, telling police or medical personnel your precise location.

But even cell phones that don't have a GPS can be used to track your location, as you'll see in an illustration later in this chapter.

There are many privacy issues related to location tracking. For example, in December 2005, federal judge Gabriel Gorenstein, in the Southern District of New York ruled in that the federal government could legally monitor anyone's location via his cell phone without having to obtain a warrant. More frightening still, the judge said that the government didn't even have to show probable cause, meaning any evidence of criminal behavior. All the government has to do, the judge ruled, is claim that information obtained by tracking someone might be somehow "relevant" to a criminal investigation.

It's not only the government that snoops on your location. The *Chicago Sun-Times* newspaper found in January 2006 that private companies were selling information about the locations of private individual cell phone calls over the Internet. They were selling the information to anyone willing to pay and weren't informing the people whose information was being sold. So, for example, if a woman was living in a shelter for battered women and her abusive husband wanted to find out where she was, all he had to do was fork over the money.

Although location tracking is no doubt a great convenience, it also represents one of the most significant potential invasions of privacy today.

How Global Positioning Satellites Work

1 To understand how GPS works, you first need to understand the concept of *triangulation*, which allows you to determine exactly where you are if you know your distance from three points. Let's say you know you're 75 miles from Boston. You could be anywhere on this circle, which has Boston in its center.

2 Now suppose you also know that you're 170 miles from New York. Drawing a second circle with New York as its center, you now can be on either point A or B, where the two circles intersect.

3 Finally, you know you're 20 miles from Hartford. You draw a third circle with Hartford in the middle, and you know your precise location. With GPS systems, though, you'll know your distance not from points on Earth, but from satellites circling above it. So, when you know your distance from one satellite, you can be anywhere not on a circle around it, but in a sphere around it. The three spheres intersect at two points, so, theoretically, there are two possible points where you can be. However, one of those points is in space, so you can use distance measurements from three satellites to determine where you are. However, for greatest accuracy, and to get information such as your altitude, you need to measure your distance from four satellites.

4 To find your location, you'll need a GPS handset. The handset calculates your distances from four satellites and, based on that, can determine your location on Earth to within a few feet.

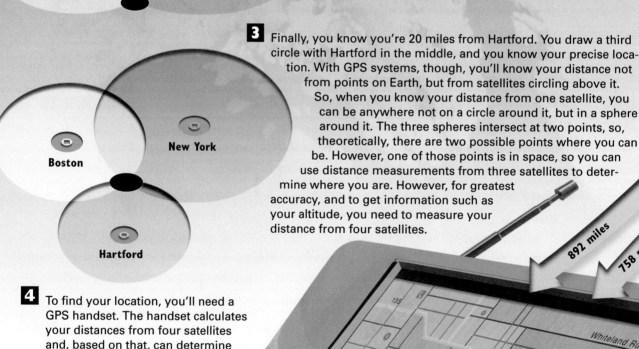

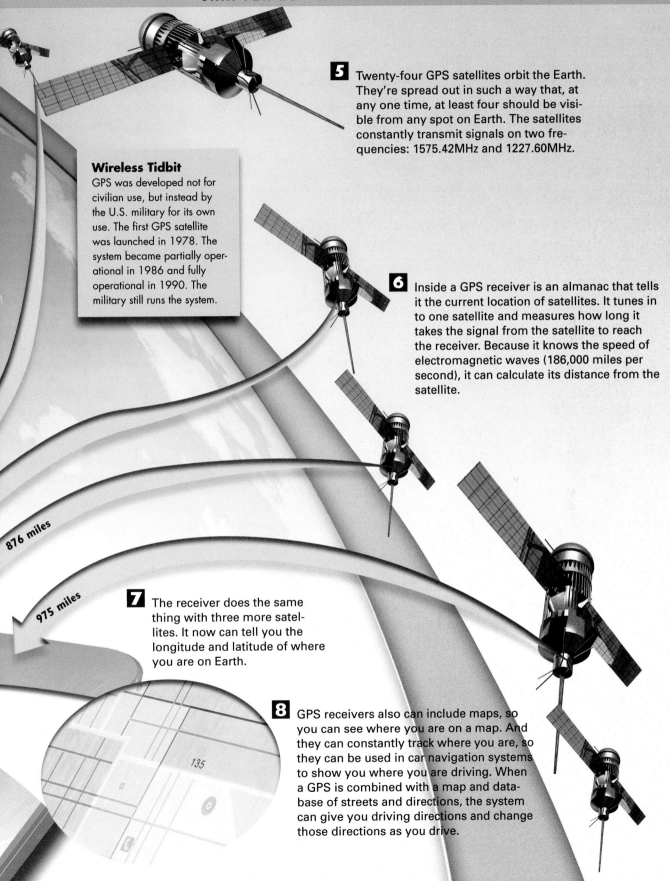

5 Twenty-four GPS satellites orbit the Earth. They're spread out in such a way that, at any one time, at least four should be visible from any spot on Earth. The satellites constantly transmit signals on two frequencies: 1575.42MHz and 1227.60MHz.

Wireless Tidbit
GPS was developed not for civilian use, but instead by the U.S. military for its own use. The first GPS satellite was launched in 1978. The system became partially operational in 1986 and fully operational in 1990. The military still runs the system.

6 Inside a GPS receiver is an almanac that tells it the current location of satellites. It tunes in to one satellite and measures how long it takes the signal from the satellite to reach the receiver. Because it knows the speed of electromagnetic waves (186,000 miles per second), it can calculate its distance from the satellite.

876 miles

975 miles

7 The receiver does the same thing with three more satellites. It now can tell you the longitude and latitude of where you are on Earth.

135

8 GPS receivers also can include maps, so you can see where you are on a map. And they can constantly track where you are, so they can be used in car navigation systems to show you where you are driving. When a GPS is combined with a map and database of streets and directions, the system can give you driving directions and change those directions as you drive.

How Cell Phone Location Tracking Works

1 Newer cell phones include GPS technology built in to them, and the locations of people with cell phones can be tracked using that. But cell phones can also be tracked without GPS technology, by using the infrastructure of the cell phone provider, as shown in this illustration.

2 When you make a call on your cell phone, the phone searches for the cell tower that has the strongest signal.

3 The phone makes a connection to the cell.

4 The cell passes this information to the cell phone company's home location register (HLR). The HLR keeps track of every user of the system and includes records of which cells they've used to make calls.

CELL 17

Home Location Register
database

- **Joe Giradi Cell 17...** • Eric Jones Cell 10...Patty Newsom
- **Jordan Black Cell 29...** • Karen Foster Cell 19...Jennifer

5 Because the HLR knows the cell being used, it knows the general location of the caller.

6 In some instances, a single cell is divided into three to six sectors. Each sector uses a directional antenna. The HLR can more precisely find the cell phone's location by determining in which sector the cell phone is.

7 As you move from one cell to another, the HLR knows that you are moving and is therefore able to track your new location.

8 Even when you don't make a call, your cell phone can track your location. Whenever your cell phone is on, it contacts the cell nearest to it and tells it its location. It does this so that, if someone makes a call to your phone, the system knows where to route the call. When your cell phone contacts the cell, that information is passed along to the HLR in the same way that the information is passed on when a call is made.

CHAPTER

26

How DNA Matching Works

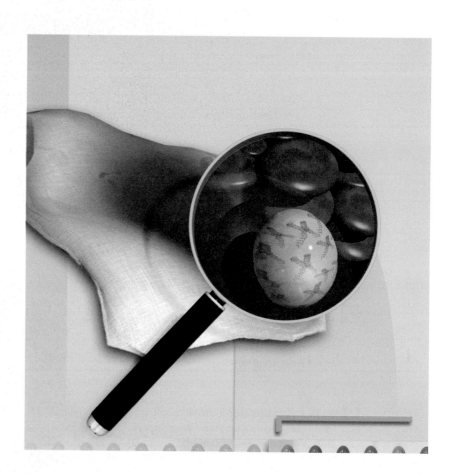

WHAT can be more private than our genes, the basic biological blueprint that makes each of use unique and human?

Genes are composed of DNA, and in them, you can read not just whether our eyes are blue or brown or our hair is red or blonde, but things less subtle than the obviously physical. For example, scientists have found that in certain people, there is a genetic disposition to shyness.

Our genes also predispose some of us to genetic diseases, such as Huntington's disease, which killed the folk singer Woody Guthrie. And they can also make it more likely that some of us will contract cancer or will be prone to high blood pressure and heart disease.

DNA is starting to take center stage in the privacy wars. There are great fears that DNA profiling can be misused by individuals, businesses, and governments. In particular, people worry that massive databases could be created of people's genetic profiles and that the information could be sold to the highest bidder and used for inappropriate purposes.

Most people don't realize it, but these databases already exist. For example, those in the military must submit genetic samples to the Department of Defense, which puts them into the Pentagon's DNA database. The database's purpose is to make it easier to identify the remains of soldiers who have been killed.

Hospitals, of course, take genetic samples as well to test for a variety of genetic diseases.

Law enforcement uses DNA profiles to help catch and convict those who commit crimes. Individual states have their own DNA databases. In 1994, the DNA Identification Act established an FBI-run national DNA database, called Combined DNA Identification System (CODIS). CODIS links together all the state databases, so someone can search the DNA database of all the states.

There are plenty of good reasons for establishing these DNA databases—they can help solve crimes, jail criminals, and help keep people healthier. But there is also a great deal of danger as well. DNA profiles have the potential to be perhaps the greatest invaders of people's privacy ever created. The most intimate parts of our lives could theoretically be sold to the highest bidder and be used to deny people jobs or healthcare or to mark them as potential future criminals.

Barry Steinhardt, the director of the American Civil Liberties Union's Technology and Liberty Program, pointed to some of these concerns when he testified before Congress against CODIS, "While DNA databases may be useful to identify criminals, I am skeptical that we will ward off the temptation to expand their use."

Will Steinhardt be right? It's still too early to know. The issue has yet to be decided in court, and the use of DNA profiles is in its infancy, apart from their use by law enforcement. Only the future will tell....

How DNA Matching Works

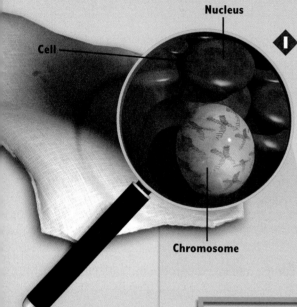

Cell

Nucleus

Chromosome

1 There are several methods of performing DNA matching. This illustration shows how restriction fragment length polymorphism (RFLP) is used to match the DNA at a crime scene to a suspect's DNA. First, DNA is extracted from blood, saliva, semen, tissue, or hair. The DNA is found only in the nucleus of a cell, so it must be extracted from one of these sources. If the DNA is being taken from a crime scene, it must be cleaned up because it is often contaminated by dirt and debris. In some instances, the DNA must be extracted from cloth, clothing, or some other material at the crime scene.

RFLP

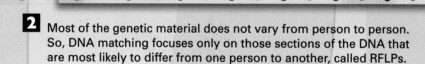

2 Most of the genetic material does not vary from person to person. So, DNA matching focuses only on those sections of the DNA that are most likely to differ from one person to another, called RFLPs.

DNA

Restriction enzymes

DNA strand

3 These DNA fragments are extracted from the rest of the DNA using "restriction enzymes." The enzymes cut DNA at either side of the RFLPs, separating the RFLPs from the rest of the DNA.

4 The lengths of the DNA fragments vary from person to person, and the length of the RFLPs is the basis of DNA matching. But the RFLPs are so small that they cannot be seen, so before a match can be made, their relative sizes need to be depicted visually, in a process called *gel electrophoresis*. The DNA is put into a gel mold, and an electrical charge is applied. DNA has a negative charge and is attracted to the positive charge on the opposite side of the mold. As the DNA fragments move over time, they leave a distinctive ladder pattern, although it can't be seen with the naked eye. To make the pattern visible, a radioactive probe and X-ray film is used and a photograph is taken of the pattern.

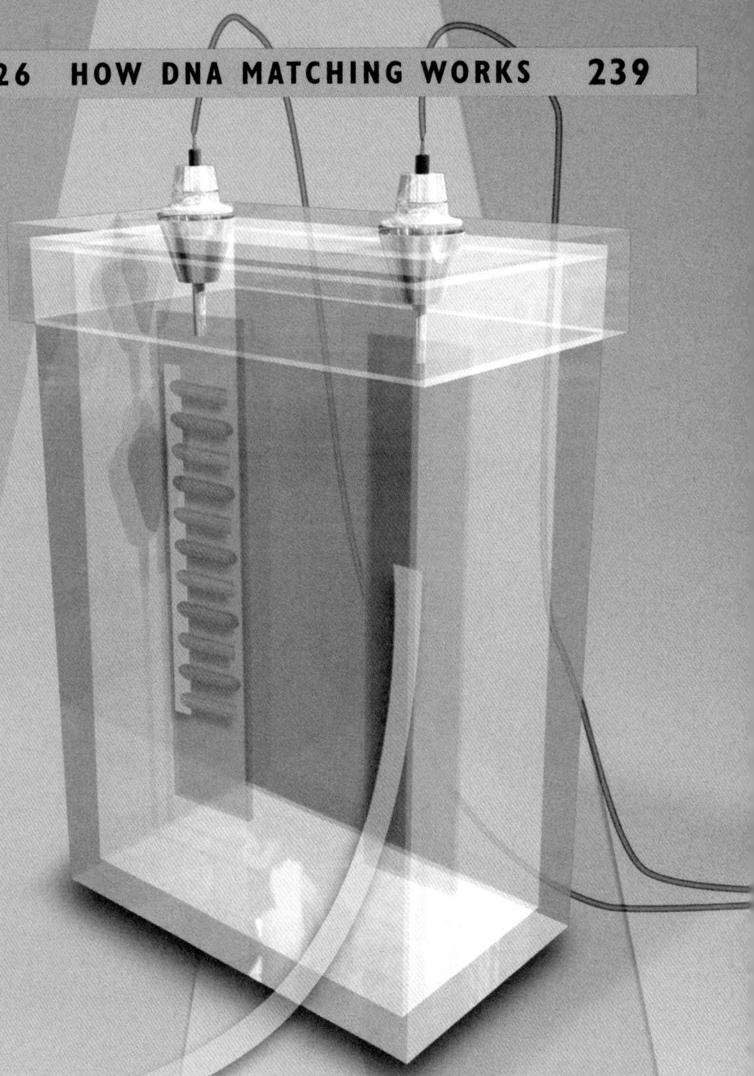

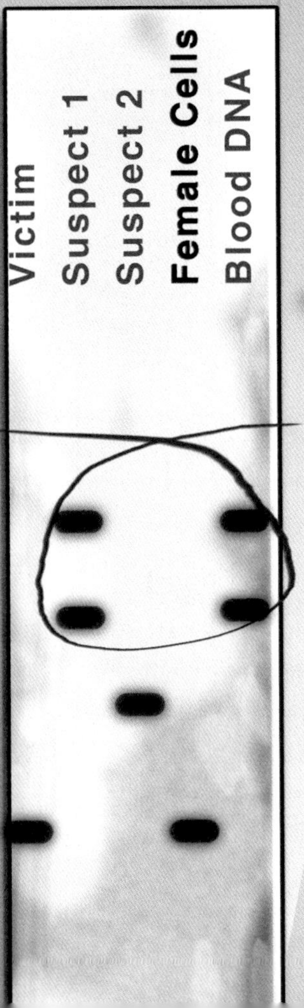

Victim
Suspect 1
Suspect 2
Female Cells
Blood DNA

5 The DNA pattern is now matched against the patterns of the victim and the suspect. Multiple probes and X-rays are taken, usually four or five. When the DNA of a suspect for all probes matches that of the DNA found at the crime scene, the suspect is arrested.

The Dangers of DNA Profiling

1 There are many reasons DNA profiles are built for someone; they don't all have to do with criminal matters. For example, someone might have DNA testing performed to see whether she is a carrier of the gene of a certain genetic disease.

2 Privacy advocates worry about the dangers of the widespread use of DNA profiling. Among their greatest fears is that DNA profiles will be compiled into a large database that can be used for business and government.

You're fired!

3 One concern is that employers would demand access to DNA profiles. If they discovered that a potential employee might be more prone to certain diseases, they might not hire him, might reassign him, or might even fire him.

Application denied!

4 Another worry is that health insurance companies will refuse to offer insurance to people who are predisposed to certain genetic diseases or disorders.

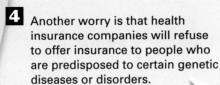

5 Privacy advocates also worry that law enforcement personnel may inappropriately use DNA profiles—for example, by saying that certain genetic profiles would predispose people to criminal behavior and then constantly watching those people or arresting them for crimes in which they were not involved.

6 Another concern is that the database information would be sold to the highest bidder and then the most personal aspects of people's lives would be up for sale.

CHAPTER

27

How Airport Scanners and Screening Systems Work

THERE was a time, not that many years ago, when an airline journey was a relatively simple affair. You made reservations, showed up at the airport not that much ahead of when your plane was supposed to take off, strolled through a metal detector, and went on your way.

Then came the September 11, 2001 terrorist attacks on the World Trade Center and Pentagon, and the world changed—including airline travel.

Security now takes central stage in the check-in process. New screening equipment has been added, security lines have become long, security procedures have become more complicated, and travel has become a much-more difficult affair.

Those changes are the obvious ones. Behind the scenes, there has also been much change, as well as some turmoil. And there has been a national debate over the rights of privacy versus the need to protect against future terrorist attacks.

The federal government has been working on a comprehensive passenger-screening system to better identify would-be terrorists. But privacy advocates are warning that many of these systems pose dangers to the very rights the government is supposed to be upholding.

A particularly controversial proposal was called Computer Assisted Passenger Prescreening System (CAPPSII). It would have rated every airline passenger according to his level of risk by tapping into commercial and government databases, including those run by the FBI, CIA, and National Security Agency (NSA).

Critics contended that there were many problems with the system. They claimed there was no way for people to know whether they were being rated fairly because they would not have access to the databases and data sources used to rate them. They said that if they were rated as a high risk, they could in essence be banned from airline travel, possibly forever, with no recourse to appeal. And they worried that the government would launch new surveillance programs to gather increasing amounts of information about people, so it could feed the CAPSSII system with as much data as possible.

Proponents of the program countered that there would be strict controls so people's privacy would not be invaded and that the system would be error-free. And they say it would help keep America safe well into the future.

The CAPSSII system, as of this writing, has not been put into effect, although there is a chance that it—or a similar program—will eventually be used.

How Airport Scanners Work

1 Most airport metal detectors are based on a technology known as *pulse induction (PI)*. In a PI system, a coil of wire on one of the sides of the detector functions as both a transmitter and a receiver.

2 The coil creates brief, powerful pulses of electrical current. Each pulse of current creates a short-lived magnetic field. Typically, the coil creates 100 pulses per second, although some systems create more than 1,000 pulses per second.

3 If a piece of metal is in the detector, the pulse creates a magnetic field in the object that is the opposite of the field of the pulse.

Coil

BEEEEEEEEBEEEEEEEEEP!!

Sampling circuit

INTEGRATOR

4 At the end of each pulse, the pulse reverses its polarity (positive becomes negative and negative becomes positive), which creates a very sharp electrical spike. When metal is in the detector, this spike is larger because of the extra energy in the metal's magnetic field.

The spike lasts a few microseconds. (A *microsecond* is a millionth of a second.) This spike makes another current, called a *reflected pulse*, go through the coil, lasting for about 30 microseconds. When metal is in the detector, this reflected pulse is larger because the metal causes the spike to be larger.

5 The metal detector contains a sampling circuit that measures the length of the reflected pulse. It compares the length of the pulse to the length the pulse would normally be if no metal was present. If the pulse is longer, it means that metal is present.

6 The sample circuit sends the information about the reflected pulse to a device called an *integrator*. The integrator amplifies the weak signal sent by the sampling circuit and sends it to an audio device that beeps, indicating that metal has been found.

How Airport Terrorist Tracking Systems Work

1 There are a variety of proposals for how to screen passengers to ensure none are terrorists or potential terrorists. This illustration shows how a controversial one called Computer Assisted Passenger Prescreening System (CAPPSII) would have worked. As of this writing, it has not been put into effect, but there are proposals to use similar programs. The program has been criticized for violating people's privacy rights and civil liberties.

2 When a passenger books a flight, he will be asked for more information than he currently provides. He will have to provide his full name, date of birth, home address, and home telephone number.

3 The airline reservation system will send that information to the CAPPSII system.

4 The CAPPSII system will look through combined, multiple databases that include information from commercial sources, such as credit agencies; information from federal and state agencies; and information from intelligence agencies, such as the CIA, FBI, and NSA.

5 The CAPPSII system will calculate a score about that person, which will be used to categorize him into one of three categories: green, yellow, or red.

The category will be sent to the airline reservation system. When the person checks in and receives a boarding pass, the pass will include encoded data that identifies him as being a green, yellow, or red risk.

Risk
Contact security

CAPSII
security

Contact security

Hold Joe Smith for further questioning

NORMAL

ADDITIONAL SCREENING

SUSPECT

6 A green risk will receive only normal screening.

7 A yellow risk will receive extra screening, such as having a wand passed over him and other methods of screening.

8 A red risk will be met and questioned by law enforcement personnel and may be detained or arrested.

CHAPTER
28

The Federal Government, Privacy, and Electronic Surveillance

MUCH is made about the dangers to your privacy from hackers, identity thieves, and businesses. But the greatest danger to your privacy comes not from any of them, but instead from the federal government and its massive bureaucracies and intelligence and law enforcement bureaus. From the moment you are born until the moment you die, the federal government gathers information about you.

Much of this information is required for you to get services—you must pay taxes, you may get benefits such as Social Security or student loans, and so on.

In addition to this kind of information, law enforcement and intelligence agencies have long gathered information about people. They do this to fight crime and protect the country, but on many occasions, critics claim, they have gone well beyond what they should be allowed to do. In the 1960s and 1970s, for example, both the FBI and CIA were cited for massive invasions of people's privacy and for investigating and prosecuting people who were doing nothing more than exercising the rights granted to them in the Constitution.

A variety of laws were passed to curb such abuses. But in recent years—especially after the terrorist attacks of September 11, 2001—the government has dramatically expanded its surveillance of people inside and outside the United States, and many people say that intelligence agencies once again are violating people's privacy and civil rights.

Many critics say the Patriot Act, passed in the wake of the terrorist attacks, has gone a long way toward violating the privacy rights of U.S. citizens. It gives the government enormous leeway in getting people's personal records without telling them, and without having to cite any evidence of a crime. Under it, the government can seize library records, financial and business records, medical records, information about Internet usage and more, with little or no oversight.

Also controversial has been President George W. Bush's decision to let the super-secret National Security Agency (NSA) tap phone calls and the Internet use of American citizens without first getting a warrant to do so. There is a well-defined legal procedure for such taps, with secret courts that allow them, and presidents have used them for years. But President Bush's decision to bypass the courts has been extremely controversial and, as this book goes to press, Congress had planned to hold hearings on the matter.

Two of the more controversial programs for gathering personal communications are the Carnivore program run by the FBI and the Echelon program run by the NSA. The Carnivore program was used to wiretap people's Internet connections. It has since been discontinued, but the FBI still uses similar technology.

The existence of Carnivore was acknowledged by the FBI, but the NSA doesn't acknowledge the existence of its Echelon data-gathering operation, which is the largest data-gathering operation in the world. It literally listens in on the world's communications and stores information it believes is relevant. We don't know exactly how the program operates because that is classified, but based on public records, we can show an illustration of its basic outlines.

How the NSA's Echelon Spy System Works

Telsat

1 The NSA's Echelon system is a top-secret way to intercept and interpret telephone, email, Internet, fax, and other electronic communications all over the world. Because the precise nature of the way it works is classified, we don't have an exact picture of it, but based on public resources, this illustration shows the general outlines of how it works.

2 Listening stations throughout the world point satellite dishes at the international telecommunications satellites (Intelsats) that most countries use. A ring of Intelsats hovers stationary above the equator, each of which handles tens of thousands of simultaneous phone calls, email messages, faxes, and other communications. The stations are pointed at different satellites and intercept every communication in their targeted satellites.

Microwave network

Undersea cable

3 Intelsats carry much of the world's telecommunications traffic, but not all of it. There are also undersea cables, land-based systems, land-based microwave networks, and regional telecommunications satellites. Echelon taps into each of those in different ways. For example, Echelon may tap directly into the undersea cables at the points where they emerge from the sea. It might tap into microwave networks by placing listening stations somewhere along the microwave route.

Telsat

4 The data captured by Echelon is separated into two streams, encrypted and unencrypted communications. The encrypted communications are sent to powerful computers that decrypt the communications and translate it back into its original language.

5 Both streams are sent to dictionary computers at the listening centers. The dictionary computers are powerful computers, most likely supercomputers, that search through every message for special keywords that have been programmed into the system—for example, specialized jargon used in the nuclear and bioweapons industries, names of terrorist leaders, and so on. Each dictionary has a different set of keywords. In some instances, keywords are provided to the NSA by a foreign intelligence agency. For example, a British intelligence agency might ask that keywords that are connected in some way to the Irish Republican Army be included.

Every piece of communication that has a keyword is put into the Echelon system permanently and is given special codes. In addition to keyword codes, it has other codes as well—for example, the name of the Dictionary computer that processed the communication, such as Cowboy.

Supercomputer

6 The keyworded communications are sent via secure, encrypted communications links to regional Echelon headquarters, where communications experts sift through the communications using powerful computers in search of useful intelligence. They then pass that intelligence to agencies that might find it useful, both inside and outside the United States.

Regional Echelon Headquarters

COWBOY BOMB NOW!!

Listening station

How the FBI's Carnivore System Worked

1 Before it was disbanded, the FBI used a system called Carnivore to track people's Internet use, including reading their emails and seeing which websites they visited. The data-gathering portion of Carnivore was a Pentium-based system on which the Carnivore packet-sniffing software ran. No keyboard or monitor was attached to the computer, so no one at the Internet service provider (ISP) could make use of it.

2 The computer was attached via a dedicated phone line and a 56K modem to the FBI offices. The FBI ran an off-the-shelf program called pcAnywhere to enable it to remotely control the Carnivore software and computer. The dedicated connection was not connected to the Internet, and all the data was encrypted, using both pcAnywhere's encryption and other encryption programs.

Dedicated phone line

3 FBI agents have the right to only monitor someone against whom the Bureau has obtained a wiretap warrant. The warrant also might require that it gathers only certain types of information about that person—for example, only his email messages. The FBI used the Carnivore software to set filters that filtered out all the data the FBI didn't want and focused only on the data it did want. So, for example, the FBI set a filter that said only to track packets to and from a particular person or only to examine his email or email and web usage.

Save all packets to and from IP 168.2.9.100

```
1 00001   1101001
  100 110   001 01
 10 11 0   011000
  100001    10001
 10110 11  001  10
 1001 1 1   100100
 110010 1   001000
```

Discard All other packets

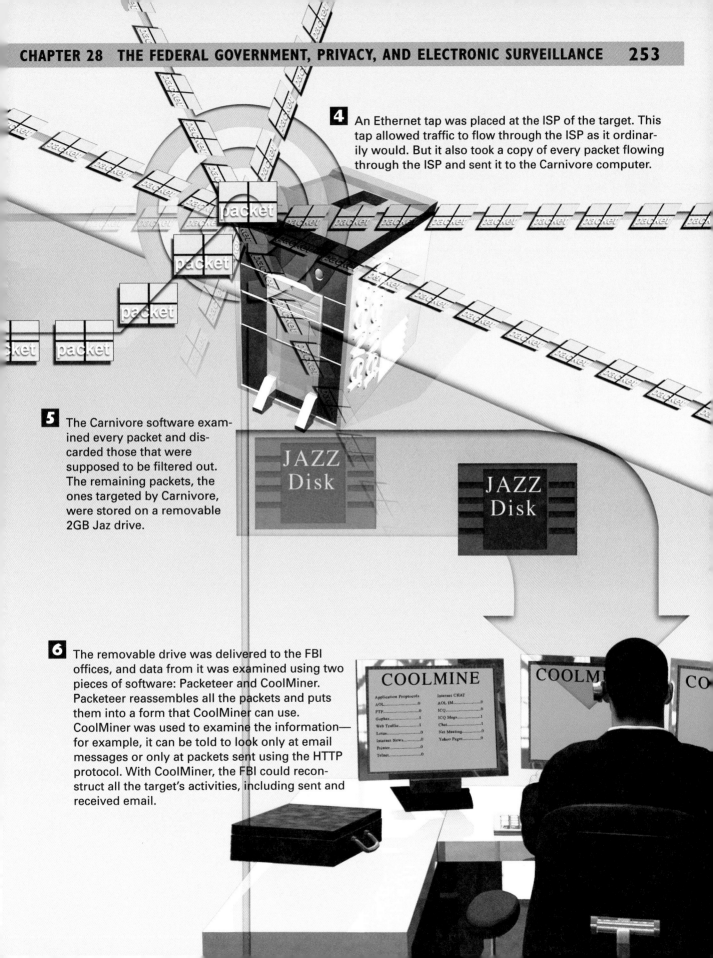

4 An Ethernet tap was placed at the ISP of the target. This tap allowed traffic to flow through the ISP as it ordinarily would. But it also took a copy of every packet flowing through the ISP and sent it to the Carnivore computer.

5 The Carnivore software examined every packet and discarded those that were supposed to be filtered out. The remaining packets, the ones targeted by Carnivore, were stored on a removable 2GB Jaz drive.

6 The removable drive was delivered to the FBI offices, and data from it was examined using two pieces of software: Packeteer and CoolMiner. Packeteer reassembles all the packets and puts them into a form that CoolMiner can use. CoolMiner was used to examine the information—for example, it can be told to look only at email messages or only at packets sent using the HTTP protocol. With CoolMiner, the FBI could reconstruct all the target's activities, including sent and received email.

How the Patriot Act Can Invade Your Privacy

1 As this book went to press, the controversial Patriot Act was being debated in Congress. So this illustration shows some of the primary dangers of the original Patriot Act. The final law, however, may be somewhat different from what is represented here.

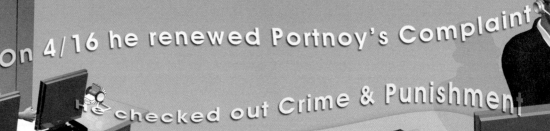

On 4/16 he renewed Portnoy's Complaint

He checked out Crime & Punishment

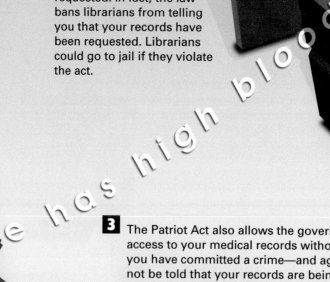

2 Under the Patriot Act, the U.S. government can gain access to your library records without evidence that you have committed a crime—and you will not be told that your records are being requested. In fact, the law bans librarians from telling you that your records have been requested. Librarians could go to jail if they violate the act.

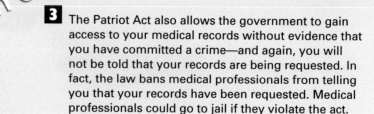

He has high blood pressu

3 The Patriot Act also allows the government to gain access to your medical records without evidence that you have committed a crime—and again, you will not be told that your records are being requested. In fact, the law bans medical professionals from telling you that your records have been requested. Medical professionals could go to jail if they violate the act.

4 The Patriot Act allows the government to seize a wide variety of your financial and business records from banks, credit agencies, and other financial institutions. Again, you will not be told the records have been requested, and anyone who tells you that they were requested could be jailed.

5 The Patriot Act allows the government to get access to various Internet communications without having to show probable cause or having to get a court order. For example, it can get records that detail your web surfing habits, such as searches you do on Google.

6 The act lets the government search your home without telling you. It can break into your home and office, take photos, and seize information without your knowledge.

CHAPTER

29

How Wiretapping and Lie Detectors Work

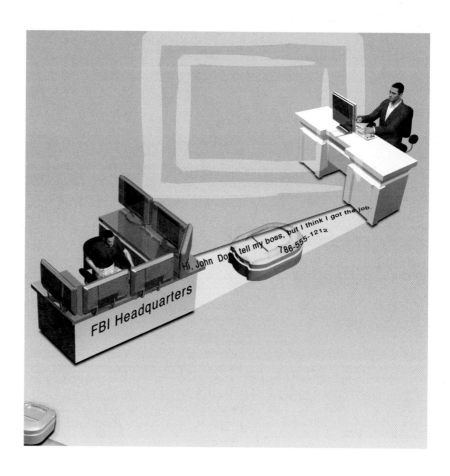

THROUGHOUT the history of the United States, one of the greatest political tensions has been that which balances personal privacy against the need for law enforcement to protect individuals and the country as a whole.

That tension has been with us from the very earliest days of the Republic. The Founding Fathers were extremely cognizant of it, and the Bill of Rights was, to a certain extent, a way to balance the rights of privacy against the rights of the federal government that was outlined in the U.S. Constitution.

The world is a more dangerous place than it was in the late eighteenth century, and technology has made it far easier than ever before for law enforcement to investigate personal details of people's lives.

Two of the most controversial techniques used by law enforcement are wiretapping and lie detectors, formally called *polygraphs*. Both of these techniques invade people's privacy yet are also needed by law enforcement personnel to stop and solve crimes.

Wiretapping is the more controversial of the two because of its intrusive nature. It allows law enforcement to listen in on all of a person's conversations via telephone and to tape those conversations.

Because of the intrusive nature of wiretaps, wiretaps typically require that law enforcement personnel first go to a judge before a tap can be installed, and reasons must be shown why the tap is necessary. Different judges interpret the laws and needs for taps differently, so some judges are more likely to issue taps than others.

The passage of the controversial U.S. Patriot Act expanded and loosened the use of wiretaps, though. Critics say that this act allows the government to ask for taps on literally anyone in the country, not just those suspected of crimes. The law does not require that the government show that the person for which it is requesting the tap actually be relevant to a criminal investigation. In addition, it expands the definition of a wiretap, so that multiple telephones can be tapped if it is suspected the person being tapped may use more than one telephone.

Lie detector tests, formally called *polygraphs*, are controversial for a different reason. In the public imagination, lie detector tests are scientifically rock-solid and can provide definitive proof of a person's guilt or innocence or whether a person is lying in answer to questions.

In real life, though, things are not so cut and dried. The tests rely on a trained person to interpret the results and are notoriously inaccurate. It is easy to get false positives and false negatives. In addition, people can use a variety of techniques to fool the tests.

Because of that, the tests are usually inadmissible in court. But they are still used and are sometimes used by private businesses that ask people to take lie detector tests before being hired.

How Wiretapping Works

Wiretapping, legally allowed to be carried out by federal, state, and local law enforcement agencies, is covered by the federal Communications Assistance for Law Enforcement Act (CALEA). But the techniques used by illegal wiretappers—people who want to listen in on your conversations—is done very differently, and in a lower-tech manner, than those done via CALEA. This illustration shows typical ways in which illegal wiretapping is carried out. The next illustration shows how wiretapping is done via CALEA.

1 The copper wires inside a telephone—one covered with red insulation and the other with green—carry the fluctuating electrical current that represents the sounds waves of your voice and the voice of the person who is talking to you over the telephone.

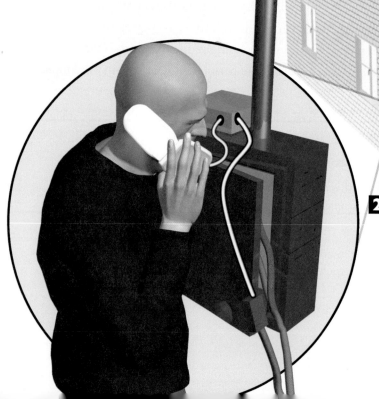

2 Someone cuts the phone line leading into your home, exposing the green and red wires. He then splices wires into it, attaching a second telephone or, more commonly, a tape machine to it. He is sure to keep the existing connection intact, however. In this way, your conversations can be listened to without your knowledge.

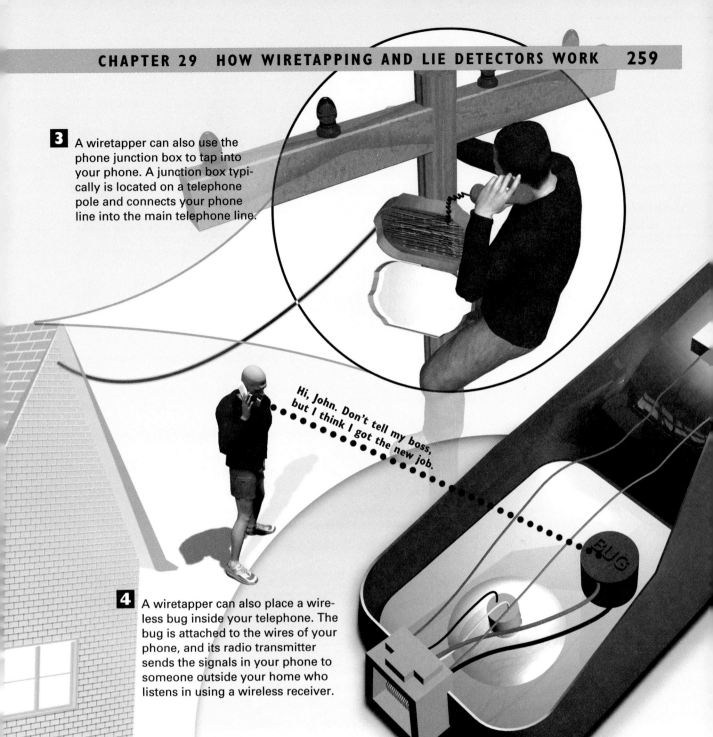

3 A wiretapper can also use the phone junction box to tap into your phone. A junction box typically is located on a telephone pole and connects your phone line into the main telephone line.

Hi, John. Don't tell my boss, but I think I got the new job.

4 A wiretapper can also place a wireless bug inside your telephone. The bug is attached to the wires of your phone, and its radio transmitter sends the signals in your phone to someone outside your home who listens in using a wireless receiver.

BUG

How Legal Wiretapping Works

CALEA requires that communications providers allow law enforcement officials to be able to listen in on phone conversations and get information about those phone calls, but only when the law enforcement agency has gotten approval for the tap.

1 The law enforcement agency goes before a judge and presents reasons a wiretap is needed. If the judge approves, a legal document or order is delivered to the communications provider.

2 A specially authorized person at the communications provider logs in to a system specifically set up for CALEA-approved wiretaps. A number of systems are sold by various manufacturers, but all of them tap into the routers and switches that make up telecommunications networks.

3 All calls on the communications network are routed digitally over switches and routers. The system used for taps connects to a central point in the network, over which all communications travel.

4 The tapping system captures two primary pieces of information about the call—the actual voice transmission itself (often referred to as *call content information [CCC]*) and data associated with each call, such as the phone numbers at both ends of the call (often referred to as *call associated data [CDC]*).

CCC LOG: HI JOHN...
DON'T TELL MY BOSS
BUT I THINK I GOT THE JOB

CDC LOG: 786-555-1212

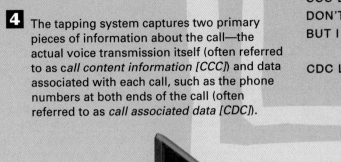

FBI Headquarters

Hi, John. Don't tell my boss, but I think I got the job. 786-555-1212

5 The CCC and the CDC information are sent over special secure routers to the law enforcement agency.

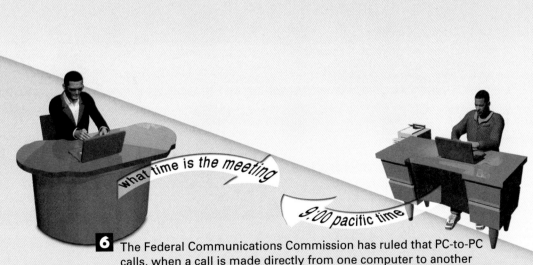

what time is the meeting

9:00 pacific time

6 The Federal Communications Commission has ruled that PC-to-PC calls, when a call is made directly from one computer to another over the Internet using Voice over Internet Protocol (VoIP) software such as Skype, is subject to CALEA. But as of this writing, no technical way has been devised to tap in to those calls.

How Lie Detectors Work

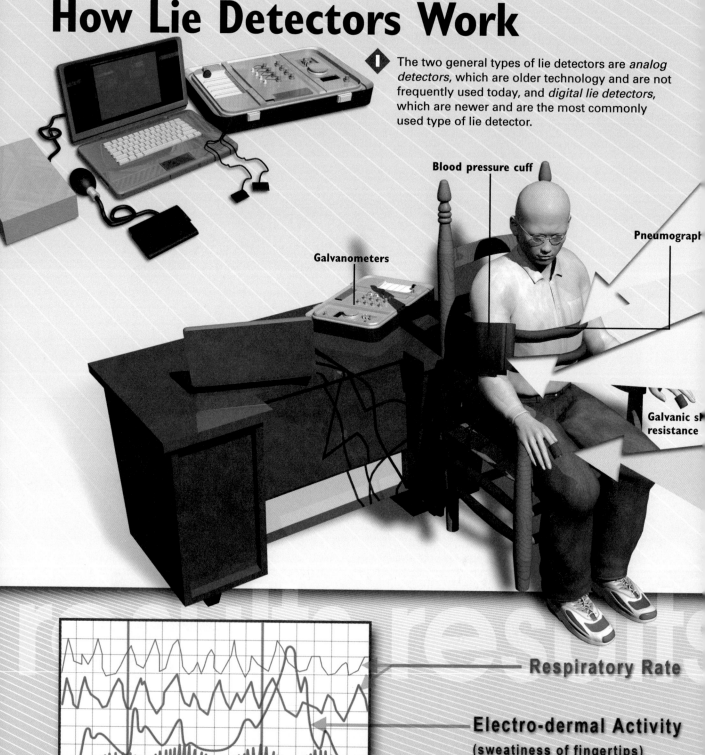

The two general types of lie detectors are *analog detectors*, which are older technology and are not frequently used today, and *digital lie detectors*, which are newer and are the most commonly used type of lie detector.

Blood pressure cuff

Pneumograph

Galvanometers

Galvanic skin resistance

Respiratory Rate

Electro-dermal Activity
(sweatiness of fingertips)

Blood Pressure / Heart Rate

-44   -33

2 When someone is given a lie detector test, various tubes and wires are attached to him to measure his physiological responses to questions. To measure the respiratory rate, two rubber tubes filled with air (called *pneumographs*) are put around the person's abdomen and chest. As the chest and abdominal muscles expand, it displaces air inside the tubes. A lie typically results in a higher respiratory rate.

In an analog lie detector, the tubes are attached to a bellows, which in turn is connected to a mechanical arm. That arm is in turned connected to an ink-filled pen that records the respiratory rate on scrolling paper.

In a digital lie detector, a transducer converts the measurements of the displaced air into digital signals that are fed into a computer. The computer uses that information to calculate the person's respiratory rate.

3 To measure blood pressure and heart rate, a blood-pressure cuff is applied to the person's upper-right arm. Tubing goes from the cuff to the lie detector. In an analog lie detector, the tubing is connected to a bellows, which is connected to an ink-filled pen that records the blood pressure and respiratory rate on scrolling paper. In a digital lie detector, a transducer converts the information into digital signals that are fed into a computer. The computer uses that information to calculate the blood pressure and heart rate. A lie typically results in higher blood pressure and a higher heart rate.

4 *Galvanic skin resistance (GSR)*, also called *electro-dermal activity*, is in essence a measurement of the amount of sweat on someone's fingertips; it is measured as well. The theory is that when someone is placed under stress, he sweats more. Galvanometers are connected to two of the person's fingers and measure the ability of the skin to conduct electricity—the more sweat there is, the better the skin conducts electricity. In an analog lie detector, the fluctuations are recorded on scrolling paper, while in a digital lie detector, they are recorded in the computer. A lie typically results in greater GSR.

5 The examiner running the lie detector tests asks the subject a series of questions. He asks control questions, as well as questions relevant to the crime being investigated. The control questions are general questions that the examiner uses as a baseline against which he will compare answers to the questions about the crime.

After the test is complete, the examiner interprets the results and reports on whether the person lied about answers to certain questions.

Lie detector results can be misinterpreted, and people can use techniques to fool the test—for example, taking sedatives before the test, putting antiperspirant on their fingertips, and other measures. Because of this, test results are usually not admissible in court, except under very strict guidelines.

Index